Architectural Guide
Katowice

Architecture since 1945

Architectural Guide
Katowice

Architecture since 1945

Jakub Bródka

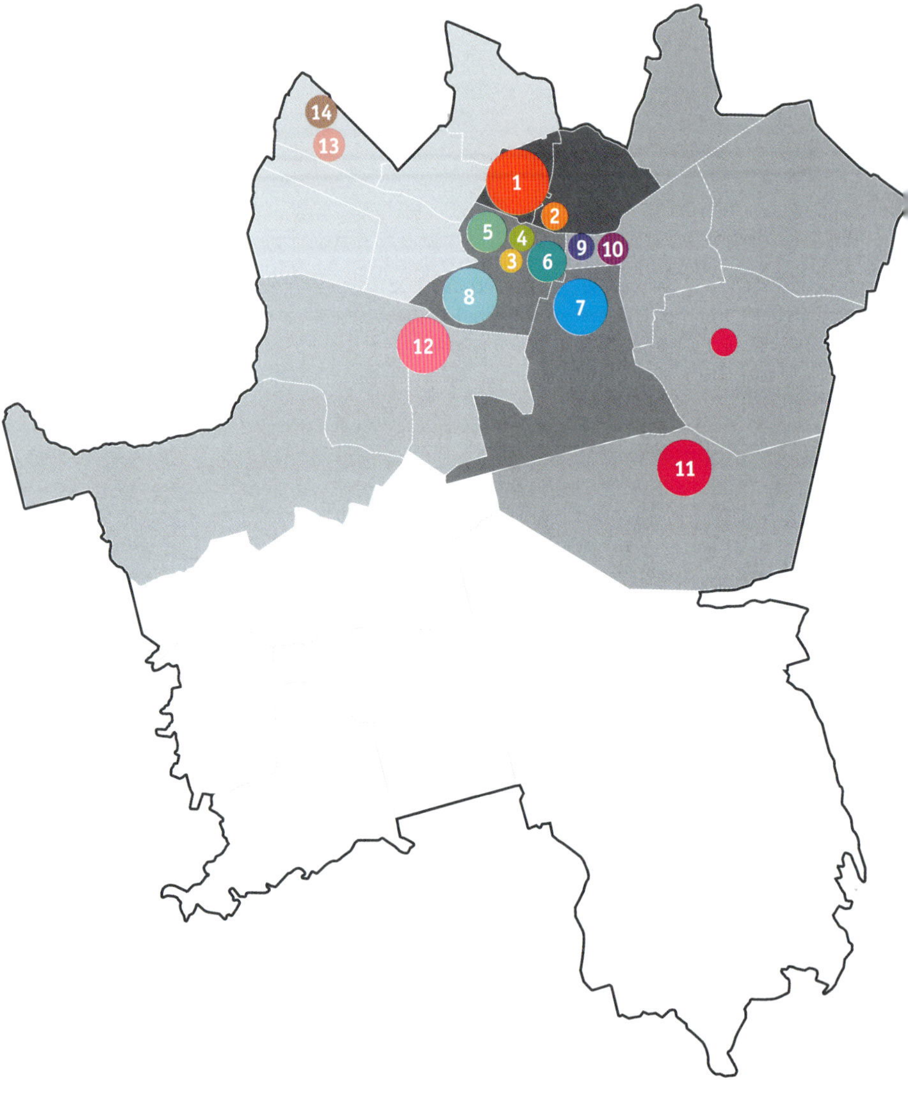

Contents

Foreword

Dr.-Ing. Marcin Krupa
Mayor of the city of Katowice

Despite being a relatively young city, Katowice boasts many architecturally interesting buildings. The history of Katowice is clearly marked by the influences of various cultures, wars, and insurgencies. The development of industry has also left its mark, visible in large influxes of people and changes in the functioning of the city. All this has been reflected in the character of the city's urban development.

In the post-war years the architects who worked in Katowice did not lose their momentum; on the contrary, they created works that still impress today with

their innovativeness and novelty. Suffice it to mention the city's most recognisable icon, Spodek Arena, which has been a venue for sports competitions and cultural and business meetings for more than 50 years. We also have 'stars' and 'corncobs' – tall apartment blocks of striking appearance that form housing estates of unique design.

Katowice's flair, often expressed in original designs, is also evident in contemporary projects. The Polish National Radio Symphony Orchestra building, the Silesian Museum, and the International Congress Centre, built in recent years on the site of a former coal mine near Spodek, are new landmarks in Katowice. The neighbouring KTW office buildings with their distinctive cuboid volumes and the Silesian Film School building, which combines history with modernity, are also examples of contemporary architectural ideas present in the fabric of our city.

Authors of architectural projects realised in Katowice today not only follow global trends but also frequently refer to the history of the region, creating an image of a city which, while fit for the twenty-first century, is careful not to forget its own heritage.

In the foreground: a part of the Culture Zone; in the distance: Koszutka District

iStockphoto (paweł.gaul)

Three generations of architecture in the city of Katowice.
View from Korfantego Avenue

Introduction

The idea of an architectural guide to the contemporary architecture of Katowice came about as a result of a combination of two circumstances. The first was an ever-growing interest in the history of contemporary architecture with particular emphasis on the heritage of the communist period. In recent years I have been frequently asked to give tours of the city or provide insights into the architecture and urban planning of post-war Katowice, which I have gladly done. It was especially pleasing that these inquiries came not only from local residents of the city or other parts of the country but also from international visitors considering a trip to Katowice. This gave rise to the idea of developing this topic in such a way as to explain the historical and spatial context and the conditions influencing the development of the city's architecture as fully as possible also to foreign readers, who are perhaps unfamiliar with the specific realities of Poland in the second half of the twentieth century. The second circumstance has a personal basis: as an inhabitant of Katowice and an architecture enthusiast professionally involved in its research and popularisation, I felt an inner need to systematise, round out, and make available the information I had gathered over the years about the space of my city. Preparing this guide has also been an opportunity to subjectively draw attention to a group of buildings which have not yet been extensively described, if they have been described at all, and which, in my opinion, constitute an interesting and valuable source of knowledge about Polish architecture both of the post-war period and constructed after the Polish People's Republic became the Republic of Poland on 31 December 1989.

I would like to emphasise that this publication is not the first that sets out to familiarise and understand the post-war architecture of Katowice. I will mention here three interesting publications that have appeared in recent years. An undoubtedly valuable contribution in terms of popularising the topic was a book published in 2020 in the form of a guide to architecture of 1945–1989 in the Silesian Voivodeship titled *Spodek w Zenicie* (Spodek at its Zenith) by Anna Syska. The author describes 26 buildings from Katowice. A monograph titled *New Katowice. The Form and Ideology of Polish Post-war Architecture, Based on the Example of Katowice (1945–1980)*, published in 2019 by Aneta Borowik, is a reliable academic study resulting from extensive historical and archival search. The third publication I would like to mention is the series 'Domy i gmachy Katowic' (Houses and Edifices of Katowice), which was published under the editorship of Grzegorz Grzegorek in two volumes in 2013 and 2016. This series reveals in a very accessible way the history of the city's most distinctive buildings built from the nineteenth century to the first decade of the twenty-first.

Architectural Guide Katowice describes a total of 120 buildings completed between 1945 and 2025. The author's aim was to have approximately the same number of buildings representing each of the two historical eras (1945–1989 and 1990–2025), and this goal has been achieved. Selecting projects for this book meant tackling two problems: giving as complete as possible an overview of projects in terms of typology of function (division into residential, academic, educational, public and commercial, culture and sports, and religious functions) and the issue of historical changes to the city's administrative boundaries. In the case of the first problem, I adopted the classic urban guide model, whereby objects are grouped into areas that constitute individual districts or settlements. This has a functional rationale: when exploring the city, it is easier to quickly access the information you require within a single chapter. Meanwhile, an appendix to the edition contains a list of projects with typological and chronological information. The second problem mainly concerned projects located in Silesian Park, which today is officially a part of the city of Chorzów. However, until the mid-1960s this park complex, construction of which began in 1950, was inside the boundaries of Katowice, a state of affairs which persisted until the exchange of land that took place between the two cities during the construction of Osiedle Tysiąclecia (Millennium Housing Estate). In deciding to include the buildings located in the park in this study of the architecture of Katowice, I also took into account the supra-local character of the park, the fact that it does not belong to any of the districts of Chorzów, and its historical and spatial connections with Millennium Housing Estate.

I would like to thank all who contributed to the creation and publication of this book, including various institutions and DOM publishers. In particular, I would like to thank Dominika Śliwińska, the author of the contemporary photographs in this guide, for her fruitful cooperation. Thanks are also due to Michał Godziek and Marek Pęczak for their technical cooperation in preparing the drawings included in the book. For their invaluable support and belief in the project, I would like to thank Prof. Magdalena Żmudzińska-Nowak, Dr Magdalena Wałek, Dieter Paleta, Ryszard Jurkowski, Dr Tomasz Konior, Przemysław Czernek, and, for their constant support and motivation, my dear parents and friends.

The architect Jurand Jarecki (second from right) with contractors at the construction site for Skarbek Department Store

How to Use This Guide

This guide consists of three parts. In addition to an 'author's introduction' explaining my motivation for taking up the topic and outlining the basic assumptions and problems encountered in the course of developing it, the introductory part of this book includes two essays. The first is a synthesised historical and spatial overview of Katowice since its foundation. The second, titled 'Architecture and Planning during the Communist Period in Poland', describes conditions that affected the shaping of space in Poland during the communist period (1945–1989). For the sake of greater readability, both essays have been structured on the basis of the adopted periodisation. Given the guide's temporal scope (from 1945 onwards), I deemed such a selection of subject matter necessary in order to complement the information provided in the main part of the book, which is only a small part of the spread of Katowice's architectural history.

The second part is a description of 120 projects, contained in six chapters. Each of chapters 1–5 refers to one conventional area of the city: the north, the centre, the east, the south, and the

west. The individual parts are divided into sub-areas according to the actual administrative division of Katowice (by district) and, in some cases, additionally for logistical reasons related to visiting the city. The sixth chapter discusses the lost heritage of the second half of the twentieth century. It presents the most valuable demolished buildings. As in the case of existing buildings, their locations are also taken into account. Each of the six chapters opens with historical introductions relating to the individual areas. In addition, practical descriptions of the proposed walking routes are included, along with commentary. Below its name, each project has abbreviated information including its address, years of construction (where the initial date is taken as the year the project was designed and the final date is the year it entered use), and the names of the author or team of authors. The numbering of the projects is consistent with the numbers given on the overview maps for each area.

Part three of the guide is an appendix containing an index of buildings ranked by type and chronology and an index of architects and design offices.

Kattowitz.

1

Kattowitz

Friedrichsplatz

LUCKHARDT

BENZ-AUTOMOBILE

2

3

KATOWICE. Ogólny widok

1. View looking from near today's Warszawska and Starowiejska streets. Postcard, 1872
2. View of Market Square, looking north. Postcard, 1905
3. South part of the centre with the interwar 'skyscraper' visible in the distance at
   the corner of today's Żwirki i Wigury and Skłodowska-Curie streets. Postcard, 1938

Historical and Spatial Overview of Katowice

Any attempt to outline a synthetic history of a city is inextricably linked to a fundamental question: since when has the city described been a city? From a historical perspective, in the case of the relatively young Katowice, the answer is the year it was granted city status: 1865. By then, however, Katowice had already had a history of more than 250 years – first as a small hamlet around an iron forge in the municipality of Bogucice (mentioned in historical documents in 1580), then as an independent village called 'Katowice' (still within the municipality of Bogucice, from 1614 forwards). A reminder of Katowice's early industrial origins can be found in the city's coat of arms, which has an image of a hammer powered by a waterwheel – the same as was found in Kuźnica Bogucka. Over the course of the seventeenth and eighteenth centuries, the village of Katowice changed hands as many as 20 times, and consequently also its membership of Silesian principalities subject to the Kingdom of Bohemia and the Habsburg monarchy. In 1742, as a result of the Silesian Wars, the municipality of Bogucice and its subordinate villages were incorporated into the Kingdom of Prussia. The beginning of the nineteenth century brought a significant increase in the population living in this industrial village. The number of residents was steadily increasing when peasants in Silesia were enfranchised in the late 1820s and early 1830s. The transfer of property (coal mines, ore mines, and zinc and iron works) from the industrialist Franz Winckler to Katowice in 1839 was another factor that influenced the village's development as it became an important industrial and administrative centre. Also significant was the inclusion of Katowice in the planning of the railway connection between Breslau and Myslowice, which opened in 1846. The same year saw the opening of the first hotel, located on Market Square. Ten years later, the first brick Evangelical church was consecrated on what is today Warszawska Street. One of the administrators of the Franz Winckler estate was Friedrich Grundmann. Together with the doctor Richard Holtze, Grundmann lobbied for Katowice to be granted the status of city; this was finally granted in 1865, crowning efforts made by German industrialists and merchants, who saw great commercial potential in Katowice due to its favourable location right next

View of the Baildon Steelworks. Lithograph, mid-19th century

to the Prussian-Russian border. The new city had a population of almost 5000. The granting of city status by King William I Hohenzollern of Prussia opened a new chapter in the dynamic economic and spatial development of Katowice. However, the following 150 years of its existence were marked by a constantly changing geopolitical context. To help understand this history full of twists and turns, it is worth first putting in chronological order in the form of an overview the most important facts about Katowice.

- 1742: as a result of the Silesian Wars, the municipality of Bogucice, together with the village of Katowice, was incorporated into the Kingdom of Prussia.
- 1850: the village of Katowice separated from the municipality of Bogucice to become an independent industrial village.
- 1865: Katowice was granted city status by the King of Prussia.
- 1871–1918: the Kingdom of Prussia became part of the German Empire. 1914–1918: World War One, the collapse of the German Empire.
- 1918–1921: the Inter-Ministerial Ruling and Plebiscite Commission, headed by the French general Henri Le Rond, took over management of

Katowice. Establishment of the Polish and German Plebiscite Commissariat. 1919: the First Silesian Uprising. 1920: the Second Silesian Uprising. 1921: the Silesian plebiscite. 1921: the Third Silesian Uprising. The Council of Ambassadors of the major powers approved the division of Upper Silesia: Katowice became part of Polish territory.

- 1921–1939: Katowice was a city of the Second Polish Republic. 1939: the outbreak of World War Two and the incorporation of Katowice under German administration.
- 1939–1945: Third Reich. 1945: capitulation of the Third Reich and the entry of the Red Army into Katowice.
- 1945–1989: People's Republic of Poland (PRL). 1953–1956: Katowice was renamed 'Stalinogród'.
- Since 1990: Republic of Poland. 2004: accession to the European Union.

Katowice's complex history, which has included, among other things, changes in nationality and accompanying changes in propaganda, translated into the creation of a wide variety of architecture in the city in each of the above periods. A general characterisation of the development of Katowice's space and

View of today's Warszawska Street from the tower of the Evangelical church. Postcard, 1910

the architecture created in it is likewise best presented using chronological ordering of information. I take the year 1850, when Katowice became an independent village, as the starting point for this analysis. This is also the period from which the oldest relics of buildings in the city have survived.

1850–1918

Even before Katowice was granted the status of city in 1865, a clear structure of main streets corresponding to today's Korfantego Avenue, 3-Maja Street, and Warszawska Street and intersecting at the site of today's Market Square had formed. Brick buildings started to be erected along the east-west axis. These included the Neo-Romanesque Evangelical Church of the Resurrection (1858; arch.: R. Lucae), the Neo-Gothic Catholic Church of St Mary (1870; arch.: A. Langer), and nearly 200 brick residential buildings in the form of apartment houses and industrialist's villas completed by 1872 (along today's Warszawska Street). The granting of city status led to Katowice being declared the seat of the district administration, which involved the construction of official buildings, such as the district office building (1876; arch.:

Evangelical church on today's Warszawska Street before the extension of 1899–1902. Photograph from the end of the 19th century, author unknown

Kattowitz.   Marthahütte.   Rawabach.

View of the former Marta Steelworks on the River Rawa (right), with the Great Synagogue (no longer extant) visible in the distance. Postcard, 1908

R. Hannig). Slightly south of today's Warszawska Street, the Neoclassical railway station building in today's Dworcowa Street entered use in 1859; it was significantly extended between 1906 and 1908. Imposing educational institutions were also built: the Neo-Gothic Royal School of Building Crafts building (1901; arch.: A. Weiss; today: the Academy of Music), the Neoclassical first city grammar school building (1872; arch.: J. Gestewitz; currently: Grammar School No. 8) and the Neo-Gothic second city grammar school building (1900; arch.: M. Grünfeld, J. Perzik; currently: Grammar School No. 1). Important cultural buildings included the Eclectic City Theatre on Market Square (1907; arch.: C. Moritz). An impressive example of the use of the Neo-Gothic style was the Great Synagogue, located in today's Mickiewicza Street (1900; arch.: M. Grünfeld; burnt down in 1939).

1919–1921

In the first years after the end of World War One, Europe was gripped by an economic and construction crisis. In addition, social unrest and the unclear situation before the Silesian plebiscite were not conducive to new investments in this short period of time; investment projects were generally limited to renovation work on neglected residential buildings.

1922–1939

Katowice's incorporation into Poland resulted in intensive measures to set up a properly functioning public administration and in an influx of civil servants and intelligentsia into the city. There was rapid population growth, also due to the incorporation of the neighbouring boroughs of Bogucice, Dęb, Ligota, and Brynów into the city. The authorities of the established Silesian Voivodeship spared no expense in erecting both modern public buildings and housing for the new workers arriving from other parts of the country. They were guided as much by functional needs as by a pro-national cultural narrative. New development plans full of momentum were being drawn up at a rapid pace. Officials and planners saw the area south of the existing railway line as a priority for development and as a suitable place to which to move the functional city centre. At the end of the 1920s the Silesian Parliament Building (1929; archs.: L. Wojtyczko, P. Jurkiewicz, K. Wyczynski), at the time the largest building in Poland, entered use. Built in the historicist Modernist style, this monumental building on Sejmu Śląskiego Square continues to serve its function to this day. Almost simultaneously, a start was made on building Catholic churches, including a cathedral, also in the spirit of classicising Modernism (completed in 1955; archs.: Z. Gawlik and F. Mączeński), and a Functionalist garrison church in today's Skłodowska-Curie Street (1933; arch.: L. Dietz d'Arma). The turn of the 1920s and 1930s was also marked by experiments with the use of steel construction, providing opportunities to increase the height of the buildings. These were so successful that steel-framed buildings began to be constructed in Katowice. The most interesting examples include: the eight-storey Professors' House of the Silesian Technical Scientific School at the corner of today's Wojewódzka and Kobylińskiego streets (1932; arch.: E. Chmielewski); the commercial and residential building of the tax office, popularly known as 'the Skyscraper' because of the record-breaking height (60 metres) of its tallest segment at the time of its construction (1934; arch.: T. Kozłowski); and a Functionalist private villa in Bratków Street (1931; arch.: T. Michejda). The 1930s abounded in construction of luxurious apartment houses, interesting examples of which can be seen in the area of PCK, Rymera, Jordana, and Skłodowskiej-Curie streets. Renowned architects, such as Karol Schayer (6 ul. PCK, 24 Dąbrowskiego, 60 al. Korfantego), were often employed to design them. Schayer was the author of the ultra-modern Silesian Museum building, whose vast scale gave it a national as opposed to merely local importance. Its construction began in 1936 and immediately aroused great interest both because of its design (it was the largest steel-framed building in the country) and its interior layout, which broke with the traditional concept of museum space. The use of a photocell-activated escalator and air-conditioned rooms also stirred excitement. Unfortunately, the opening ceremony, scheduled for 1940, did not take place due to the outbreak of World War Two and the country's occupation by the Nazis.

1939–1945

When the German army entered the city, many buildings were devastated, including the Great Synagogue, which was set on fire. When Katowice was incorporated into the Third Reich, it became the seat of the administration of the German province of Upper Silesia. The new authorities not only rejected the realisation or completion of building projects that had been commenced but actually caused their destruction. Such was the fate of the modern, as yet unfinished Silesian Museum building: it was completely demolished between 1941 and 1944 (only the residential wing of the complex was left standing; its current address is 5 Kobylińskiego Street). The occupiers carried out actions aimed at obliterating all traces of Polish culture. The monuments to the Silesian insurgents were demolished, and façade details, including the Polish eagle, were removed from the Silesian Parliament building.

1945–1989

After the Soviet army entered Katowice and a provisional government was established, the city officially became the capital of the Silesian Voivodeship again. With the advent of the People's Republic of Poland, the central authorities prioritised Katowice's demographic and spatial development as an important industrial centre. As early as 1946, directions for the redevelopment and expansion of the central areas were outlined. By the beginning of the 1960s, several urban planning and architectural competitions had been held to select proposals for redevelopment of the city centre: programmatic principles and aesthetics were changing; in the first half of the 1950s Socialist Realism had been the ruling style (about which more in the next section). Eventually, a concept of developing the city centre northwards relative to the historical Market Square took shape. This was implemented by the end of the 1970s. At the same time, new residential districts and housing estates, such as Koszutka, Osiedle Tysiąclecia, and Osiedle Paderewskiego, were built around

The hoist tower of the Warszawa shaft of the former Katowice Coal Mine,
now part of the Silesian Museum

iStockphoto (ewg3D)

the city centre. Subsequently, the 1980s brought a gradual economic slowdown and a decreasing number of large-scale state investment projects. Individual buildings from 1945–1989 are described in this guide and are therefore not cited in this brief overview.

1990–2025

The end of communism in Poland and the transition period brought significant changes in terms of new investments, design guidelines, working conditions for architects, and construction and the quality of its execution. Private companies and clients accounted for an increasing share of the procurement market for design services, leading to an increase in the number of emerging private architecture studios. Investments ceased to be centrally managed; the role of investors was taken over by local governments. The exchange of experience and increasing access to technology and modern building materials allowed architects to propose increasingly daring designs that were in line with global trends. The breakthrough year was 2004, when Poland joined the European Union. Increased cooperation between the countries of the European community fostered steady improvement in the competence of Polish architects. EU funds played a huge role in spatial development and increased the number of prestigious projects implemented throughout the country. In Katowice a good example of use of such funds is the Culture Zone.

National Digital Archives (NAC)

Silesian Museum building under construction, 1939

Silesian Digital Library

Silesian Museum building being demolished, 1942

Architecture and Planning During the Communist Period in Poland

In view of the time frame adopted in this guide, it seems necessary to introduce the reader to the characteristics and conditions affecting architecture and urban planning during the historical period of the People's Polish Republic (1945–1989). The working conditions for architects and planners until the country's political transformation in 1989 and the advent of the free market economy were significantly different from those we know today. After World War Two the economy and other areas of the state came under central control. Architects had the opportunity to work professionally within state institutions, which over time began to specialise in the services they provided. In the province of Silesia the first state planning institution was Miastoprojekt, which started operating in Katowice in 1948. Over the years other planning institutions were established: Inwestprojekt specialised in residential construction projects, and other planning offices were also established to create projects for the needs of various industries, including Biprohut, Bipromet, and Energoprojekt. Until the 1980s private design offices were basically non-existent.

Pracownia Projektów Budownictwa Ogólnego (PPBO) in Katowice, run by the architects Henryk Buszko and Aleksander Franta, was an exception. PPBO was a hybrid of a studio structured similarly to a state design office and a design studio run by a strong creative hand. This guidebook describes how PPBO carried out a dozen interesting realisations of projects in the late 1960s and early 1970s.

If we are to characterise the architecture of the communist period in Poland, we may divide it into different temporal stages. In each of these stages architectural creativity took a different form.

1945–1949

In the years immediately following the end of World War Two, the focus in the devastated part of the country was on clearing the rubble, cleaning up, and, where possible, rebuilding partially damaged buildings. Intensive work was also carried out aimed at reconstructing buildings of symbolic significance (such as the Royal Castle in Warsaw) destroyed by the occupiers. There was huge

Central Department Store in Warsaw (1948–1951) in the 1960s

demand for local housing. The new buildings were, in architectural terms, a continuation of the Modernist trend which had been interrupted in 1939. Examples of buildings from this period are the Central Department Store (1948–1951; archs.: Z. Ihnatowicz, J. Romański) and the headquarters of the Supreme Supervisory Chamber (1946–1949; archs.: M. Leykam, J. Hryniewiecki) in Warsaw and the Okrąglak Department Store in Poznań (1948–1954; arch.: M. Leykam). An interesting example of a housing estate from this period is Koło II in Warsaw (1947–1951; archs.: H. and S. Syrkus). This state of affairs persisted until June 1949, when the Conference of Party Architects in Warsaw proclaimed a new aesthetic in architecture and art: Socialist Realism.

1949–1956

The condemnation of all manifestations of the Avant-garde in architecture, including Constructivism and Functionalism, was linked to the intensification of the political regime (Stalinism). The idea of Socialist Realism originated in the Soviet Union and involved promoting national values by drawing, in architectural composition and aesthetics, upon historical, usually Classical, models. Under this doctrine architecture was to be accessible to all citizens, including the working class. Architects were required to embody these postulates by proposing monumental, often axially (symmetrically) composed edifices finished with details, sculptures and, in many cases, wall paintings in the style of Socialist Realism. Examples of buildings characteristic of this period include the Palace of Culture and Science in Warsaw (1952–1955; arch.: L. Rudniew), the Palace of Zagłębie Culture in Dąbrowa Górnicza (1851–1958; arch.: Z. Rzepecki), Marszałkowska housing estate in Warsaw (1950–1952; archs.: J. Sigalin, S. Jankowski), Nowa Huta residential district in Cracow (1949–1955; arch.: T. Ptaszycki), and the A housing estate in Tychy (1951–1953; arch.: T.T. Todorowski). The ideas of Socialist Realism remained in force in the country until October 1956, when, following the political 'thaw' and the end of Stalinism, they were officially criticised and condemned as distorted.

Marszałkowska housing estate in Warsaw (1950–1952), 1952

Kino Kijów and Hotel Cracovia in Cracow (1959–1965); photograph from the 1960s

1957–1969

The break with the Socialist Realist style resulted in an enthusiastic return to Modernism and the Avant-garde. Architects immediately took advantage of the opportunity in their creative work to return to drawing on the latest technical knowledge and modern artistic forms and effects. The rapidly increasing number of architectural competitions and commissions within state design bureaus fostered the creation of high-class public and residential buildings, which, from the perspective given by passing time, have become known as icons of Polish post-war Modernism. The mid-1960s saw the development of large-scale residential construction, which was linked to the implementation of prefabrication technology. This period brought icons of late Modernist architecture, such as the Jubilat department store in Kraków (1959–1969; arch.:

J. Saniecka), Zenit department store in Katowice (1959–1962; archs.: M. Król, J. Jarecki), Supersam department store in Warsaw (1962; archs.: J. Hryniewiecki, M. Krasińki), the rotunda of Panorama Racławicka in Wrocław (1961–1966; archs.: E. and M. Dziekoński), Spodek Arena in Katowice (1964–1971; archs.: M. Gintowt, M. Krasinski), Hotel Cracovia in Cracow (1959–1965; arch.: W. Cęckiewicz), Hotel Harnaś in Bukowina Tatrzańska (1966–1969; archs.: L. Filar, P. Gawor, J. Pilitowski), the Zawodzie sanatorium district in Ustroń (1966–1988; archs.: H. Buszko, A. Franta), the Sady Żoliborskie housing estate in Warsaw (1959–1964; arch.: H. Skibniewska), a residential and commercial complex on Grunwaldzki Square, and the so-called 'Manhattan' residential complex in Wroclaw (1967–1970; arch.: J. Grabowska-Hawrylak).

1970–1980

Edward Gierek's appointment as first secretary of the PZPR Central Committee in 1970 made him the country's most important decision-maker. The 1970s are often referred to as the 'Gierek decade' and in the popular consciousness evoke positive associations related to the opening up of the country and its economy to the West and cooperation with countries outside the so-called 'Eastern Bloc'. The construction sector grew as materials and technologies were imported: this decade saw the construction of prestigious cultural, sports, and infrastructure facilities but also numerous religious buildings, which continued into the 1980s. Examples of buildings constructed during the Gierek decade include the passenger terminal at Warsaw-Okêcie Airport (1973–1975; archs.: J. and K. Dobrowolscy), the Central Station building in Warsaw (1972–1975; archs.: A. Romanowicz, P. Szymaniak), the bus station in Kielce (1975–1984; arch.: E. Modrzejewski), the LIM office and hotel skyscraper in Warsaw (1977–1989; arch.: J. Skrzypczak; now: the Marriott Hotel), and the opera house in Bydgoszcz (1973–2006; archs.: J. Chmiel, A. Prusiewicz).

1981–1989

As the country took on more foreign debt, the end of the 1970s brought growing social discontent and the beginning of a crisis in the economy and in construction. In the 1980s many of the ambitious intentions that stemmed from the previous decade of success were either postponed or completed in truncated form. The way in which architects worked also began to change: state planning offices ceased to be the only possible workplace, as the authorities began to allow the establishment of private design practices. This gradual decentralisation resulted in increased creative freedom for architects: the younger generation especially began to abandon the design forms of late Modernism in favour of the aesthetics of Postmodernism, which they had observed in their Western neighbours. The fruits of this period are buildings such as the Higher Theological Seminary in Cracow (1983–1996; archs.: D. Kozłowski, M. Misiągiewicz, W. Stefański), the church on the Popowice Estate in Wroclaw (1980–1995; arch.: W. Jarząbek), and Brama Słońca, a residential complex in Tychy (1980–1983; archs.: Z. Łojewski, K. Wejchert).

Central Railway Station in Warsaw (1972–1975); photograph from the late 1970s

Brama Słońca (the Gate of the Sun), a residential building in Tychy (1980–1983); photograph from the mid-1980s

North Katowice: Koszutka District

1

North Katowice: Koszutka District

The history of Koszutka District dates to the seventeenth century, when this was a colony of the nearby village of Bogucice (today a district of Katowice). The first homestead buildings were located on a tributary of the Rawa River, between today's Grażyńskiego and Morcinka streets. Most of the buildings erected at that time were wooden cottages with thatched – or, more rarely, shingled – roofs. The hamlet's noticeable development at the beginning of the nineteenth century was caused by the growth of the mining and metallurgical industry, mainly in the area of Bogucice, Wełnowiec, and Dąb (today these are also districts of Katowice). On the right side of today's Korfantego Avenue there were, among others, two zinc works, Fanny and Franz, which, after a later merger, operated until 1903 before being subsumed into the Marienhof manor complex. The buildings of the complex existed until the early 1960s, on the site of what is today the Spodek sports and entertainment arena. At the turn of the twentieth century, the character of Koszutka's buildings changed significantly: in place of wooden houses, the managers of the industrial plants erected brick multi-family buildings– so-called 'familoki' – for their employees. In 1924 Koszutka, together with the municipality of Bogucice-Zawodzie, was incorporated into Katowice, which, following the plebiscite of 1922, was already Polish. Despite the difficulties caused by numerous sinkholes, development of the western frontage of today's Korfantego Avenue began at the end of the 1920s. Prominent among these developments were rental apartment houses designed by eminent architects such as Karol Schayer and Tadeusz Łobos. The parcelling out of plots for individual housing, mainly on the east side of the district (on today's Topolowa, Klonowa, and Wierzbowa streets) resulted in the development of a villa colony with interesting examples of Functionalist architecture. Such villa buildings can also be seen on Górnika Street.

Spatial development between 1945 and 1989

The political reality of the country after the end of World War Two brought a completely new chapter in the city's spatial

Development plan for Koszutka District for 1949–1952

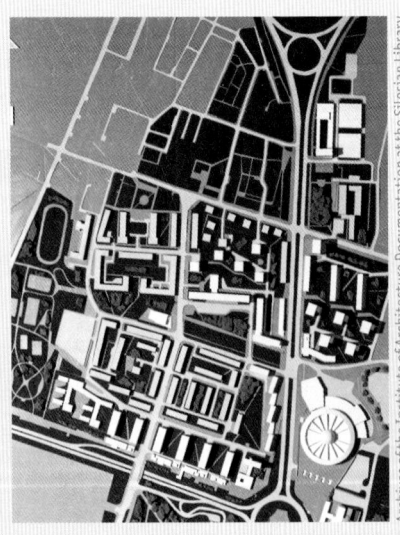

Development plan for Koszutka District for 1960–1962

Archives of the Institute of Architecture Documentation at the Silesian Library

Archives of the Institute of Architecture Documentation at the Silesian Library

history. As a developing industrial and academic centre, Katowice began to rapidly gain new inhabitants attracted by the possibility of employment. As a result, the construction of the city's first post-war housing estate, which gave rise to an inner-city residential district, began in the late 1940s in the area of Koszutka. Its development had two stages. The first comprised the design and construction of the housing estate then called 'J. Marchlewski' between 1948 and 1956. Designed for 20,000 inhabitants, this estate was intended to cover an area of approximately 66 hectares between today's Chorzowska and Słoneczna streets. Based on assumptions consistent with the aesthetics of Socialist Realism, the development was to consist of groups of low-rise (generally 3–4-storey) linear buildings arranged in symmetrical layouts and U-shaped buildings encompassing green courtyards. The decision to opt for low-rise buildings was also based on concerns about what was technologically possible given the sinkholes that occur in Koszutka; these worries were resolved following the completion of the eight-storey Coal Industry Studies and Projects Office building on Grunwaldzki Square (016) in 1955. Approximately 60 per cent of the development was built on the basis of the implementation plan of 1949. The mid-1950s brought a decision to update or amend the district's development plan, a task which was entrusted to Marian Skałkowsky, Stanisław Kwaśniewicz, and Mieczysław Król, who designed many of the later buildings described in this guide. The development of the new plan for the district coincided with the official break with Socialist Realism in Poland in 1956, which allowed architects to return to creating in the Modernist style. This moment marked the beginning of the second stage of the systematic development of Koszutka, which lasted until almost the end of the 1970s. At that time a design was developed for the first tower-type building in Upper Silesia. The design was replicated five times in the area between today's Sokolska, Misjonarzy Oblatów, and Aleja Korfantego streets (006). Construction of this complex marked the beginning of other developments of this type not

Model of development of Koszutka
District, 1962

only in Katowice but also in other cities in the province. Almost simultaneously, a start was made on construction of another innovative residential building in the district: an 11-storey residential complex with a gallery-corridor layout (015). This not only closed off the east front of Grunwaldzki Square, but was also intended to serve as a distinctive, imposing landmark at the entrance to Koszutka District. On the east side of Korfantego Avenue, meanwhile, another complex was under construction for almost a decade: five 13-storey residential tower blocks (014) were completed at the beginning of the 1970s. In addition to residential buildings grouped into urban complexes, Koszutka also contained interesting one-off buildings designed individually as supplementary (008 and 009). At the beginning of the 1980s an architectural competition was held to design an experimental residential complex in the area around Owocowa and Jesionowa streets. This complex was also intended to function as a residential exhibition (called 'EXPO-DOMKAT'), but the systemic changes affecting the country at the end of the decade prevented the realisation of anything but the first stage of this neighbourhood development (011).

It is estimated that in the late 1960s and early 1970s Koszutka District had a population of approximately 15,000. Educational and sports facilities, as well as recreational and cultural facilities, were important additions to its functional programme. In 1962 a modern school complex (002) opened in the vicinity of the Blue Blocks complex. The first example in the country's history of a school with a pavilion-like configuration, this made a stark contrast with the compact buildings erected hitherto not only in Koszutka but also in Katowice in general. Nearby, on the opposite side of today's Grażyńskiego Street, a district house of culture was erected; this likewise consisted of interconnecting low pavilions (003). The construction of the glazed Kosmos Cinema building, which has since been rebuilt, added a distinctive structure closing off the green Grunwaldzki Square from the west side (017). A very important landmark for the city in terms of composition and image is the Spodek sports and entertainment hall (021), whose rounded body presents excellent views when seen both from the north section of Korfantego Avenue and the roundabout. Headquarters of state institutions and research institutes have also been incorporated in Koszutka's

An example of a Functionalist 1930s villa on Wierzbowa Street

Family, a monument from 1963 by J. E. Kwiatkowski, Grunwaldzki Square

development structure. In addition to the aforementioned building of the Coal Industry Studies and Projects Office at Grunwaldzki Square, it is worth mentioning the single-storey atrium pavilion of the PPBO (General Building Design Office) on the corner of Sokolska and Misjonarzy Oblatów streets (007). The same studio, headed by the architects Henryk Buszko and Aleksander Franta, has designed many buildings that are now considered icons of post-war Modernism in the Silesian Province. In the north part of the district, on the east side of Korfantego Avenue, are the seats of two important research centres: the buildings and halls of the Central Mining Institute and, located behind the Słoneczna Loop, the ZETO Electronic Computing Technology Plant, designed in the first half of the 1960s (010).

Spatial development between 1990 and 2025

The three decades that have elapsed since the country's political transformation have not resulted in significant new urban developments in this district. The end of the 1990s and the beginning of the 2000s brought reconstructions and modernisations that changed the original appearance of some communist-era buildings, including buildings that before the changes had constituted valuable testimony to design skills and technological capabilities. In the years 1993–1994 the pavilion of Elegancja Fashion House (020) was completely rebuilt in order to house a new bank headquarters, as was the former commercial pavilion of the Radio and Television Services Company at what is now 56 Korfantego Avenue. The iconic Kosmos Cinema (017) also underwent controversial reconstruction in the years 2004–2006; the designer of the reconstruction project was awarded the Concrete Cube anti-award. A large proportion of the residential buildings underwent thermo-modernisation, which in many cases resulted in changes to the original colour scheme or the covering up of finishing details.

In 2021 construction of a complex of six residential buildings began on the north side of the Solar Loop. One of these buildings, a 36-storey structure designed by HRA Architekci on the axis of Korfantego Avenue, will be the district's new focus and salient feature. The remaining buildings will be 15 storeys high. Construction work is scheduled for completion in 2026.

View from Korfantego Avenue, next to Grunwaldzki Square, of Spodek Arena and later high-rise buildings

View from Korfantego Avenue of a late 1950s residential tower block and a 1990s commercial pavilion

'Blue Blocks', residential complex with commercial pavilions

001 B

ul. Grażyńskiego 7–13
Stanisław Kwaśniewicz
1958–1963

rchives of The Institute of Architecture Documentation at the Silesian Library

Blue Blocks owes its name to its original colour scheme, which, combined with the triangular balcony motif and sail-like railings, gave this eight-storey complex a strong whiff of the avant-garde at the time of its construction. The buildings have since undergone a change in colour palette, and the only remaining blue elements are the balcony railings. The complex consists of six buildings. Due to category-4 mining damage, each building has been divided into three segments connected by two glazed expansion joints illuminating the internal staircases. This

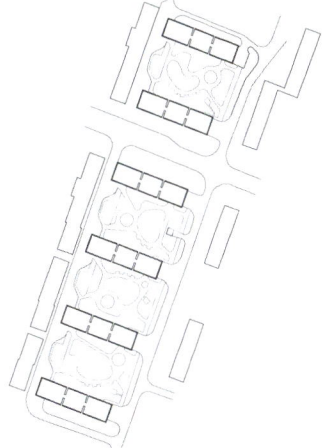

Małgorzata Malanowicz

solution was adopted as a prototype for linear buildings, recommended for use in areas prone to mining damage. Each of the standard floors contains 12 two- and three-room apartments, ranging in size from 33 to 64 square metres. Each apartment has a separate, well-lit kitchen. In 1965 a row of multi-storey commercial and service pavilions designed by Jurand Jarecki was added between the residential buildings and Chorzowska Street. These pavilions stood out thanks to elaborate typography in the form of colourful neon signs.

rchives of The Institute of Architecture Documentation at the Silesian Library

School complex

ul. Grażyńskiego 17
Stanisław Kwaśniewicz
1958–1962

002 **B**

This school complex is situated between today's Grażyńskiego and Chorzowska streets, in the vicinity of the Blue Blocks residential buildings (001). Originally comprising both a primary school and a high school, the campus featured shared recreational and sports facilities. Its groundbreaking architectural design created a stark contrast with the solid structures of the neighbouring residential complexes in Koszutka District. The school complex was envisioned as an arrangement of intimate two-storey pavilions connected by segments containing corridors and sanitary facilities. Each pavilion has a distinctive arrangement of windows, with large aluminium windows on the first floor. The main building facing Grażyńskiego Street is extended by a connecting structure accommodating locker rooms, a common room, a library, administrative offices, and an auditorium. The campus' pavilion-type layout represented a pioneering approach to school building design in Poland. However, over time, the buildings' original textures and colour palette have been obscured beneath insulation and plaster, to the detriment of the complex's initial aesthetic charm.

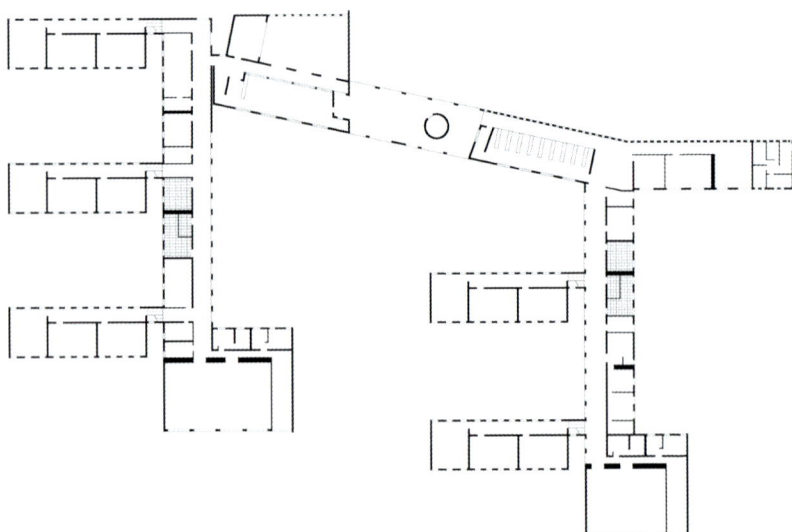

1

Koszutka District Community Centre

003 B

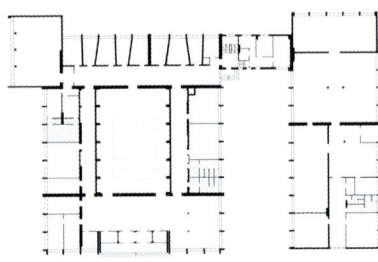

ul. Grażyńskiego 47
Wacław Lipiński
(Miastoprojekt – Katowice)
1965–1969

Located between Grażyńskiego Street and Alojzy Budniok Park, this building essentially consists of two single-storey rectangular sections. The first, notably more expansive, section houses a concert hall with facilities and administrative spaces; the ceiling above the concert hall is elevated. The second segment contains a library with a reading room. The two parts are connected on the north side by a narrow link containing technical and utility rooms. A green, longitudinal atrium is located between the library and the concert hall. The selection of textures and finishing materials used for the façade is noteworthy. Stone cladding, reminiscent of brickwork in its proportions, is embedded in exposed reinforced-concrete frames. An intriguing feature is the roofing design for the entrance areas of both sections, which takes the form of zigzag-shaped reinforced-concrete canopies.

Residential complex

ul. Sokolska 68–74,
ul. Okrzei 2–6
M. Szymanowski,
Zofia Garlińska-Hansen
1952–1954

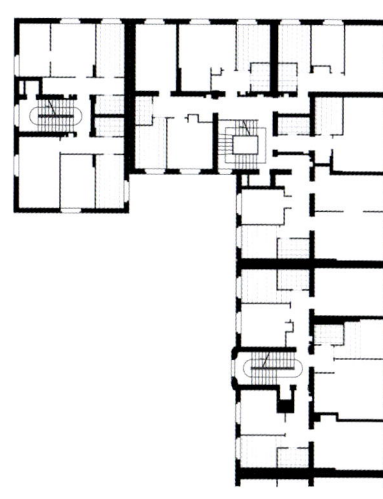

Located between Sokolska, Okrzei, and Dunikowskiego streets and abutting Gustaw Holoubek Square from the south, this residential complex was designed by the State Urban Construction Design Office in Warsaw. Symmetrically composed about the north-south axis, its plan takes the form of two Ls and a straight section. Due to the fact that the terrain slopes towards the south, the number of residential floors varies from five to seven. The apartments have from one to three rooms, separate kitchens, and floor areas of between 32 and 68 square metres. An interesting feature is the mixed communication system: as well as from internal staircases, some apartments are accessible from external galleries overlooking the courtyard and located above arcaded walkways. On the Sokolska Street side, ground-floor spaces were designated for commercial use. The seven-storey building on Okrzei Street originally contained a kindergarten with a fenced garden on the south side. This complex is a good example of a housing estate that embodies the architectural principles of Socialist Realism, especially in terms of its urban layout and exterior detailing.

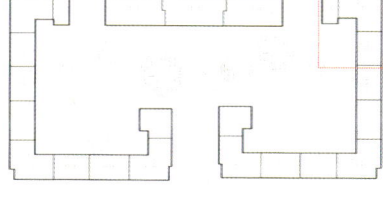

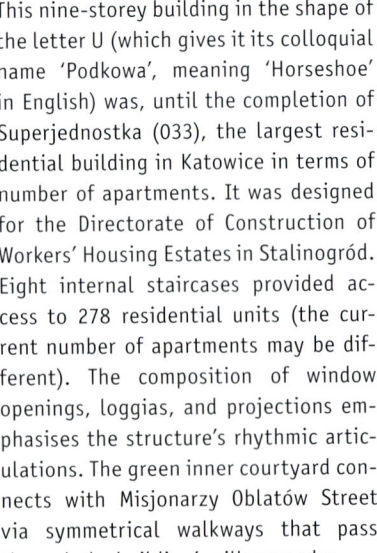

'Podkowa', residential building 005 B

ul. Okrzei 1–15
Włodzimierz Łubkowski
1955–1958

This nine-storey building in the shape of the letter U (which gives it its colloquial name 'Podkowa', meaning 'Horseshoe' in English) was, until the completion of Superjednostka (033), the largest residential building in Katowice in terms of number of apartments. It was designed for the Directorate of Construction of Workers' Housing Estates in Stalinogród. Eight internal staircases provided access to 278 residential units (the current number of apartments may be different). The composition of window openings, loggias, and projections emphasises the structure's rhythmic articulations. The green inner courtyard connects with Misjonarzy Oblatów Street via symmetrical walkways that pass through the building's pillar arcades.

Residential complex of tower blocks ↓ → 006 B

ul. Sokolska 61,
ul. Broniewskiego 1, 1A, 1B, 3
Mieczysław Król
1956–1960

Innovative not only for the district but also for the entire region, this complex of five residential tower blocks breaks with the aesthetics of Socialist Realism. The tower blocks were designed under a plan developed at the turn of 1955 and 1956. Setting new directions for the district's development and co-authored by

Mieczysław Król, the project envisaged replacing linear, low-rise buildings with loose arrangements of compact and taller buildings. The first of the complex's completed tower blocks (and at the same time the first of its kind in Silesia) received numerous awards and distinctions. These were justified not only by the towers' utilitarian and aesthetic qualities but also by their construction: their simple volumes with no projecting parts made them suitable for areas at risk of mining damage. Their design was held up by the then authorities of the Katowice Voivodship as a prototype solution, and many other buildings in Katowice and neighbouring cities were later realised on its basis. Each building has ten storeys, the topmost of which was originally intended as a laundry and drying room with a terrace. There are three types of apartment: one-room with a kitchenette and a floor area of 21 square metres, one-room with a separate kitchen and a floor area of 37 square metres, and two-room with a separate kitchen and a floor area of 54 square metres.

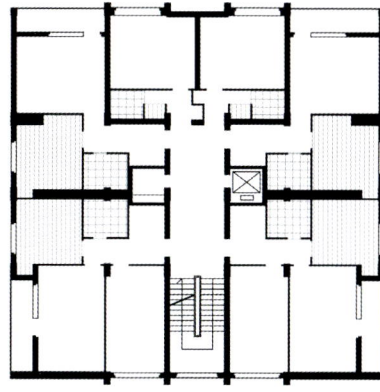

Former PPBO design office pavilion

007 B

ul. Misjonarzy Oblatów 19
Henryk Buszko, Aleksander Franta
1959–1960
MUS Architekci
2021–2022 (redevelopment)

On the west side of the intersection of Sokolska and Misjonarzy Oblatów streets is a one-storey building with a square plan. Today it no longer has the original finishing materials (including light silicate brick) designed by architects Henryk Buszko and Aleksander Franta in the late 1950s and early 1960s for their architectural studio PPBO (the General Building Design Office). It was here that they and their team developed several hundred designs for buildings, many of which are now considered icons of Polish post-war Modernist architecture, including the 'star' and 'corncob' building types , the Tysiąclecia Housing Estate in Katowice, the pyramid-shaped centres at Ustroń-Zawodzie sanatorium, and buildings in Silesian Park. All this building's rooms are arranged around a square, glazed atrium, which served as a resting place for the workers during breaks from work. Combined with the building's large exterior windows, this guaranteed two-way illumination for each part of the studio. The atrium contained a small fountain and an area of greenery. The modern, minimalist interior design was complemented by functional solutions, including electrical sockets built into the floor. The converted building now houses a private legal services firm.

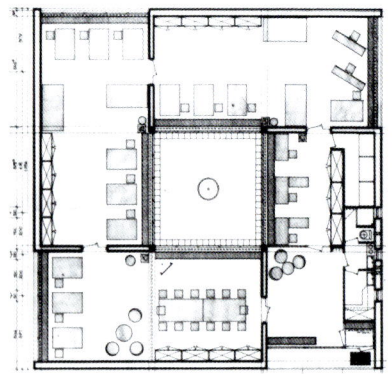

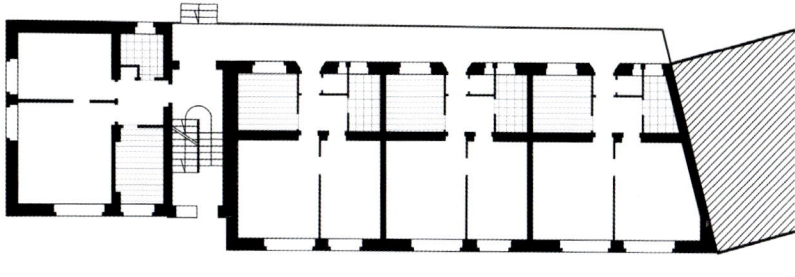

Katowice City Hall archives,
prepared by Marek Pęczak

Residential building

ul. Misjonarzy Oblatów 2
Tadeusz Łobos
1948–1949

This three-storey building is one of the first residential structures erected after World War Two in Koszutka District. It was built in the style of post-war Functionalism for the employees of the National Bank of Poland on a plot adjacent to a corner building from the 1930s. There are four two-room apartments with well-lit kitchens and floor areas of 44 square metres on each floor. One is accessible from the internal staircase, while the other three are accessed from an open gallery overlooking the courtyard. On Broniewskiego Street, to the north of this building, are five identical residential buildings completed in 1949. Together with the house on Misjonarzy Oblatów, they constitute the National Bank of Poland residential complex designed by Tadeusz Łobos.

Infill residential building

al. Korfantego 62–64
Jurand Jarecki
1958–1960

This five-storey residential building was designed in 1958 for the Directorate for the Construction of Workers' Housing in Katowice. The project posed a unique challenge, said its author, Jurand Jarecki, due to its location next to a multi-family house designed by Karol Schayer in 1937 – a notable example of Katowice's Functionalist architecture. To add complexity to the straightforward, box-like structure of the new building, Jarecki introduced a dynamic rhythm by incorporating obliquely slanted loggias and balustrades. Following the occurrence of mining damage, the building was divided into two segments, each with a staircase providing access to two apartments per floor. All the residential

units are three-room apartments with a floor area of 55 square metres, a separate kitchen, and a dining nook equipped with a window. The ground floor of the building has three spacious services and workshop rooms. The attic accommodates a laundry room with a drying area, while the basement contains an emergency shelter.

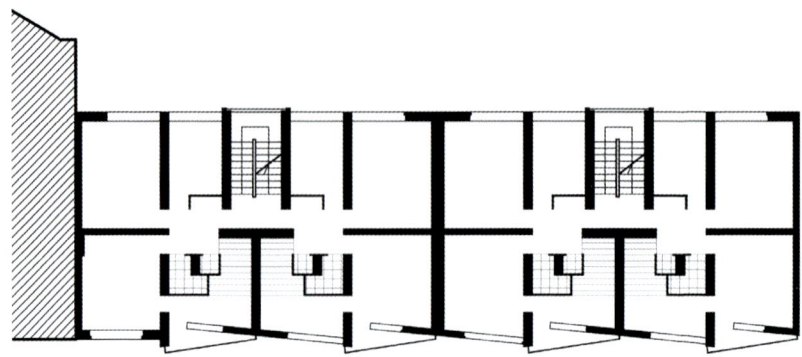

Department of Electronic Computing Technology (ZETO) headquarters

010 B

ul. Owocowa 1
Henryk Buszko, Aleksander Franta (PPBO)
1967–1969

The Department of Electronic Computing Technology (ZETO), a state-owned information technology enterprise, had branches in the country's largest cities. The commission to design the headquarters building on Owocowa Street was given to the PPBO architecture office. The complex consists of four pavilions connected by a communication segment and a recreational terrace. The four-storey pavilions originally housed office spaces, a conference hall, and a library. The computer room was located in a two-storey pavilion adjoining the others on the north side. Between it and the upper hall of the office section was a recreational terrace, which was accessible from the adjoining relaxation room, which was connected to the library with a reading room. Sanitary facilities were located near the staircase. The basement contained utility rooms, a garage for three cars, and a generator supplying power for the computing machines. The façade composition is cohesive, featuring large aluminium windows with geometric divisions in a black-and-white colour scheme. On the neighbouring parcel to the north is the Statistical Office building, also designed at more or less the same time by Henryk Buszko and Aleksander Franta. The two buildings form an aesthetically harmonious ensemble.

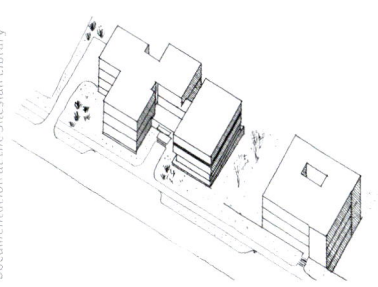

Archives of the Institute of Architecture Documentation at the Silesian Library

Archives of the Institute of Architecture Documentation at the Silesian Library

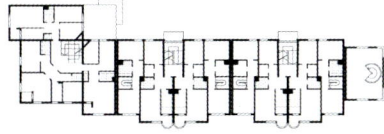

EXPO-DOMKAT, experimental residential complex

011 B

ul. Owocowa 4a,
ul. Jesionowa 10–14
Jan Pallado, Aleksander Skupin
1984–1991

Opposite the ZETO building (010), at the junction of Owocowa and Jesionowa streets, is an interesting housing complex that is part of a much larger, not fully realised, project called 'Experimental residential complex EXPO-DOMKAT'. This model housing complex was to be made up of various buildings, the design concepts for which had been commended and received awards in a nationwide competition. A different team of architects was to be responsible for each stage of the complex's construction. The only realised part of the complex, commissioned by the Central Mining Institute in Katowice, consists of three segments housing 34 flats with different layouts. The middle segment has two-storey flats with independent entrances from the street and separate gardens. The ground floor of the outermost segment facing Owocowa Street additionally housed two commercial premises. The complex's footprint and finishes make a clear break with the Modernist aesthetic of the 1960s and 1970s. The onlooker's eye is drawn to the design of the balconies and loggias and the presence of bay windows covered with pitched roofs or gables. The exterior walls are clad in grey clinker bricks, broken up with bricks of a brown or yellow colour. The elaborate canopies over the staircase entrances on the public side of the courtyard are also notable.

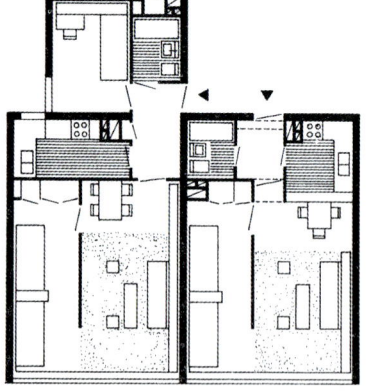

Experimental residential building

012 B

al. Wojciecha Korfantego 65
Józef Miksa, Stanisław Makomaski, Juliusz Szczurkowski
1963–1965

An important event in the context of the region's housing history was the construction of an 18-storey residential building at the intersection of W. Korfantego Avenue and Katowicka Street. Built for employees of the Staszic Coal Mine, it was the first building in the region to utilise innovative sliding formwork technology. While the design of the sliding formwork used in Katowice was based on architectural solutions devised for a prototype sliding-formwork building in Warsaw, the architects improved the process by which the floors were constructed, assembling them simultaneously with the pouring of the monolithic walls. The building has 173 two- and three-room apartments, served by three elevators and an enclosed staircase located in a central communication core. This construction

Archives of the Institute of Architecture

method allowed very rapid construction, with one floor being completed per day. The façade rhythm is characterised by strips of glazing and irregularly spaced loggias. The cost-effectiveness of construction and the swift pace of work contributed to this project's success. In the 1960s a start was made on constructing an almost identical building in the centre of Sosnowiec.

'Houses with Noses', residential complex

ul. Ordona 10–16
Mieczysław Król
1961–1964

This complex consists of two elongated eight-storey buildings situated in the second and third lines of development to the east of Korfantego Avenue. Each building is divided into four sections. In each section a staircase and an elevator provide access to four two-room apartments on each floor. The south section deviates from this pattern. Longer than the other sections, it accommodates two two-room apartments and two three-room apartments with south-facing loggias on each floor. On the buildings' ground floors are garages and entrances to utilities infrastructure. The buildings' elevations are enriched by distinctive trapezoid, reinforced-concrete balconies that taper on the outer side. These balconies extend beyond the façade plane to a distance of two metres.

![photograph of residential high-rise buildings behind a curved concrete structure with stairs]

Residential complex of five high-rise buildings

 014 B

ul. Ordona 20–22, 20a–22a,
al. Korfantego 55
Mieczysław Król
1961–1970

To the north of the Spodek (Saucer) complex (021) is a group of five buildings, arranged in two rows of two and three, designed to accommodate approximately 2060 residents. At the time of construction, these were the tallest residential structures in the city; they served as the architectural backdrop for the entertainment and sports arena. Each 13-storey building consists of 132 one-, two-, and three-room apartments, served by two staircases and two elevators. Garages and technical rooms are located on the buildings' ground floors. Due to potential risks associated with mining-related damage, the buildings are set on a foundation slab of reinforced concrete. The construction follows monolithic reinforced-concrete technology. The initial choice of façade colours aimed to visually break up the massive structures by using light-coloured strips to separate the individual floors, thus emphasising horizontality.

'Galeriowiec' residential building

015 B

pl. Grunwaldzki 4
Mieczysław Król
1957–1962

Colloquially known as 'the gallery building', this nine-storey residential building consists of two parts connected at a right angle. The south part, parallel to Morcinka Street, is a sequence of one- and three-room apartments accessed from an external, open, gallery corridor. The lowest floor of this part of the building is given over to glass-fronted commercial spaces with windows facing the pedestrian passage, while the top floor (in the form of a recessed pavilion) houses a laundry with drying rooms. The second part has a central double-loaded corridor with identical, two-room apartments on either side of it. Connecting the two parts of the building is a communication core housing four elevators and a staircase. The choice of the building's size and layout was largely influenced by the desire to create a green forecourt for the existing Coal Studies and Industry Office building (016). A preceding version of the development plan for this district assigned this plot of land to a four-storey residential building. The city's decision-makers accepted Mieczysław Król's proposal to increase the size of the planned structure, freeing up space to create the public space now known as 'Grunwaldzki Square'.

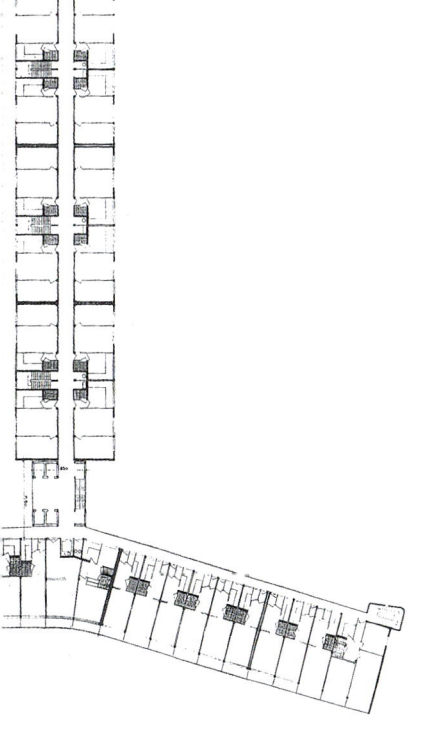

Administration and office building

pl. Grunwaldzki 8–10
Janusz Ballenstedt
1951–1955

016 B

The scale of this building, which measures 145 metres in length and was designed for the needs of the Coal Studies and Industry Office, made it a pioneering structure in Koszutka. Its successful completion alleviated planners' concerns regarding risks of damage due to mining activity and thus became a supporting argument for the subsequent introduction of taller buildings in this district. Housing offices, the main building was originally six-storey with an imposing double-height main entrance hall situated in a monumental columned portico facing Grunwaldzki Square. On the north side, a pavilion housing an auditorium was added in the first half of the 1960s.

Kosmos Cinema

ul. Sokolska 66
Stanisław Kwaśniewicz, Marian Skałkowski, Jurand Jarecki
1959–1963
Jacek Machnikowski
2004–2006 (redevelopment)

The cinema building which currently stands on Sokolska Street with its front elevation facing Grunwaldzki Square has an exterior appearance which has virtually nothing in common with its original façade, which was extremely modern for its time. The first conceptual drawings for the project date to as early as 1956. The idea was to create a building that would both be a spatial counterpart to the compact surrounding development and provide a sense of lightness and transparency to the greenery round about. A two-storey building was created, with the upper storey cantilevered over the ground floor. A neon sign with the cinema's name was placed above the entrance. The fully glazed east (front) elevation fronted the spacious double-height foyer. The distinctive interior owed its character to the artwork of the original staircase and the geometric polychromy created by Zbylut Grzywacz. This was lost when the building underwent major reconstruction. It is worth noting that Kosmos was the first cinema in the city with a screen adapted for showing widescreen films.

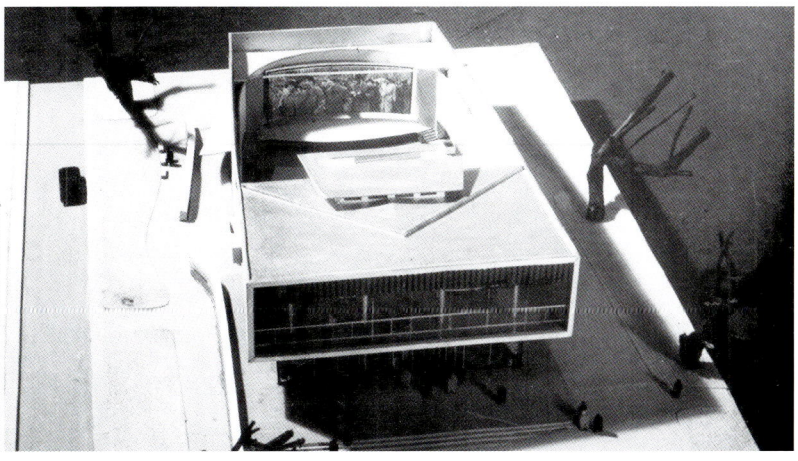

Residential building

018 **B**

ul. Gustawa Morcinka 1–3A
Mieczysław Król
1958–1960

Located on Morcinka Street, this five-storey residential building features distinctive top and bottom floors. The ground floor windows are covered with a layer of evenly spaced louvers providing illumination for the technical rooms, workshops, and adjacent stairwell rooms. Additionally, the ground floor accommodates commercial spaces. The building consists of three identical segments, each served by a stairwell with no elevator. The three-room apartments with separate kitchens have identical layouts and a usable area of 57 square metres. The apartments' balconies are on the south side of the building. The top floor houses a laundry room and drying rooms with access to loggias and small terraces that are partially shielded from the street by walls pierced with distinctive

square openings. Combined with the finishing touches on the ground floor, the north façade provides an aesthetically interesting backdrop to the greenery of Grunwaldzki Square.

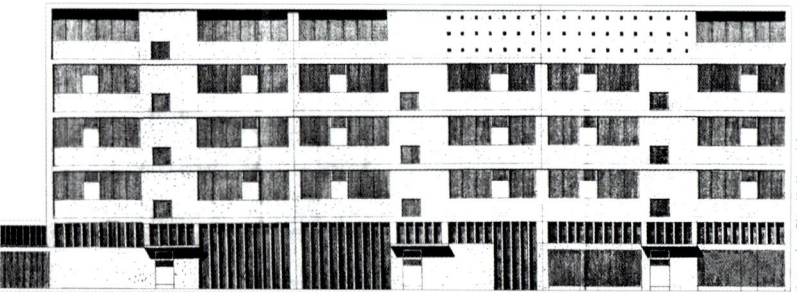

Residential complex with commercial pavilion ↑

019 B

al. Korfantego 34–42
Mieczysław Król
1958–1962

A series of three identical seven-storey residential buildings, each with six apartments per floor. The apartments have two or three rooms and a well-illuminated kitchen. Waste chutes are located in the staircase wells, next to the elevator shafts. Thanks to the way the sanitary-kitchen and ventilation shafts have been laid out, the ground floors are almost entirely free of structures, creating wide passages through to the other side of each building. The south façades are designed as openwork loggias facing the green spaces between the blocks. The three buildings are connected on the side overlooking what is currently Korfantego Avenue by a single-level pavilion containing commercial services, adjoining which is a structure of lightweight steel which serves as a roof for a pedestrian walkway.

Residential building with communication gallery and commercial pavilion ↙ ↓

020 B

ul. Grażyńskiego 5
Marian Skałkowski
1962–1965

This eleven-storey, rectangular building standing right next to General Jerzy Ziętek Roundabout, at the intersection of Korfantego Avenue and Chorzowska Street, was originally designed as a complex consisting of a gallery building linked to a two-storey commercial pavilion containing Elegance fashion house. Today, following comprehensive reconstruction of the pavilion in 1999 for use as a bank, the two sections lack aesthetic cohesion. The gallery building houses exclusively two-room apartments, with windows facing both north and south. The apartments are individually accessible from an external gallery, adjacent to which is a striking, glass-enclosed core housing a staircase and an elevator. At the end of the gallery is a semi-open emergency staircase.

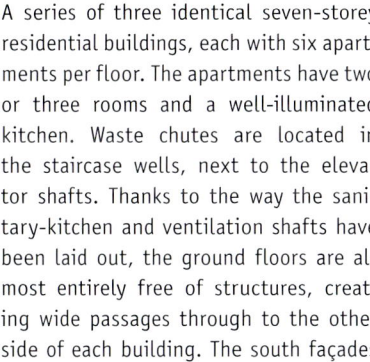

'Spodek' (Saucer) Arena

al. Korfantego 35
Maciej Gintowt, Maciej Krasiński,
Andrzej Żórawski (construction)
1959–1971

021 B

The entertainment hall complex situated at General Jerzy Ziętek Roundabout is one of the most recognisable architectural icons in Katowice and the entire Silesian-Zagłębie region. Its nickname, 'the Saucer', derives from the distinctive shape of the main building, which houses an events and sports arena capable of accommodating up to 11,500 spectators (including 7776 fixed seats and additional seating in retractable and add-on sections). The conceptual design was the victor in a nationwide architectural competition held in 1959. After a multiphase design process, construction commenced in 1965. The building was completed and opened to the public in 1971.

The complex comprises several interconnected structures. Adjacent to the main arena on the north side is a hexagonal structure containing an ice rink with seating for 2500 spectators, accessible via a striking incline. Connected to the ice rink building are, in order: a hotel with a restaurant and a ground-level swimming pool, a sports arena with seating for 500 spectators, and medical facilities. The unique construction of the main building – the arena – is particularly noteworthy. Its hanging roof consists of 120 cable trusses anchored in a concrete ring encircling the stands. The total roof span with no internal support is 126 metres. The roof supports a dome with skylights weighing 360 tons. Due to its impressive parameters and overall architectural expression, this complex garnered significant attention beyond the country's borders even as it was being built.

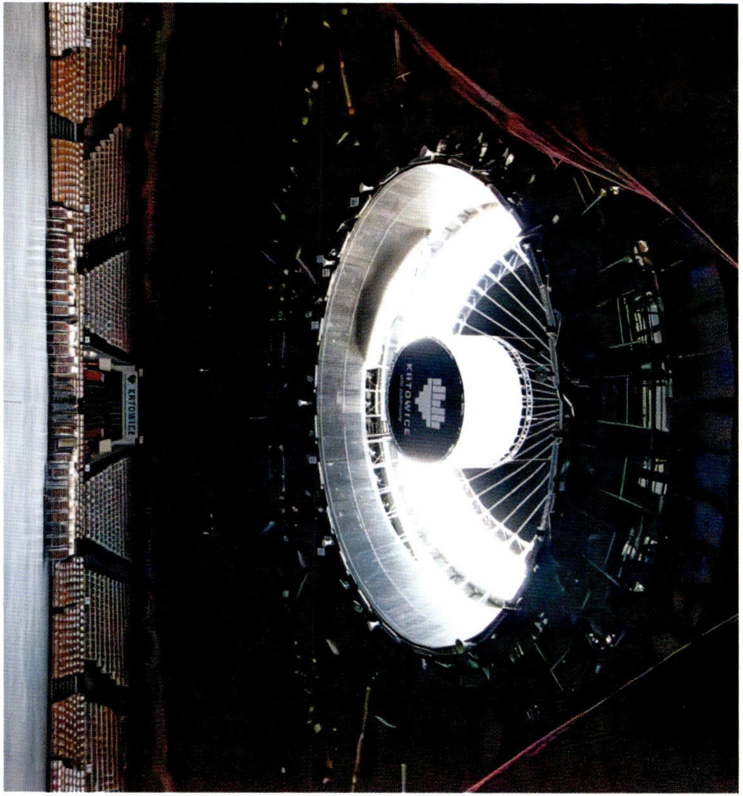

Archives of the Institute of Architecture Documentation at the Silesian Library

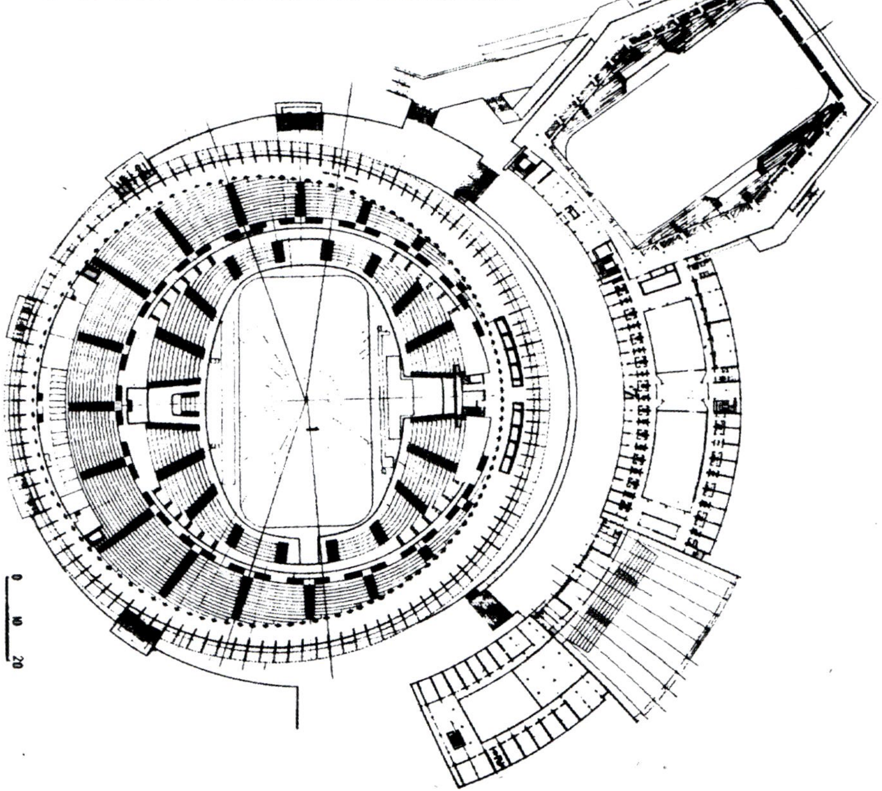

North Katowice:
the Culture Zone

North Katowice: the Culture Zone

The Culture Zone area, which is a contemporary spatial landmark in Katowice, boasts a long industrial history. It has been created as a result of revitalisation of this site and, in part, the infrastructure of Katowice Coal Mine. The mine's history dates to the first half of the nineteenth century: coal deposits were discovered in the vicinity of what is today the downtown of Katowice in 1823. Initially, the mine operated under the name 'Ferdinand' in honour of the Prussian monarch of the time. In the second half of the nineteenth century the mine experienced intensive development. In 1889 a joint-stock company was established, with Hubert von Tiele-Winckler as its main shareholder, to own the mine, which operated from 1922 under the polonised name 'Ferdynand'. The company survived through to the interwar period. In 1936 it changed its name to 'Katowice' and in 1937 became part of the Mining and Metallurgical Interest Community, owned by Polish capital. During occupation by the German Reich, it was incorporated into the Reichswerke Hermann Göring concern under its former name 'Ferdinand'. After World War Two, under the rule of the Polish People's Republic, the mine was nationalised and became part of the state mining and metallurgical combine. The Katowice Mine was one of the most important industrial plants in the region. The political transformation and restructuring of heavy industry led to the gradual closure of many industrial plants. This was also the fate of the Katowice Mine, which finally stopped mining in 1999. The beginning of the twenty-first century brought a lively discussion of the correct

Riegler Riewe Architekten

Model of the Silesian Museum at the time of the architectural competition

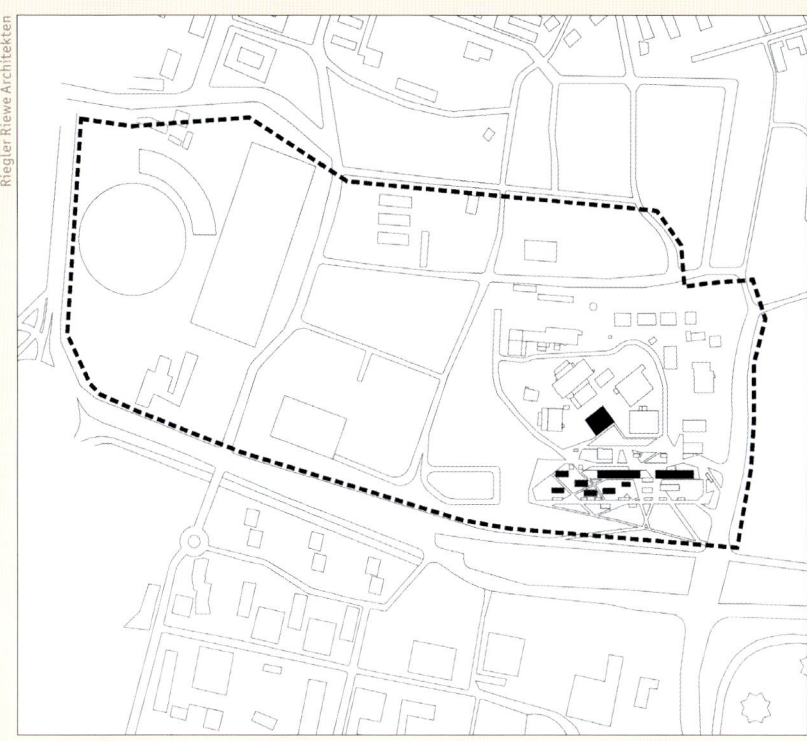

Riegler Riewe Architekten

Development scheme for the Silesian Museum in the context of the Culture Zone, 2007

direction for development of post-mining areas: between 2001 and 2004 a number of conferences of planners, architects, and city officials were held, leading to an outline of a functional concept for the area. This assumed, among other things, the construction of the first of the buildings of the future Culture Zone: the Silesian Museum (024).

Creation of the Culture Zone and its spatial development

Obtaining formal approval of the concept for developing the post-mining areas into a Culture Zone was an initiative of the Regional Operational Programme for 2007–2013, approved by the Board of the Silesian Voivodeship. Among listed projects of supra-local importance was the construction of a new headquarters for the Silesian Museum, along with accompanying facilities with cultural functions. Provision was also made for, among other things, the construction of a large concert hall and an exhibition centre. An important stipulation was the functional and aesthetic coherence of the entire

area. This led to the adoption of a loop pattern for the traffic system of new roads surrounding the new development of the Cultural Zone in 2007. At the same time, the primacy of pedestrians over motorised traffic was manifested in the provision of footbridges to allow pedestrian communication in the most heavily travelled directions. In parallel with construction of the Silesian Museum complex (completed in 2015), two other important buildings were erected: the headquarters of the National Polish Radio Symphony Orchestra (023) and the International Congress Centre (026). These three institutional buildings entered service in 2014 and 2015. At the same time the implementation of the Culture Zone in its original urban scope was completed. A year later, however, two other construction projects started in parallel, initiated on the two edges of the area by KTW, a private investor. These were the office complex on the site of the former DOKP office building (119) and the Pierwsza dzielnica residential complex (025), whose scale led to objections from the then management of the neighbouring Silesian Museum.

KTW office complex

022 D

al. Walentego Roździeńskiego 1
Medusa Group
2016–2022

At the intersection of W. Korfantego and W. Roździeńskiego avenues, overlooking the roundabout and the Culture Zone, stands a complex of two office skyscrapers. This is not the first high-rise structure in this prestigious location: it was built on the site where a 1960s building belonging to the District Directorate of State Railways was purchased by TDJ Estate and demolished in 2015. Designed by a team led by the architects Przemo Łukasik and Łukasz Zagała, the two towers are of different heights. The shorter tower (KTW I) is 66 metres high with 14 above-ground floors. Completed in 2018, it consists of two rectangular prisms stacked and offset from one another. The second tower (KTW II) follows the same principle but is composed of three rectangular volumes with a total height of 133 metres (31 above-ground floors). Both buildings are clad in panels of blue-tinted selective glass, with technical floors concealed by a black tensile-cable mesh. Centrally located reinforced-concrete communication cores house staircases and 6 and 12 high-speed elevators. Below the complex, three underground levels were constructed to accommodate technical rooms and a garage with capacity for 460 cars for use by both towers. When the taller tower was completed in 2022, it was the tallest building in GZM Metropolis (the metropolitan association of 41 contiguous municipalities in the Silesian Voivodeship of Poland).

Headquarters of the National Polish Radio Symphony Orchestra

023 D

pl. Wojciecha Kilara 1
Konior Studio
2008–2014

To the west of the Silesian Museum complex stands another significant structure in the Culture Zone: the headquarters of the National Symphony Orchestra of Polish Radio. The idea behind constructing this new building was associated with the orchestra's local needs: the conditions at its previous location in the building at plac Sejmu Śląskiego 2 (072) were less than optimal. An international architectural competition held in 2008 resulted in selection of a concept designed by architect Tomasz Konior and his team. The rectangular, cuboid structure is part of a spatial layout which constitutes

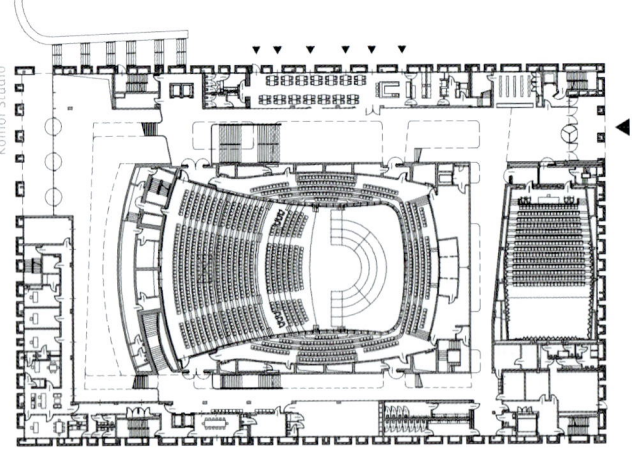

Konior Studio

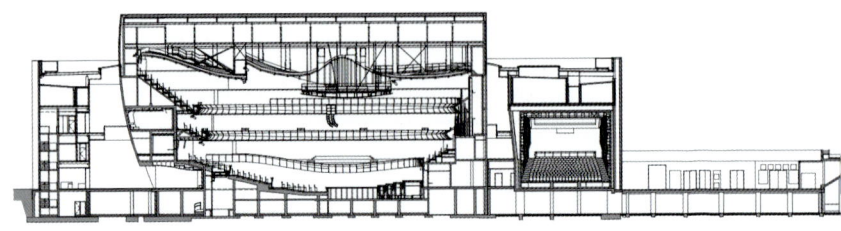

Konior Studio

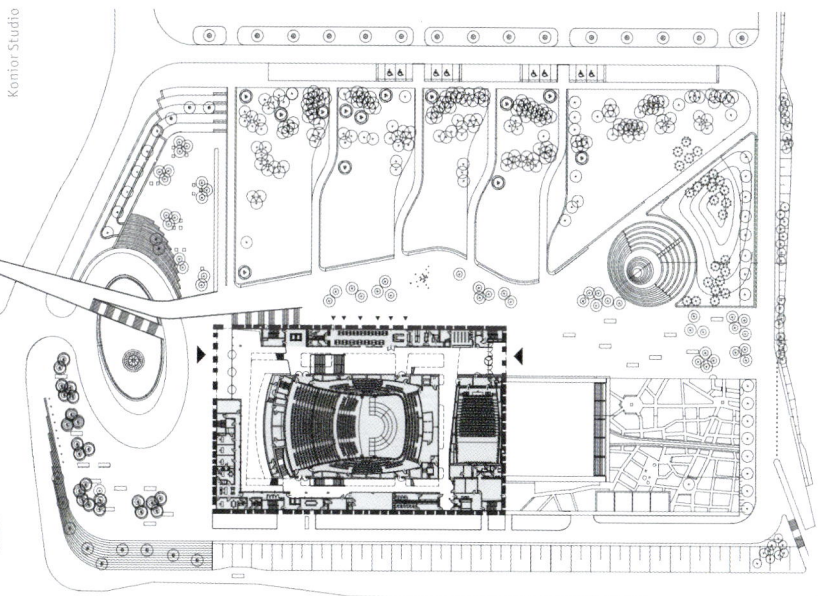

Konior Studio

the central point of the Culture Zone. Carefully selected external elements and thematic zones include musical playgrounds, an open amphitheatre, and a labyrinth based on the urban layout of Katowice. The building is characterised by a rhythmic façade with 80 vertical shafts housing acoustic installations, which simultaneously serve as niches for vertical bands of windows. The colour and texture of the façade bricks are noteworthy: the niches are red and glossy, creating a contrast with the rough brown bricks covering the exterior surfaces of the shafts. The spaces are grouped into three concentric zones. The outer zone houses a set of office spaces, practice rooms, dressing rooms, guest rooms, and a chamber concert hall. The central zone features a spacious foyer with access to the concert hall and two main entrances (east and west) located at different levels. The internal zone comprises a vineyard-style concert hall designed for an audience of 1800. Particularly interesting are the largest organs in the country, installed in the concert hall and completed in 2023. The building's underground part includes a garage with 150 parking spaces for employees and musicians, with access from the technical courtyard, which is lower than the level of the surrounding gardens.

Konior Studio

The new complex of the Silesian Museum

024 D

ul. Tadeusza Dobrowolskiego 1
Riegler Riewe Architekten
2007–2015

The history of the Silesian Museum dates to 1929. Originally located in a Functionalist building designed by Karol Schayer which was demolished during World War Two, the museum has moved twice since its establishment – to an eclectic building at 3 W. Korfantego Avenue and now to this new complex in the Culture Zone. The current incarnation consists of several interconnected structures with underground levels in the revitalised grounds of the former Katowice Mine. Its design, developed by an Austrian architectural studio, emerged as the winner of an international design competition held in 2007. Eight glass-clad, cuboid structures are strategically arranged to harmonise with existing historical buildings belonging to the mine. The above-ground levels house an entrance hall with a café, as well as administrative and office spaces. These levels are built over an underground portion containing exhibition spaces with a floor area of approximately 6000 square metres, conference rooms, a 320-seat auditorium, collection warehouses, a library, and a museum shop. The three lowest levels contain underground parking with 232 parking spaces. The complex's programme also includes two post-mining buildings (with plans for adapting others of the 16 preserved buildings). These house a restaurant and museum workshops. An essential element of the ensemble is the restored tower of the former Warszawa Mine shaft, which, following the addition of an elevator, has become a fully accessible observation tower. The carefully designed landscaping, including greenery, pathways, and street furniture, integrates the components of the new Silesian Museum Complex.

Riegler Riewe Architekten

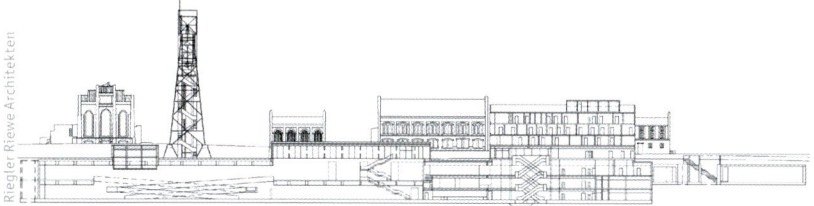

Residential complex

025 D

ul. Henryka Mikołaja Góreckiego
11–15
Medusa Group
2016–

Abutting the Culture Zone to the north and located between Góreckiego and Dobrowolskiego streets, a residential complex is being developed by TDJ Estate on disused post-industrial land.

The complex will consist of nine square, tower-like buildings of two types. On the front line of development on Góreckiego Street there will be three 12-storey structures, linked to one another by a roof at ground-floor level. Behind them, six buildings of the second type, with 17 above-ground floors, will stand in a scattered formation. At the time of writing this guide, five buildings have been completed: three of the shorter type and two

of the taller type. The 12-storey build-ings have eight apartments on each of their identical standard floors and four penthouse-type apartments on their top floor. The 17-storey buildings accom-modate ten apartments on each stand-ard floor, with the two top floors hav-ing higher-standard apartments. In both cases, communication is taken care of by elevators and a staircase located in the centrally positioned reinforced-concrete core. Three of the 12-storey buildings have services and commercial spaces on the ground floor, one of which spaces is earmarked for a local kindergarten. The spaces between the buildings are cov-ered by a roof with openings to facilitate the growth of trees.

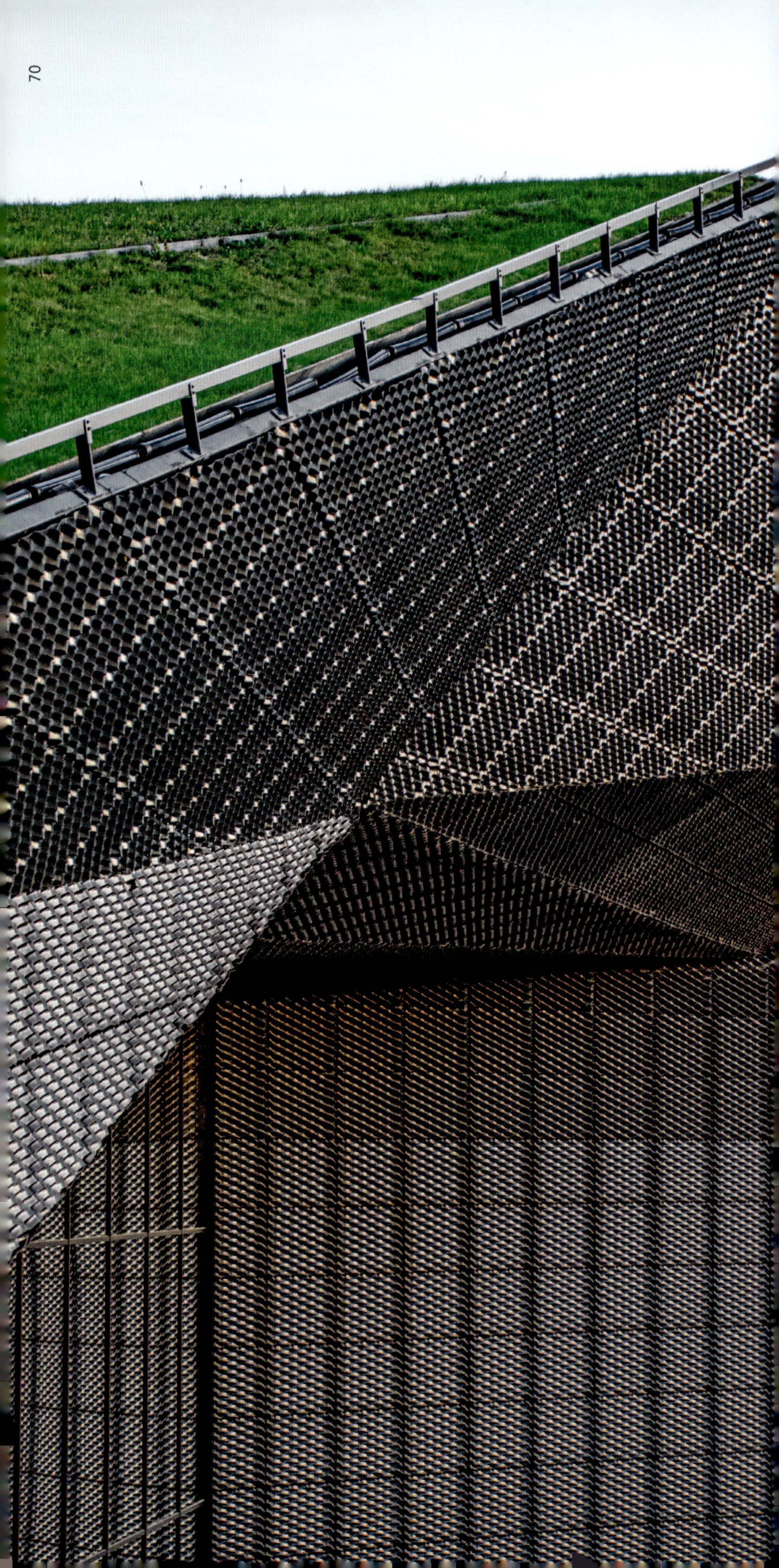

International Congress Centre

pl. Sławika i Antalla 1
JEMS Architekci
2008–2015

026 D

Between the National Symphony Orchestra of Polish Radio building and the 'Saucer' arena complex stands the International Congress Centre. As with the other buildings in the Culture Zone, the concept for the congress centre was selected through an international architectural competition. This rectangular building has its longer sides aligned on the north-south axis. Its cuboid shape is cut in two by a distinctive deformation of the green roof. The deformation creates an irregular valley that reproduces the historical path leading to Bogucice and opens up a scenic view of the 'Saucer' arena. A covered observation terrace with numerous seats is located on the upper part of the green roof. The building's glass façades are covered with a black tensile-cable mesh. Currently the largest congress centre in the country, the International Congress Centre is primarily a venue for exhibitions and conferences. In 2020–2021 it served as a temporary hospital for COVID-19 patients. The centre has two main entrances, located on different levels. The west entrance, facing the forecourt of the 'Saucer', leads to level 'zero', where the main foyer, a 570-seat auditorium, kitchen facilities, and conference rooms capable of being combined into a larger space are situated. The first floor contains the east entrance, additional conference rooms of various sizes, and a multifunctional hall capable of accommodating 12,000 people simultaneously. The hall is adjacent to a strip of office spaces, located in close proximity to the loading area and technical courtyard. Access to the technical courtyard is from the northwest side, next to the service area for the 'Saucer' complex.

026

The Centre:
Market Square

3

The Centre: Market Square

Buildings had already started to go up around the central square, later known as 'Rynek' (Market Square), long before Katowice was granted the status of city in 1865. The square is located at the intersection of historical routes connecting Bogucice, Szopienice, Mysłowice, Brynów, and Mikolow. The middle of the nineteenth century saw the first systematic regulation of roads and streets. Buildings important to the community began to emerge around the square. The first hotel was built here opposite the existing village inn. As more and more brick buildings were erected around the square and apartment blocks rose towards today's 3go Maja Street and Warszawska Street, the square became Katowice's main square. In 1871 the surface was compacted and paved. On its north side the square had a passageway leading to what was then Schloss Strasse (part of today's Korfantego Avenue). The east frontage of Market Square housed important functions: first, the administration of the Tiele-Winckler family estate; then, from the 1870s forwards, in the same building following its adaptation, the city hall; and, since 1907, the Municipal Theatre (now: the Stanislaw Wyspianski Silesian Theatre). The west side of Market Square was occupied by an inn until 1864, when the inn collapsed and was replaced with a brick building. At the end of the nineteenth century Market Square was subject to further modernisation when a tram link was routed through it, connecting the line from Katowice to Mysłowice with the east-west line that extends to what is today Liberty Square. Throughout almost the entire first half of the twentieth century, as development of the square continued, the infrastructure of Katowice Market was modernised

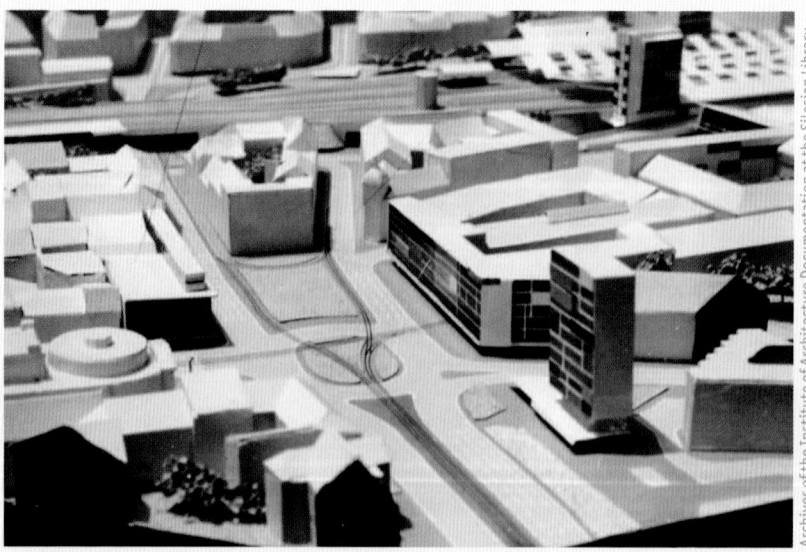

Model of a spatial development concept around Market Square, 1958

Archives of the Institute of Architecture Documentation at the Silesian Library

Drawing of a development concept for Market Square and the axis of Korfantego Avenue, 1962

(under Prussian, Polish, and even German rule). Not a single building was damaged during the military occupation itself; a number of buildings, however, were lost in 1945, shortly after the end of World War Two, when the entire south side consisting of almost-100-year-old apartment blocks, together with the Welt and De Prusse hotels, burned down.

Spatial development between 1945 and 1989

The urgent need to organise Katowice's central square was recognised as early as 1946, when a planning competition for its regulation was held. It is worth noting that the competition was conducted before Socialist Realism came into force; this meant that proposals submitted were in keeping with the aesthetics and philosophy of pre-war Modernism. One of the entries, by Zygmunt Majerski and Julian Duchowicz, envisioned the creation of a wide, imposing urban artery extending north from Market Square. This urban planning idea was in fact adopted at the beginning of the 1960s, when a start was made on large-scale reconstruction of the city centre along the axis of Red Army Avenue (today's Korfantego Avenue). The period up to 1958 was marked by frequent urban planning and architectural competitions. It may be noted that many of the proposed elements became the basis for development of the final concept for the reconstruction of the city's downtown from the late 1950s and early 1960s forwards. The shape of Market Square had until this moment undergone little change, with the exception of the clearing of plots where buildings had burned down in 1945 and construction of a new building, the so-called 'Zieleniak House', on one of the

Drawing of a residential and office building on Market Square, 1947

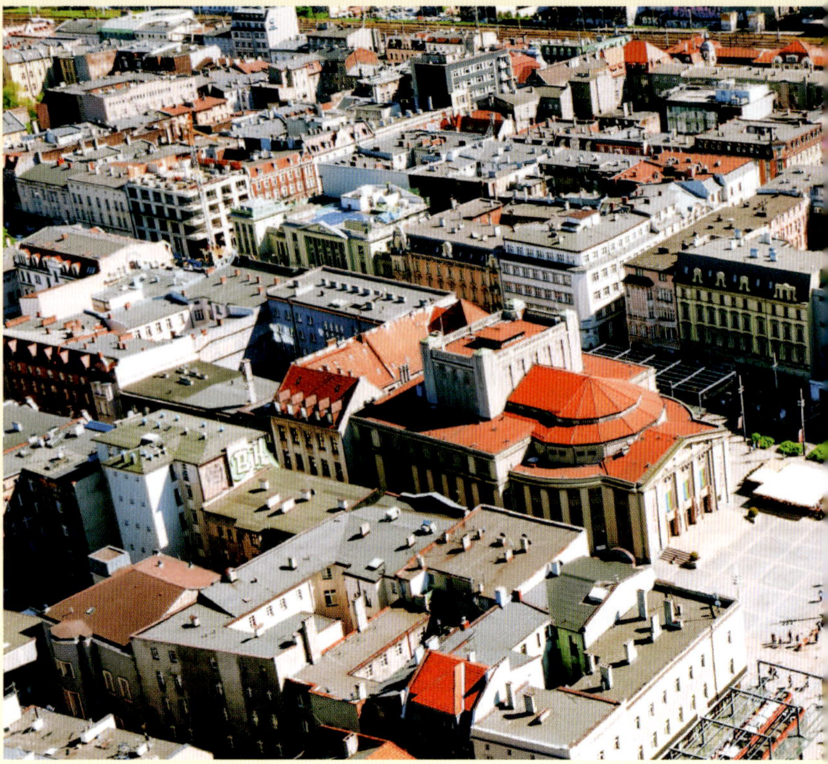

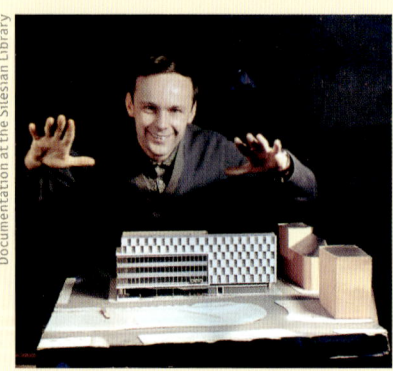

View of Market Square today, looking southeast

acquired plots of land in 1948 (027). The Socialist Realist period, between 1949 and 1956, saw continued interest in the idea of connecting Market Square with a planned artery along which some of the city's most important buildings were to be located, including the opera house, the library, city hall, and downtown residential blocks. In the mid-1950s demolition was carried out in preparation for realisation of this Socialist Realist programme. Shortly afterwards, however, came the so-called political 'thaw', putting an end to Socialist Realist ideas in planning, architecture, and art. The city's architects and planners revised their development plans; from 1958 to the end of the 1970s new development took the form of buildings in the style of late Modernism. This period saw the completion of the modern Zenit department store (028), the Press House (029), and the Skarbek department store (030), designed a decade later, on Market Square.

Archives of the Institute of Architecture Documentation at the Silesian Library

Architect Jurand Jarecki with a model of the Zenit department store, 1959

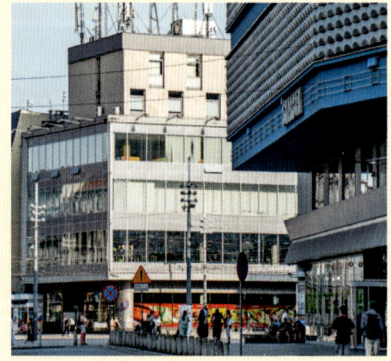

Department stores: Zenit (in the background) and Skarbek

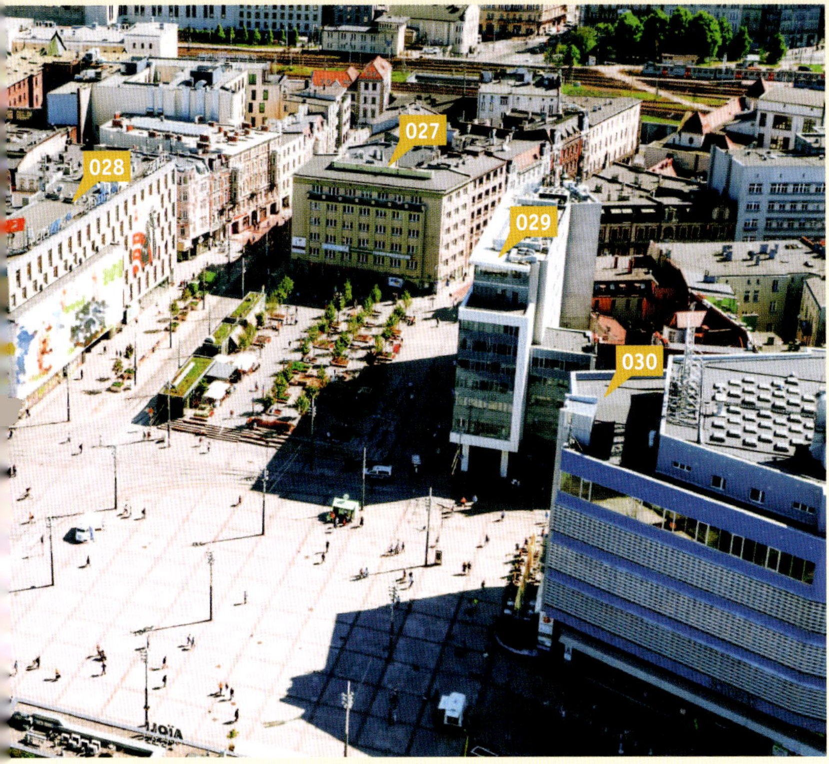

iStockphoto (pawel.gaul)

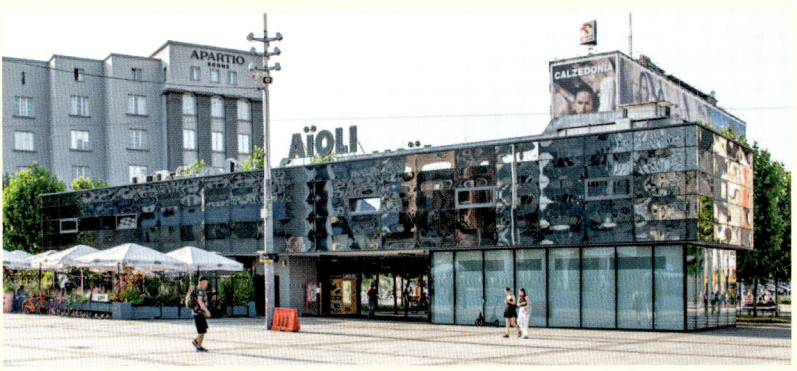

Spatial development since 1990

Following the end of the communist period, two competitions were held, in 1996 and 2006, to redesign Market Square and its axis leading north to the roundabout. Neither idea was proceeded with. It was not until 2010 that a project for reconstruction of the square was adopted. This involved changes to the layout of the tram routes; installation of fountains, flower pots, and kiosks; and, north of Market Square, the covering over of the Rawa River and the creation of shallow, regulated watercourses in its course. The work was completed in 2016. Controversy arose over the development of the north border of Market Square with a two-storey, glass-roofed pavilion housing public toilets, as well as service and food establishments. Entering use in 2017, this structures obscures the view of the Korfantego Avenue axis as seen from Market Square.

Commercial pavilion on Market Square, built across the axis of Korfantego Avenue

Office building with former residential function

Rynek 13
Julian Duchowicz,
Marian Śramkiewicz
1947–1948

One of the first residential buildings constructed in Katowice after the end of World War Two. Designed prior to the imposition of Socialist Realism in architecture, this is an example of post-war Functionalism. The investor and initial owner was the entrepreneur Aleksander Zieleniak from Katowice, who commenced its construction before regulations prohibiting private construction initiatives within the city limits were introduced. The six-storey building completes the row of buildings on Świętego Jana and Pocztowa streets facing Market Square. The main entrance is symmetrically positioned in the middle

of the façade facing the square. On the ground floor are two commercial premises (six were originally planned). On the second, third, and fourth floors there were office spaces that the investor planned to rent out. The top floor, designed for residential purposes, contained three single-room studios, two two-room apartments, and one four-room apartment with a maid's room. All units in the building were served by a centrally located staircase with an elevator. Today the building houses offices belonging to Katowice City Hall and, on the ground floor, the city's tourist information centre.

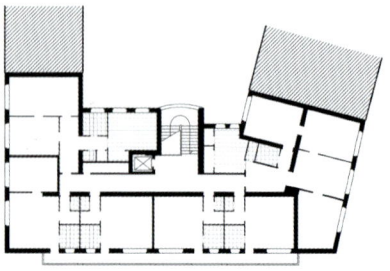

Zenit department store

Rynek 12
Mieczysław Król, Jurand Jarecki
1958–1962

Closing off the east side of Market Square, this department store was built for Społem Universal Cooperative on a plot of land between Staromiejska and Warszawska streets previously occupied by nineteenth-century buildings that had partly burned down shortly after the end of World War Two. The design of the building was selected in a nationwide architectural competition. Justifying their choice, the competition jury noted not only the proposal's modern façade design but also the apt selection of architectural forms. Due to the location of the plot on which it stands, this building had to look good when viewed not only from Market Square but also from the streets leading into the square. The architects proposed an interesting combination of two interpenetrating volumes: a seven-storey block housing office spaces with a rhythmic composition of chequerboard-style windows and a projecting, completely glazed, three-storey volume accommodating rooms for the display and sale of goods. The office part was internally connected to the sales area by a corridor on the second floor. Each part was served by independent staircases and separate entrances. The ground floor is set back from the front façade, and its corners were originally slanted; the overhangs allowed for unimpeded pedestrian flow between the streets and the square. The building has a reinforced-concrete load-bearing structure. The use of a glazed curtain wall on the retail floors, one of the first such curtain walls in the country, was a pioneering technological innovation in the Silesian Voivodeship. The suspended ceilings with built-in lighting were also innovative.

Former Press House

 029 B

Rynek 1
Marian Śramkiewicz
1960–1964
2010–2014 (redevelopment)

On the west side of Market Square, adjacent to the historical townhouses at the exit of Młyńska and 3 Maja streets, is the building that now houses Katowice City Hall. Its current form is due to a 2010–2014 redevelopment commissioned by the city magistrate to convert the building for official use. It was originally designed in 1960 as the headquarters of the district's sports associations but during construction was adapted to house the editorial offices of state newspapers such as *Trybuna Robotnicza*, *Dziennik Zachodni*, and *Panorama*. In addition, the building contained a reading room belonging to the International Press and Book Club, and the ground floor on the Market Square side housed the offices and showroom of Orbis, the state travel agency. At an early stage in the building's design it was assumed that it should be no taller than the neighbouring Zieleniak residential building (027), but a proposal for a uniform nine-storey structure with a glazed curtain wall was eventually approved. Like the Zenit department store opposite, this was one of the earliest examples of the use of the glazed curtain wall in the country. In the first years after the building was commissioned, the façade was blue in colour, but in the 1980s the original fenestration was replaced with aluminium windows with orange glazing. The cuboid, slender main segment aligned with the longer wall along Market Square used to be intersected at the height of the second storey by a retractable terrace accessible from the café (this was built over during the conversion to an office building between 2010 and 2014). The top, ninth, storey – a set-back pavilion with access to the roof terrace – had an extra storey added to it during the conversion work.

Skarbek department store

030 B

ul. Adama Mickiewicza 4
Jurand Jarecki (Miastoprojekt)
1970–1975

Built on the axis of today's Warszawska Street, on a trapezoid plot between 3 Maja and Mickiewicza streets, the Skarbek department store is one of the most striking buildings in Katowice, thanks to both its size and the original plasticity of its façade. In a radical departure from the approach embodied in Zenit department store (028), completed more than a decade earlier, the architect proposed minimising the quantity of natural

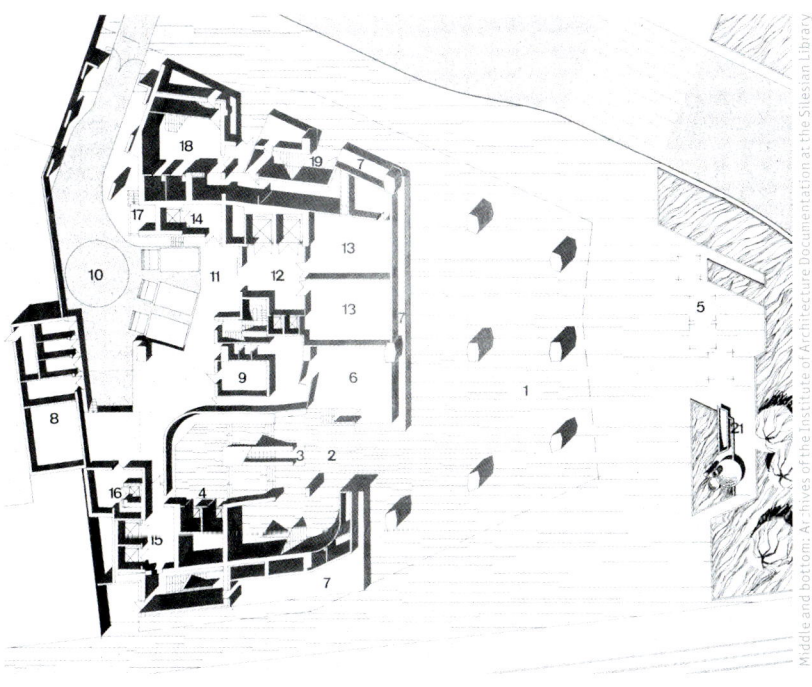

light entering the display spaces, arguing that this allowed them to be used more efficiently and would reduce overheating. As a result, approval was given to a seven-storey building with a trapezoid ground plan and a number of dynamic curves. Due to the location on a busy pedestrian thoroughfare, the ground floor of the building was originally left almost entirely free. Above it, a set-back storey was intended for use as a self-service grocery shop. The following three storeys contain open display and retail spaces, which have only small hinged windows in the exterior walls. These spaces were air-conditioned from the start. They are covered in an exterior element that gives this building its unique character: an aluminium structure of openwork cladding in the form of fish scales, developed in accordance with a French patent. Above the sales floors is a warehouse with exposed horizontal strips of

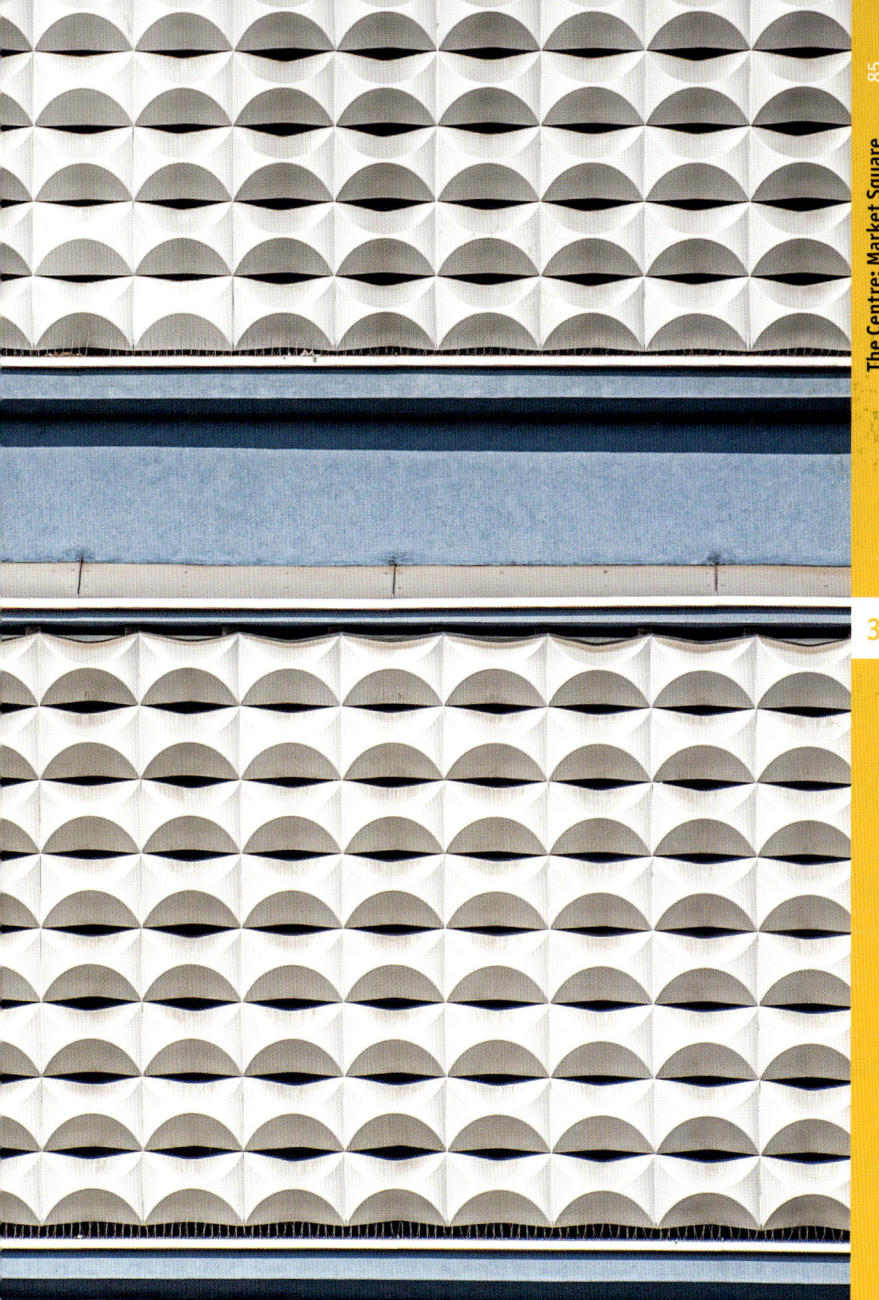

windows. On the Mickiewicza Street side of the store's main block is a wing containing office and staff rooms. Underneath it is a driveway for delivery vehicles; this leads to a small courtyard. Interestingly, a rotating platform was designed to allow vehicles to turn to face Mickiewicza Street. Almost immediately after entering use, Skarbek acquired the reputation of being a modern commercial building that set an example provided at not just provincial but also national level. It also, due to the numerous neon signs mounted on its façades, became known as the 'brightest' department store. Between 2005 and 2007 Skarbek underwent modernisation, the most visible result of which is the two external lifts located in a shaft which is visible from Market Square. The fish scales were also replaced at this time. This work was carried out with the approval of the building's original architect, Jurand Jarecki.

The Centre: Development Along Korfantego Avenue

4

The Centre:
Development Along Korfantego Avenue

Spatial development between 1945 and 1989

The first post-war spatial concepts for the development of modern Korfantego Avenue sprang from a series of planning competitions for the regulation of Market Square held over the course of the 1940s and 1950s, as mentioned in the introduction to the previous chapter. In the 1950s the north part of the city was adopted as the location of its most prestigious urban artery. Several versions were developed for building monumental neighbourhoods abutting the two sides of the artery. However, shortly after Socialist Realism fell out of favour, these concepts were dropped and in 1958 a project for development of the east side of the then Red Army Avenue was adopted. This was built on the site of the demolished buildings of the Tiele-Winckler family's grange and the adjacent park. By 1962 two buildings had been completed: a residential building with a pavilion housing a delicatessen (039) and Hotel Katowice (038). On the other side, closest to Market Square, a start was made on construction of the Separator office and services complex (031). At the same time as the east side of Korfantego Avenue was being built up, preparations were made for development of its west side. After a functional programme for the Centre-West area was

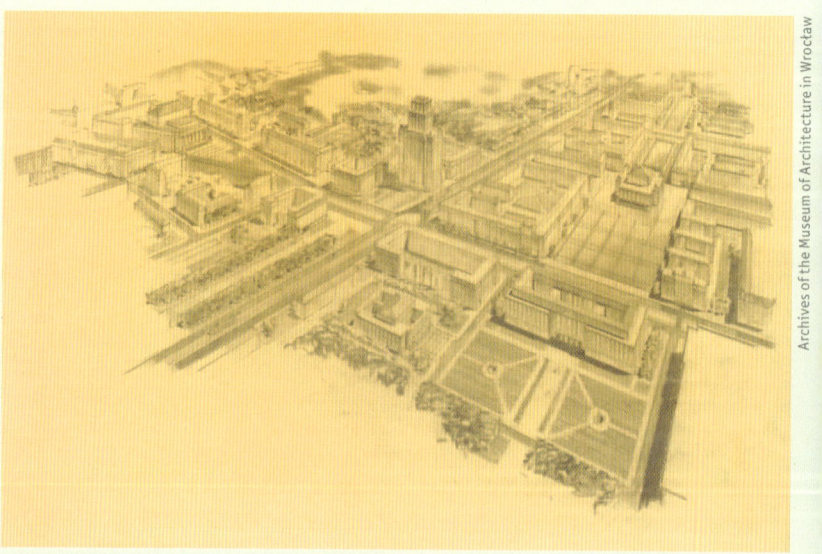

Concept drawing for redevelopment of the city centre, 1954

Archives of the Museum of Architecture in Wrocław

Development of the Korfantego Avenue axis, 1961

drawn up based on analyses, it was decided to conduct a closed urban planning and architectural competition for three teams from the Miastoprojekt Katowice design office. In 1963 planning work was carried out by teams led by Jędrzej Badner and Jurand Jarecki, Wiktor Lipowczan, and Mieczysław Król. The proposals submitted by the first and second teams involved placing the residential functions in tall tower buildings. The team led by Badner and Jarecki proposed four 16-storey buildings and three five-storey buildings of expressive artistic design based on a contrast between solid perimeter walls and glazing placed inside vertical intersections in the massing.

The team under the direction of Wiktor Lipowczan, on the other hand, proposed three 16-storey buildings with a Y-shaped plan and a mixed system of communication with external galleries in the openings of the masses on the north side and a core containing an internal staircase adjacent to two corridors on the inside. In both these proposals the tower buildings were to be accompanied by free-standing pavilions that would be easily accessible from both the residential buildings and the complex's periphery. It was the third proposal, however, designed under the supervision of Mieczyslaw Król, that in the end won the competition. This differed significantly from the others: the

Buildings on the east side of Korfantego Avenue: Hotel Katowice and Delikatesy pavilion, 1965

Model of the spatial development concept for Market Square and the axis of Korfantego Avenue, 1955

Centre-West, model of development concept by J. Jarecki and J. Badner, 1963

entire residential programme for Centre-West was condensed into one long building 16 storeys high. Provision was made for underground parking located on two sides of the structure, and service functions were placed together in a number of pavilions. This approach was justified by the architect's desire to free up as much area as possible for recreational green space adjacent to the new buildings. It was this concept that won the competition and was selected for implementation. In 1964 a master plan for this area already existed, and preparatory work began for the erection of the 'Superjednostka' ('Super-unit') (033). A year later, the plan for the emerging Centre-West complex was expanded to include a 24-storey residential building, intended as an important spatial landmark in the northwest corner of the development site, off the axis of the development of today's Korfantego Avenue (042). In the first half of the 1970s all the buildings included in the auxiliary development entered use, including a kindergarten with an interesting volume supported by round pillars (035).

Centre-West, model of development concept by L. Lipowczan, 1963

Centre-West, model of development concept by M. Król, 1963

Spatial development since 1990

The 1990s brought no significant changes to the structure of the development and organisation of traffic on the axis connecting Market Square and. It was not until 2005 that a long-term process of reconstruction of Korfantego Avenue was initiated: the tram tracks were modernised and moved (from the height of Moniuszki Street to the frontage in the east), and the avenue was partially transformed into a pedestrian promenade connecting with Market Square. This work was completed in 2015. Another change came in 2021–2022, when the space allocated to car traffic on Korfantego Avenue was narrowed by one lane to allow a row of trees to be planted on the roadway. The tram route was also greened with the help of grass strips. The changes also included buildings: in 2015 the Palace of Weddings and the Centrum services and commercial pavilion (118) were demolished. In place of the Wedding Palace, construction of Hotel Puro began in 2019, but funding for this project was held up during the Covid-19 pandemic. The plot of land where the Centrum pavilion once stood is now a parking lot.

Model of the approved development concept for Centre-West in a wider spatial context, 1964

Separator office and commercial building

031 B

al. Wojciecha Korfantego 2
Stanisław Kwaśniewicz
1962–1965

The ten-storey office building erected for the Design Office of the Mechanical Coal Processing Plant was the first new building to be built as part of the western development belt alongside Korfantego Avenue. This is a cuboid block containing office space on eight storeys supported by eight reinforced-concrete cantilevers, each ten metres high, over a two-storey arcade. The arcade provides a foreground for the main entrance to the office building with its glazed, double-height foyer. Adjacent to the entrance is a pavilion protruding in the direction of Korfantego Avenue. This originally housed Motozbyt, the state car dealership, and was modern for its time. Its ground floor contained a large show space equipped with innovative rotating devices for presenting the cars. The mezzanine above the showroom provided a glazed office for signing sales agreements. In addition, the first floor of the pavilion housed the administrative offices of Motozbyt. These were illuminated by window openings that, juxtaposed with original white and red panels, formed a distinctive façade composition.

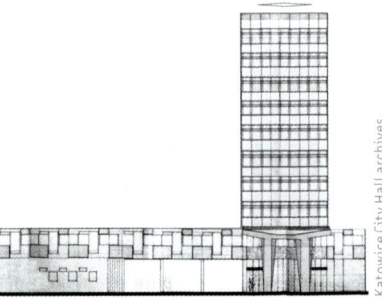

Katowice City Hall archives,

Ślizgowiec residential building with BWA exhibition pavilion

032 **B**

al. Wojciecha Korfantego 6–8
Stanisław Kwaśniewicz (Miastoprojekt)
1965–1969

Standing on the extension of the pedestrian passage on Korfantego Avenue is a complex of two buildings: a two-storey pavilion containing the BWA Art Exhibition Office and a 20-storey residential building. The two buildings complement one another in terms of contrasting spatial composition. Both were designed by the same architect. The lower of the two buildings, a cuboid block on a rectangular plan, adjoins the pavilion belonging to the Separator

building (031). Its basement houses storage for exhibits. The glazed ground floor used to contain a shop, Cepelia, on its north side. In its middle is the entrance with the technical rooms (shielded from the outside by a wall covered with glass shapes); and on its south side is the foyer. The ground floor connects with the main exhibition hall on the first floor via a spiral openwork staircase, which is worth taking a walk up. In contrast to the glazed ground floor, the exhibition floor has a windowless façade; this is enriched with a sculptural frieze by Jerzy Egon Kwiatkowski. The residential building, the vertical element in this urban composition, is located

4

on the opposite side of the pavilion. It has earned the nickname 'Ślizgowiec [the Slider]' due to the technology used in its construction, which involved a self-climbing crane, but is also known as 'the bachelor building' in reference to the surface area of its flats. The apartments here are predominantly one-room (with a floor area of 28 square metres), of which there are 12 on each floor. There are also two two-room flats (37 square metres) on each level. The two lower floors are connected to the commercial units and are separated from the residential floors by a technical floor.

![Superjednostka residential building photograph]

'Superjednostka', residential building

033 B

al. Wojciecha Korfantego 16–32
Mieczysław Król
1964–1969

The most eye-catching building on the Korfantego Avenue axis is undoubtedly the enormous residential building, commonly known as 'Superjednostka [Superunit]'. This is an important element in the project selected in the competition for the development of Centre-West from 1963 forwards; many buildings in the complex are spatially and functionally subordinated to it. The initial concept for this 18-storey building, however, was developed somewhat earlier and was based on ideas for future housing developed by the architects Zygmunt Winnicki and Wojciech Leśnikowski. The results of Winnicki and Leśnikowski's study led Mieczysław Król to include a revised and refined version of the concept of Superjednostka in his competition design for the west part of the city centre. After winning the urban planning competition, Król proceeded to develop a detailed design for the gigantic building. The planned layout of the horizontal and vertical communications, as a combination of a stairwell-based layout and a corridor layout with a full corridor only every three storeys, not only allowed savings on construction but also opened up greater freedom in the design of apartment types, which were originally to include two-storey apartments. Ultimately, no two-storey apartments were realised; they were considered too extravagant and expensive for the time. Likewise abandoned was the idea of locating a kindergarten on the top floor of the building, as in Le Corbusier's Unité d'habitation in Marseille. Superjednostka consists of three segments, each with its own separate entrance to its staircases. It is served by a total of 12 lifts. The building originally had 765 flats of various sizes (from 35 to 56 square metres) for 2823 residents. An interesting feature is the heating distribution system, which takes the form of hotplates integrated into walls to save space in the apartments. All the apartment types have kitchens with indirect lighting. The building also has an underground storey with 160 individual garages arranged on two sides of the driveway. The building's underground part is 186 metres long

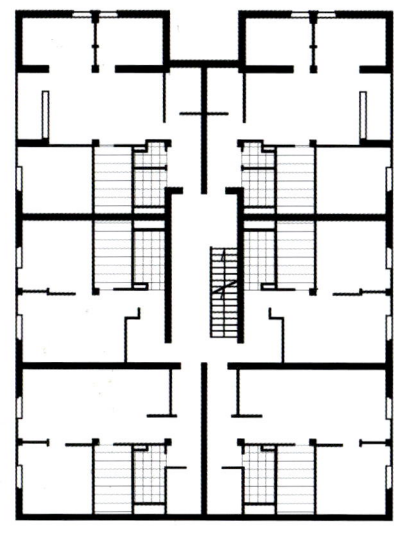

and just 17 metres wide. Superjednostka is still the largest prefabricated building in Poland. Until the 1980s it was described as the largest cooperative building in Europe.

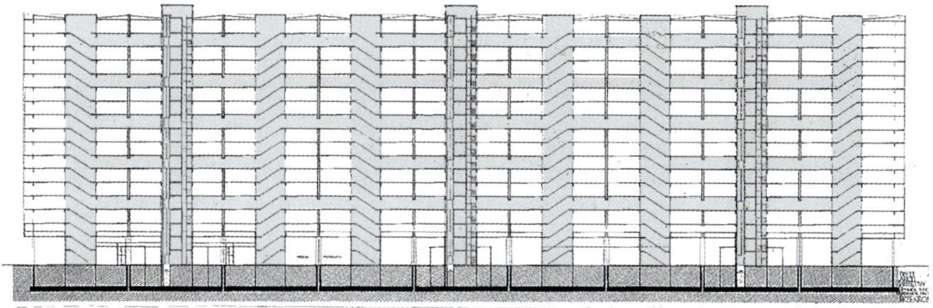

4

Junior commercial pavilion

ul. Sokolska 31
Mieczysław Król
1969–1974

034 B

The only surviving pavilion that is part of the complex of buildings conceived by Mieczyslaw Król to functionally support

Superjednostka is the Junior commercial pavilion. This extends alongside the residential unit and is cantilevered southwards beyond its edge, along the ramp leading to the underground garage. Its architecture is aesthetically similar to that of the demolished Centrum shopping pavilion, which stood adjacent to the pedestrian thoroughfare along Korfantego Avenue. The building has two storeys. Originally, part of the ground floor was occupied by a grocery shop; the remainder, including the entire second storey, was a clothing shop. The underground part contains warehouses, which were supplied from the basement of Superjednostka next door. The pavilion was built as a reinforced-concrete structure with façades in the form of precast concrete elements and plates of glass mounted on an aluminium frame.

Documentation at the Silesian Library

Kindergarten

ul. Sokolska 25
Olga Ziętkiewicz (Miastoprojekt)
1970–1973

035 B

When the idea of allocating space in the Superjednostka for use as a kindergarten was abandoned, it became necessary to build an independent facility not far away. The choice fell on a site adjacent to the Junior shopping pavilion on the west side. This square two-storey building has obviously been shaped in accordance with the principles of Le Corbusier. The ground floor is almost entirely unenclosed, with the exception of the volumes housing the staircases leading to the upper floor. On this floor groups of utility rooms and corridors are clustered around an atrium. The children's rooms are on the west and south sides and have access to a large terrace. The window openings are of different shapes on different elevations. On the north and east sides the openings take the form of variously juxtaposed geometrical figures based on the shape of an inverted letter L.

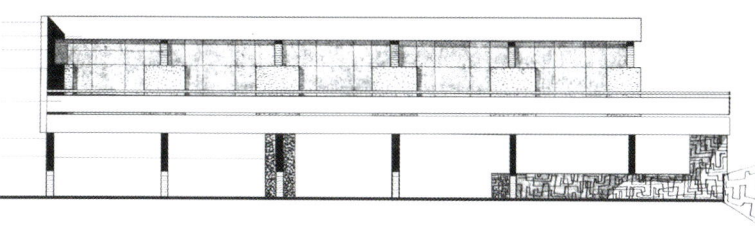

prepared by Marek Pęczak

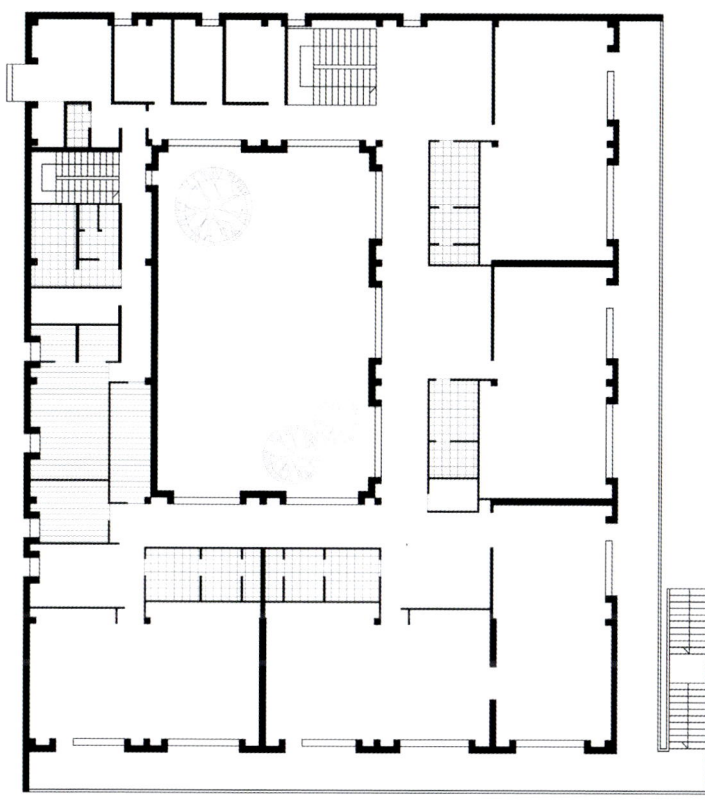

037

036 B

4

Roundabout with a half-dome structure

036 B

Rondo gen. Jerzego Ziętka 1
Wiktor Lipowczan, Jędrzej Badner
1960–1965 (roundabout)
Tadeusz Czerwiński, PBiR Mosty Katowice
2003–2006 (half-dome structure)

The roundabout at the intersection of to-day's Korfantego Avenue, Roździeńskiego Avenue, and Chorzowska Street is one of the city's most important transport inter-changes. The question of what form the intersection of the city's two main arter-ies should take was raised several times in the second half of the 1950s, lead-ing to development of diverse concepts ranging from intersections to rounda-bouts with multi-level structures. Finally, Wiktor Lipowczan and Jędrzej Badner's proposal for a two-level roundabout with a diameter of 130 metres was adopted in 1960. This has a relatively shallow under-ground part with exits directed towards the developments built on either side of Korfantego Avenue. Tram stops were placed in the middle of the roundabout. The underground passages in the form of tunnels with shopping arcades and city toilets were greeted as a sensation in the

national press, which dubbed them 'the underground salon of Katowice'. The interior design was by Wiktor Lipowczan. In the centre of the underground complex was a glass-enclosed retail space with a ring-shaped plan with a diameter of 42 metres. In his memoirs Wiktor Lipowczan, co-author of the roundabout, emphasised that the design team had been inspired by the intersection and accompanying underground service centre at Opernring in Vienna. Another chapter in the history of the site was the major redevelopment that took place from 2000 to 2005 in connection with construction of the tunnel for the Intercity Road Route, which opened in 2006. The pedestrian routes and tram stops were reorganised. The most prominent feature is now a 12-metre-high glass semi-dome containing two above-ground floors. The ground-floor level houses the Art Gallery of the Academy of Fine Arts and a maintenance centre, while the upper level is occupied by a second exhibition space and a restaurant venue with a dance club. The steel structure of the dome consists of two large circular arches and a set of smaller ribs. The outer shell has grey-blue glass panels with inserts of silver sheet metal.

Monument to the Silesian Insurgents

al. Wojciecha Korfantego /
Park Powstańców Śląskich
Gustaw Zemła, Wojciech Zabłocki
1965–1967

037 B

In the immediate vicinity of General Ziętek Roundabout is a spatially linked memorial complex. The concept for this monument was selected at the end of 1965 from among 116 entries in a nationwide competition organised by the General Board of the Association of Polish Artists and Designers and the General Board of the Association of Polish Architects. Justifying its decision, the jury noted the clear ideological value contained in the three bronze blocks symbolising the uprisings of 1919, 1920, and 1921 (aimed at making Upper Silesia part of the newly independent Polish state).

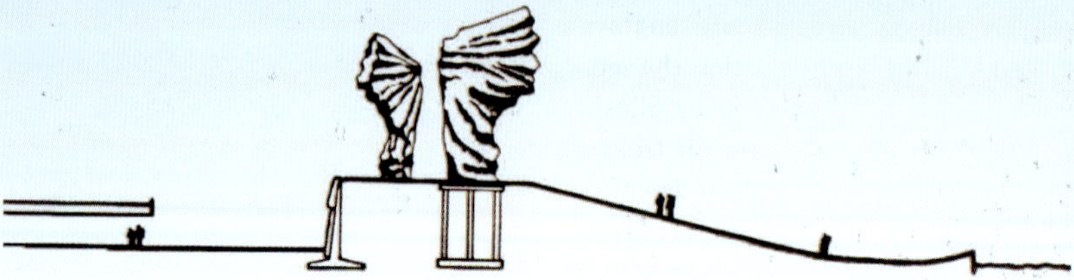

Archives of the Institute of

The site's elevation and the approach to it up a slope alongside a wall clad with massive stone slabs enhance the expressiveness of the monument, as does the way the three blocks have been angled, creating rich opportunities for lighting. During the groundbreaking ceremony, an urn with soil and ashes from the sites of the insurgencies was placed in the crypt. Granite from a quarry in Strzegom was chosen to line the slope beneath the monument; the names of the towns where the battles were fought are engraved on the slabs. On its east side the monument complex is bordered by Silesian Insurgents' Park. The stand of trees in the park is a remnant of the garden of the Tiele-Winckler 'castle', which was demolished to make way for Hotel Katowice.

Hotel Katowice

`038` `B`

al Wojciecha Korfantego 9
Tadeusz Łobos, Jan Głuch
1961–1965

In response to the need to build a new hotel in the city centre, a number of initial locations and architectural concepts were proposed as early as the 1950s. Eventually, the site of the Tiele-Winckler mansion ('castle') on the east side of today's Korfantego Avenue was assigned to this building . The design was prepared by

Documentation at the Silesian Library

Documentation at the Silesian Library

Tadeusz Łobos, a distinguished architect from Katowice with a well-known architectural oeuvre going back to the 1930s. The interior design was by Jan Głuch. The designers were confronted with the need to adapt their concept to the general development plan drawn up under Mieczysław Król for this part of the city centre, and to the dimensions of the neighbouring residential building and service pavilion (030). The hotel building consists of two interconnected parts. The lower, single-storey part with a basement houses a spacious foyer with a reception area, a restaurant for 250 people, a café and night bar, as well as kitchen facilities and a mechanical laundry. An internal atrium provides additional illumination for the foyer, administrative spaces, and the kitchens. Three lifts connect the reception hall with the ten-storey second segment containing double and triple guest rooms on either side of a central corridor. The building's façades are a calm composition of horizontal window bands, originally clad in granite slabs with geometrically patterned mosaics in the spaces between the windows. In 2023 a start was made on modernising and redeveloping the hotel so as to bring it into conformity with contemporary standards. The number of guest rooms will be reduced in favour of more space. The original granite slab façade and interior design elements have been removed.

Residential building with Delikatesy commercial pavilion

039 B

ul. Piastowska 2,
al. Wojciecha Korfantego 5
Marian Skałkowski
1959–1962

In the strip of development on the east side of Korfantego Avenue is an interesting building consisting of two interconnected blocks. The low-rise section opening onto the pedestrian area was designed to house Delikatesy, a self-service grocery shop. The first shop of

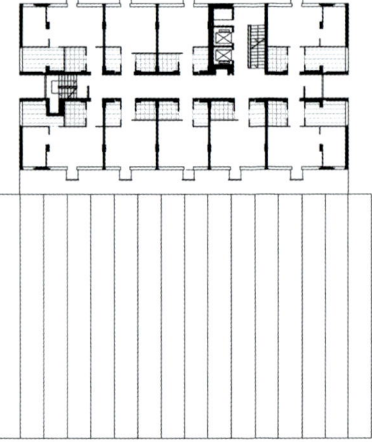

Archives of the Institute of Architecture Documentation at the Silesian Library

its kind in the city, Delikatesy was conceived as a single-space, partially glazed structure with a sales floor capable of serving up to 200 customers at a time. On the mezzanine floor are administrative offices. An interesting feature is the reinforced-concrete ceiling with its distinctive accordion-shaped arrangement of beams. Supported by eight massive load-bearing columns, the ceiling forms a 'fifth façade' which is visible from the flats in the adjacent tall segment. The latter has ten identical floors with two rows of small one- and two-room flats lining a central corridor. Each storey is served by two staircases and two lifts. The main entrance to the residential block is from Piastowska Street. The principal façades of the tall block are notable for their alternation of porte-fenêtre-type windows with longitudinal hatches. The building's original colour scheme was sandy blue with white accents; this has since been modified.

Archives of the Institute of Architecture Documentation at the Silesian Library

The Centre:
the Northwest

5

The Centre:
the Northwest

This area (currently bounded by Chorzowska Street in the north, Korfantego Avenue and Market Street in the east, the railway line in the south, and Grundmann Street in the west) has a street layout created in the early 1860s. It was then that a concept was developed to create an imposing axis running from Warszawska Street (originally: Friedrichstraße), through Market Square (Friedrichplatz) and 3 Maja Street (Grundmannstraße), to Wolności Square (Wilhelmsplatz). Until 1922 Wolności Square was named after the Prussian King Wilhelm I Hohenzollern, who had granted Katowice the status of city in 1865. Conceived as an impressive transport hub forming the local centre of this part of the emerging city centre, the square was hexagonal in shape, with five streets radiating from it. One of these is Sokolska Street (originally: Karlstraße),

which intersects with Mickiewicza Street (originally: Uferstraße; later: August-Schneiderstraße), where it originally ended its course. Sokolska was not extended further northwards until the late 1950s, when Koszutka District was built up. Today's Mickiewicza Street, which diverges from Market Square, was created by drying out part of the smelter ponds in order to create an elegant promenade. At the end of the nineteenth century it was decided to move the pond's south bank northwards to allow the construction of important public buildings along Mickiewicza Street, including the municipal bathhouse (3 Mickiewicza Street), the Great Synagogue (no longer extant), and the municipal gymnasium (11 Mickiewicza Street). At the same time, from the 1860s onwards, residential areas in the vicinity of Wolności Square and Sokolska Street were being densified. In 1872 the

The city bathhouse, the Great Synagogue, and the city gymnasium on what is today Mickiewicza Street; photo by M. Kechlitz, 1911

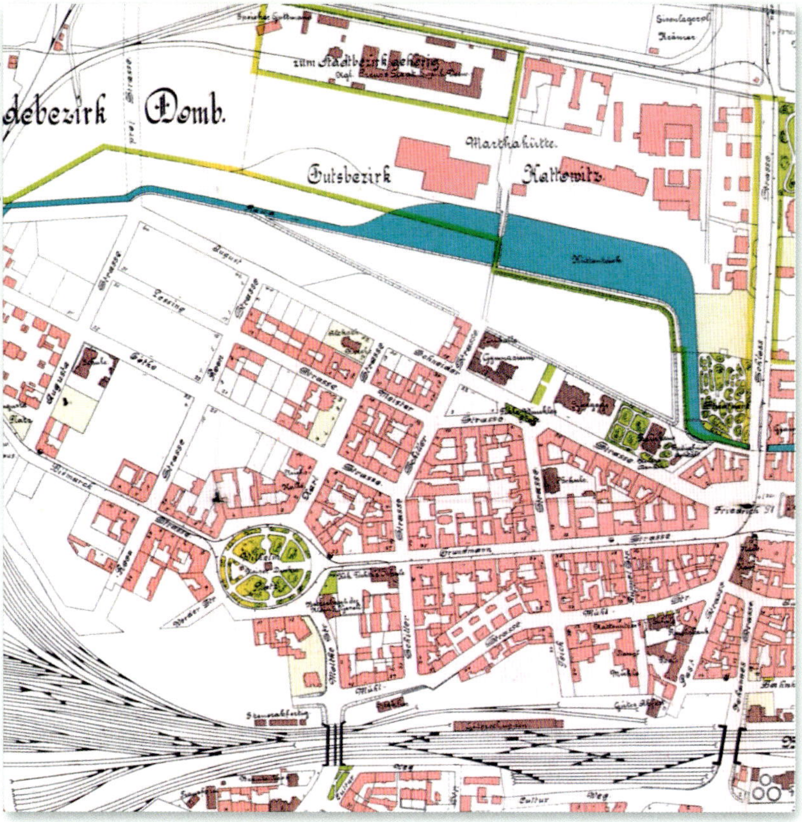

Part of a plan of the city of Katowice, 1900

construction of the Neo-Renaissance Goldstein Palace (12a Wolności Square) was completed for the owners of a wood-processing factory; today this building belongs to the city and houses the registry office. At 2 Sokolska Street is the seat of the Silesian Philharmonic (since 1945),

which owes its present form to modernisation work carried out in 2011–2014, including the addition of a superstructure. Built around 1880, this building was originally a brewery. It was converted into a choir house with a restaurant at the end of the nineteenth century. The

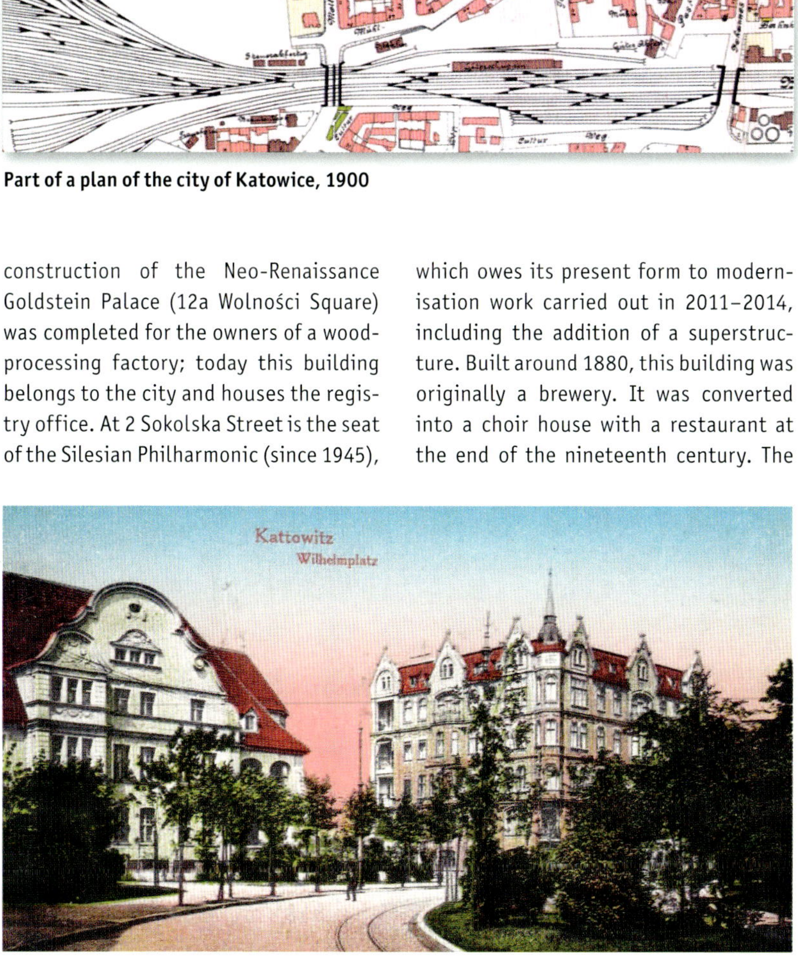

Buildings on Wilhelmsplatz (today's Wolności Square);
photographer: unknown, 1917

intensive development of the city centre and the construction of a tram line around Wolności Square also led to the demolition of the city's first Catholic church, which had stood on the site of today's square since 1860. The church was a small, single-aisle, half-timbered building that served as a temporary place of worship until the completion of the Neo-Gothic St Mary's Church (1870) at what is today 1 Szramka Square. In 1910 a public garden was created in the middle of Wolności Square to go with the Two Emperors Monument unveiled in 1898 (the monument was blown up in 1920, probably by members of the Polish Military Organisation). When Katowice came under Polish administration in 1922, construction of a new monument began immediately; this was The Tomb of the Unknown Silesian Insurgent (destroyed by the Nazis in 1939). During the German occupation an obelisk honouring the fallen soldiers of the Wehrmacht was erected in place of the tomb. This was removed in 1945, and in 1947 a memorial of gratitude to Soviet soldiers was unveiled. The sculpture depicting two soldiers was taken down in 2014 and moved to the cemetery of Soviet military war dead in Park Kościuszki. Only the empty pedestal remains. Also worth noting among the buildings in this part of the centre is the Functionalist House of the Silesian Insurgent at 3 Matejki Street (1937; arch.: Z. Rzepecki), located in the vicinity of Goldstein Palace. In addition to union premises, flats, and a restaurant, this building housed a 760-seat cinema.

Spatial development between 1945 and 1989

The years 1945–1989 brought a number of changes to the spatial structure of the northwest part of the city centre. In the first half of the 1950s planning work was initiated for a new railway station (the existing one, located on Dworcowa Street, could no longer handle the growing volume of railway traffic). Several options for the station's location were considered, including a) demolition of the nineteenth-century building and erection of a new station building in its place and b) a site at the west end of Mickiewicza Street, where the tracks and platforms would have run parallel to today's Grundmann Street. Eventually, the choice fell on a location in the vicinity of the junction of Stawowa and Młyńska streets. This led to the demolition of a row of nineteenth-century apartment blocks in order to create a vast plot of land. In 1959 an architectural competition for the new station building complex was held. The winning design (archs.: W. Kłyszewski, E. Wierzbicki, J. Mokrzyski; see 117) provided for a communication link with the existing city-centre layout and the introduction of a

House of the Silesian Insurgent with Zorza Cinema; photo by C. Datka, 1937

National Digital Archive (NAC)

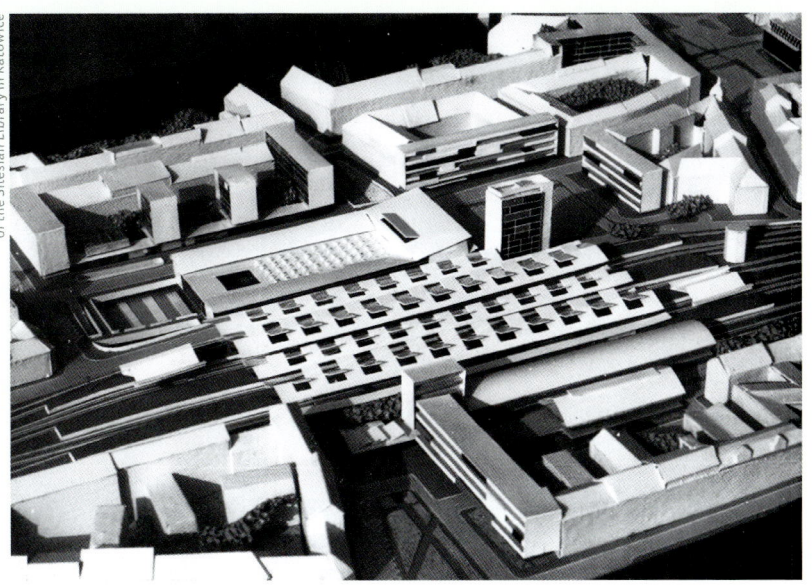

of the Silesian Library in Katowice

Photograph of one of the post-war architectural concepts for a new railway station in Katowice developed for a competition, 1959

5

clear division between vehicular traffic (cars and buses) and pedestrian traffic (for which a footbridge was built over the bus stops; Galeria Katowicka now stands in place of the footbridge – see 049). In the late 1950s and early 1960s efforts were made to extend the road system to the north in order to connect the city centre with the expanding Koszutka residential area. Drainage and elimination of the smelter ponds and demolition of the remains of the Marta Steelworks buildings led to the development of a large area abutting the east side of the Superjednostka complex, which had been under construction since the early 1960s. The second half of the 1960s brought construction projects for buildings taller than ever seen before in the city, including the 24-storey Haperowiec residential building (042) and an unrealised complex of office high-rises whose daring concepts were a prelude to the construction of Stalexport Foreign Trade Centre Complex (045) in the second half of the 1970s.

Spatial development since 1990

After the country's democratic and economic transition, the urban fabric in this part of the city was gradually supplemented with new buildings. One example is the complex of office and service buildings at the corner of Chorzowska and Sokolska streets (043), designed in the 1990s. Almost at the same time the space east of Superjednostka was densified with a glazed office building (1997; archs.: T. Bator, A. Kapuścik) and, a dozen or so years later, with a second office and services building (2012; arch.: D. Paleta). The surroundings of the railway station were significantly transformed when work started on building Galeria Katowicka in 2010, replacing a piazza with a demolished pedestrian flyover that had served as foreground for the station's passenger hall, whose original cup-shaped roof structure had not survived (117). The Supersam market hall has also been completely transformed, with a shopping mall now operating in its place and under the same name (041). Also noteworthy, given that Katowice still has very few examples of contemporary residential buildings, are two new residential projects complementing the pre-war development on Opolska Street (047, 048). Additionally, a complex of three residential and office buildings, two of which stretch to than 100 metres high, was built not far away, on Zabrska Street, between 2019 and 2024 (046).

Domus furniture store

ul. Adama Mickiewicza 7
Marian Skałkowski,
Stanisław Kwaśniewicz
1959–1963

040 B

The first modern furniture house in the region took the form of a glass pavilion with two parts that are offset relative to one other by a distance of half a storey. Designed for the Regional Furniture Trading Company in Bytom, this pavilion had a total of five exhibition levels with a combined area of 1500 square metres. The exhibition spaces were laid out in such a way that they could be reconfigured to resemble popular apartment layouts. In addition to the main exhibition hall, there were elegant, semi-open rooms where furniture-purchasing transactions could be carried out, along with a small bar. On the north side, above the unloading area, were administrative offices. The building's structure consists of a reinforced-concrete frame with façades of glass fixed between steel profiles. A standalone glazed display case stood in front of the main entrance on Mickiewicz Street. Between this case and the principal façade a canopy stretched over the main entrance. Unfortunately, neither of these elements has survived. Today, no longer a furniture pavilion, Domus houses Ślązak department store. However, despite modification of the façade divisions and finishing materials, it is still possible to make out the building's original interior layout and the principle by which its façades were shaped. As you approach on Mickiewicz Street, be sure to note the dynamic effect created by the distinctive façade plane break, introduced one third of the way along the building's width.

Supersam shopping mall

041 B

ul. Skargi 6
Konior Studio
2012–2015

The plot at what is today 6 Fr Piotr Skargi Street has a long commercial tradition that dates to the 1930s. The modern municipal market hall erected in 1936 with a steel arch structure designed by Stefan Bryla served its purpose until 2012, when it was partially demolished. This left only a section of the original pre-war structure still standing; it was incorporated into the planned new building, as requested by the Office of the Provincial Conservator of Monuments at the time. The new retail and services building, called 'Supersam' after the original 1960s shop, opened in 2015 and fills an entire street block. The main entrance area on the axis of Stawowa Street is emphasised on the façade by a recess between two massive blocks with rounded corners. Axially located entrances on the south and north sides lead to a spacious covered atrium in which four original trusses from the demolished hall from the 1930s have been exposed. The building has five floors above ground, the last two of which are occupied by a car park for 400 cars on the west side of the building. A significant part of the roof has also been used for parking spaces. The entrance to the spiral ramp is from the west elevation.

5

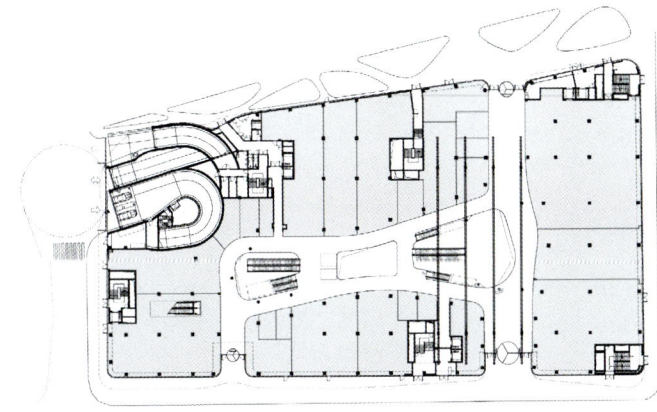

Konior Studio

Haperowiec
residential building

ul. Sokolska 33
Jurand Jarecki,
Marian Skałkowski (Miastoprojekt)
1965–1968

Visible from afar, the distinctive slender mass of this 24-storey residential building is reminiscent of a razor blade, from which it derives its nickname, Żyleta. The decision to place a tall residential building in this spot as a landmark was taken during the fine-tuning of the spatial development of the western development belt alongside Korfantego Avenue, in parallel with the construction of the Superjednostka complex. The architects adopted the principle of shaping the massing with protruding vertical strips of loggias, interestingly similar to an earlier alternative development competition design they had submitted, which lost out to the wining proposal for Superjednostka. This building's structure is a steel skeleton, the design for which was developed at Mostostal-Zabrze. Nine apartments (with floor areas of between 26 and 56 square metres) were configured on each residential floor. Each floor is served by a corridor with two staircases and three lifts. The building was intended to provide homes for 700 inhabitants. There is a two-storey basement with storage areas. Three commercial premises were planned on the ground floor. The twelfth storey above ground has communal areas for residents, including a common room and a meeting room, as well as ancillary facilities such as a laundry and a drying room. Seen from the street, this storey is distinguished by the absence of a loggia – which has the visual effect of cutting into and breaking up the building's monolithic mass. In 1970 Haperowiec was described as the tallest building in Katowice Province and the fourth tallest in the country.

Office and commercial complex

ul. Sokolska 34
Denton Corker Marshall
1997–2000

50 ul. Chorzowska
Biuro Architektoniczne MAT sp. zoo.
1998–2001

Perpendicular to Sokolska Street, a sprawling office and service complex stretching across 2 hectares consists of two buildings arranged linearly along busy Chorzowska Street. Although the construction of the two buildings proceeded almost simultaneously, the architectural concepts were developed by different design studios. The investor in both cases was the Silesian Bank Centre. The first building, at the intersection of Sokolska and Chorzowska streets, was designed by the British architects Denton Corker Marshall as the headquarters of ING Bank Śląski. It consists of two segments of varying heights: the higher, ten-storey segment houses offices for management; the lower (five-storey) segment, offices for other employees. The two parts are connected by a glazed customer-service centre and a passageway which is accessible only to bank employees. Under this is the main entrance. The auditorium has an elliptical floor plan, is located to the south of the building, and is linked to the atrium. The second building, commissioned a year later, is a commercial office building with a compact but visually unobtrusive form. It has 15 storeys, three of which are occupied by a multi-storey car park with a striking spiral ramp.

Parish church

ul. Sokolska 12
Tadeusz Łobos,
Jan Głuch
(general redevelopment)
1975–1978

044 B

The contemporary form of the church at the junction of Sokolska and Mickiewicza streets, in the style of late-1970s Modernism, is in fact the result of reconstruction of a much older church, built at the end of the nineteenth century in the Neo-Gothic style. The church originally served the Old Catholic Community, but in the 1930s the building was handed over to Catholics. In the early 1970s, following the establishment of the independent Transfiguration parish, a decision was made to extend the building. The creation of a much larger nave with the addition of a chapel, ancillary rooms, and a large choir gallery on the south side resulted in a building which appears visually squat – an impression which is reinforced by the lack of a clearly designated tower. The tower has been replaced by a pylon supporting the bells, which is connected to the body of the church by a full-height wall. The church building itself is an interesting juxtaposition of varied, cuboid masses with slender window openings. Since 2012 the church has been cared for by the Dominican Order, which began a renovation in 2022. The interior has been redesigned.

Office complex of the Foreign Trade Centre
045 B

ul. Mickiewicza 29
Djordje Grujicic
(KMG Trudbenik)
1976–1981

This complex of two skyscrapers, which originally housed the offices of the Central Office of Foreign Trade, no longer stands out for its height, which has been eclipsed by new buildings nearby, but still attracts attention for its elegance. By its very nature the Upper Silesian industrial region has always been a busy hub for foreign trade agreements. Discussions on the construction of a headquarters building for the administration and handling of such contracts had been ongoing since the first half of the 1960s. Five architectural concepts were produced for the development of this plot on Mickiewicza Street, developed in closed competitions by teams from three design offices. None of these concepts were referred to the central authorities for implementation. It was only in 1973 that an indirect investor – Intraco, a company from Warsaw – commissioned KMG Trudbenik from Yugoslavia to develop a new design, which was approved by the Ministry of Foreign Trade a year later. The chief architect was Djordje Grujicic. A foreign company was also chosen as the general contractor: IBS Industribyggnader Stenungsund from Sweden. The construction of the skyscrapers attracted considerable interest due to the technology used. In view of significant mining damage suffered by the terrain, the two 18- and 20-storey buildings were designed with a three-column structure, which was still seen as innovative in the country despite previous experiments (eg in Wrocław). The arms supporting the hanging cantilevers, attached to a reinforced-concrete shaft, are a distinctive visual accent. Inside the shafts are stairwells, lifts, and sanitary facilities, around which office spaces of various sizes are arranged. The two towers share a basement and are linked by a large atrium pavilion containing a two-storey foyer with a reception area, a restaurant, conference rooms, and services. The complex has been finished with high-quality materials. A second factor influencing comfort of use is the more generous foreign standards adopted for the dimensions of the corridors, offices, and sanitary facilities relative to those in force in Poland at the time.

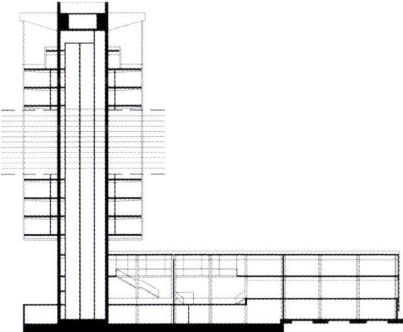

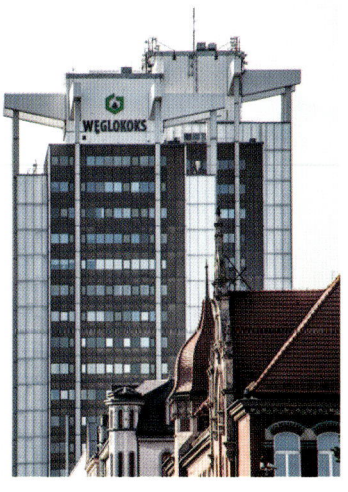

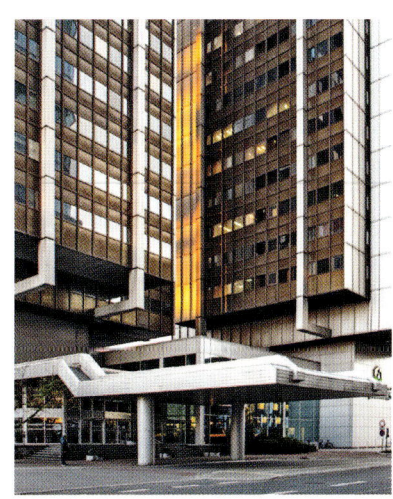

Global Office Park residential and office complex

046 B

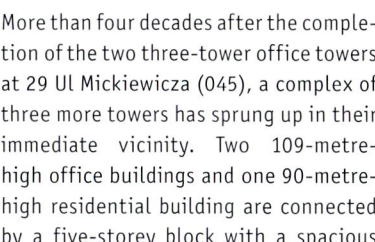

ul. Zabrska 15–20
Cavatina Holding
2019–2024

More than four decades after the completion of the two three-tower office towers at 29 Ul Mickiewicza (045), a complex of three more towers has sprung up in their immediate vicinity. Two 109-metre-high office buildings and one 90-metre-high residential building are connected by a five-storey block with a spacious atrium, which houses commercial premises and a multi-storey car park. The two underground floors contain 2138 parking spaces. Cavatina Holding, which has its own architectural design studio, was the investor in the three high-rise towers and the lower office building in this development of a city block on Zabrska Street. Together with the neighbouring towers of the Foreign Trade Centre, the Global Office Park complex sets an example of a new order of scale for development of Katowice's new business centre as it takes shape on the western edge of the city centre.

Residential and commercial building

ul. Opolska 17–19
Ostrowscy Architekci
2011–2014

047 B

Not far from the Global Office Park complex is Opolska Street, which is predominantly built up with pre-war apartment blocks. Not all the plots here, however, were filled with buildings during the twentieth century. This, combined with the relatively lower levels of car traffic on this street, make it an attractive location for new residential development. One example of such infill construction is this residential and commercial building, which occupies the space between a 1930s corner house and an urban villa in the Eclectic style. The architects respected the historical context by adjusting the height of the new building to that of the neighbouring apartment block and reduced its visual mass on its east side by stepping back the two upper storeys abutting the villa. In addition, by locating the entrance to the underground garage at the eastern boundary of the plot, they ensured a greater distance from the Eclectic-style villa. The new house has seven floors above ground level. The ground floor is given over to commercial premises. The first floor is occupied by offices. A total of 36 apartments, ranging in size from 28 to 112 square metres, are spread over the remaining floors. The underground garage has capacity for 50 cars. The onlooker's attention is drawn to the clearly accentuated main entrance set in a triple-height recess leading through to the residential area and the courtyard. The office floor has an independent entrance and staircase.

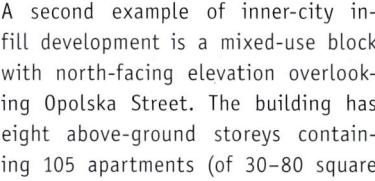

Residential
and commercial building
ul. Opolska 12
LINIA Architekci
2017–2021

048 B

A second example of inner-city in-fill development is a mixed-use block with north-facing elevation overlooking Opolska Street. The building has eight above-ground storeys containing 105 apartments (of 30–80 square metres), four two-storey commercial units, and an underground garage for 108 cars. The residential floors are served by two staircases. On the top level is a space for socialising and a communal roof terrace with a pergola and a small garden, accessible to all residents. Due to the prestigious proximity of the Silesian Philharmonic at 2 Sokolska Street, which it borders on the courtyard side, this building is known commercially as 'the House at the Philharmonic'.

Railway station and Galeria Katowicka shopping mall

 049 B

pl. Marii i Lecha Kaczyńskich 2,
ul. 3 Maja 30
SUD Architectes
2011–2014

Construction of this complex combining a railway station with underground bus stops and an adjacent shopping mall on its north and west sides began in 2010 while the demolition of the original, Brutalist-influenced station hall and pedestrian overpass (117) was still underway. The new station building is a covered walkway stretching alongside the railway tracks. On its two sides are lines of services premises and ticket offices. The main entrance, located on the axis of Stawowa Street, leads into a spacious hall with exposed reinforced-concrete structural cups that attempt to recreate the original, demolished cups. The two rows of cups extend linearly on an east-west axis before passing seamlessly

into the structure of the shopping mall, where they have also been exposed at the level of the upper shopping passageway. From the main station hall it is possible to descend by escalator to the underground bus station, which consists of through platforms with ten stops. Access to the four train platforms is provided by a series of three subways. These also lead to the south entrance to the station area from Andrew Square, which is enclosed by the original surviving original 1970s pavilion. Named 'Galeria Katowicka', the shopping mall is a private commercial investment project. This is the part of the station complex that is most visible from the downtown streets (Stawowa and 3-go Maja). It consists of four above-ground storeys and three underground storeys. Alleys of shops are arranged in a ring formation along the pedestrian route. In addition, there is a cinema on the side facing Słowackiego Street. An underground car park has capacity for 1200 cars on two storeys.

Mercure Hotel

ul. Młyńska 6
AiR Jurkowscy-Architekci
2019–2021

On the other side of the square in front of the main entrance to the railway station is a hotel built by the Mercure hotel chain. This building has ten floors above ground and closes off the city block bounded by Młyńska Street. The four-star hotel has 268 rooms, two amphitheatre-style conference rooms, catering facilities, and an underground garage with capacity for 70 cars. There is a small roof terrace on the top floor. Façades with a minimalist composition with emphatic vertical strips of windows are interrupted by vertical gardens in the form of plant walls on the west and south sides. A digitally controlled water conduit system has been incorporated in the building's walls to ensure optimum irrigation levels for the plants. With a total area of 230 square metres, this green façade is the city's largest to date.

5

The Centre:
the Northeast

6

The Centre:
the Northeast

The northeast part of the inner city is a historically and spatially diverse area. In the north it includes what used to be parkland, undeveloped until the 1960s, and the Tiele-Winckler family mansion and estate management building, built around 1840 (the mansion and farm buildings were demolished in 1976). By contrast, the development axes of today's Warszawska (originally: Friedrichstraße) and Mariacka (originally: Holtzestraße) streets in the southernmost part of this area were already experiencing rapid development in the second half of the nineteenth century. Note, however, that Warszawska is one of the oldest streets in the city: the first brick buildings were put up here even before Katowice was granted the status of city in 1865. One of these buildings was the Evangelical Augsburg Church (now 18 Warszawska Street), consecrated in 1858 and later extended. In addition to the progressively taller bourgeois apartment houses, the city's wealthy citizens began to build urban villas for themselves on Friedrichstraße. An example is the Neo-Renaissance villa of Friedrich Grundmann, completed in 1869. It survived until the 1970s and is now home to the National Bank of Poland (059). Warszawska Street was intended to be an impressive 'city salon'; hence lavish public buildings were also located along it. It is worth noting the Neo-Renaissance building of the former county office, which now houses

Evangelical church on today's Warszawska Street before its extension;
photo by L. A. Lamche, 1872

Villa Friedrich Grundmann,
demolished in the 1970s;
photo by L. A. Lamche, 1872

Silesian Digital Library, Silesian Library

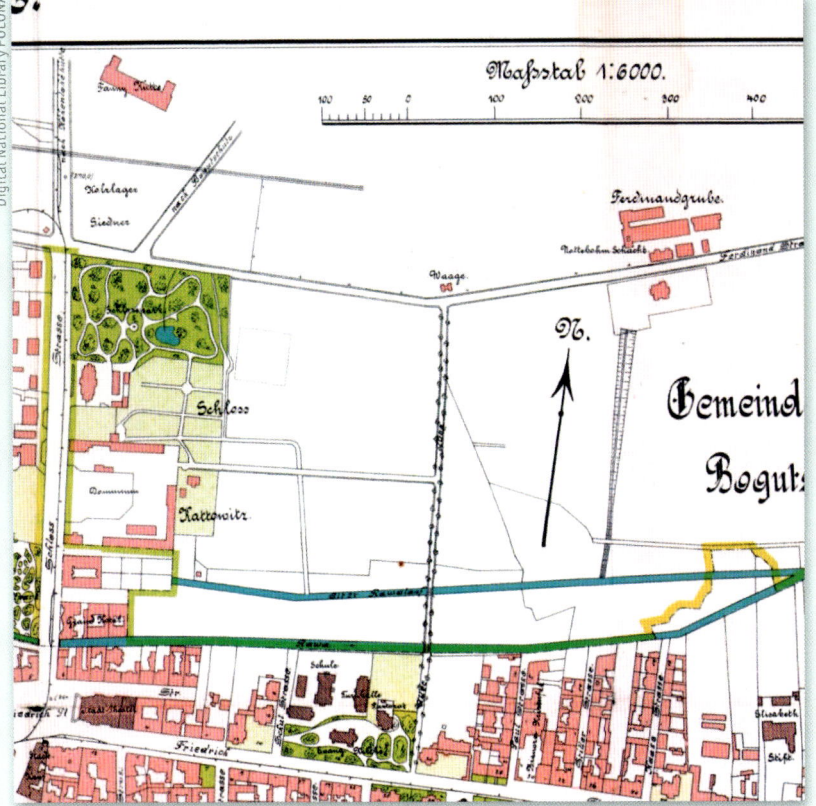

Part of a plan of the city of Katowice, 1900

6

the district court at 4 Warszawska Street (1876; arch.: Hannig) and two former bank buildings – at 7 Warszawska Street (1924; arch.: P. Jaretzki; extension of a former villa) and 14 Warszawska Street (now the library of Silesian Medical University; 1939; arch.: M. Lalewicz). Two other streets run parallel and slightly to the south: Mariacka Street (Holtzestraße) and Dworcowa Street (Bahnhofstraße). The former rose to prominence when the Neo-Gothic Catholic church of St Mary's (arch.: A. Langer) was built at its eastern end between 1862 and 1870. Dworcowa Street owes its course to the city's first railway line, opened in 1846, on which a small, single-storey station with a gabled roof was located. The station was extended several times in the second half of the nineteenth century until it reached its final form in 1906 with, among other things, an Art Nouveau waiting room and pavilions. Almost simultaneously, two hotels entered use opposite the station: Hotel Monopol (1904; arch.: L. Goldstein)

and Zentralhotel (1907). In the 1920s the station's central volume was extended twice, by a total of three storeys. In 1937 a Functionalist apartment block was built for the engineer Jan Squeder on the corner plot between today's Dworcowa and St John's streets. Some historians attribute the design of this house to the architect Karol Schayer.

Spatial development between 1945 and 1989

After World War Two, in the late 1950s and early 1960s, a number of buildings were erected in the northeast part of the city centre in the form of infill development. Notable among them are: the Socialist Realist building currently housing the offices of the Municipal Office at 4 Warszawska Street (1954; arch.: T. Łobos), the residential and services building of the former Agricultural Bank at 17 Teatralna Street (archs.: H. Buszko, A. Franta; 052), and the music school at 16

Katlowilz O.-S.
Friedrichstrasse mil der kath. Kirche

View of Friedrichstraße (now Warszawska Street) with St Mary's Church in the background; photo by J. L. R., 1913

Teatralna Street (arch.: W. Lipiński; 051). However, it was not until the early 1960s that a larger-scale construction project was initiated. In 1962 it was decided to establish a branch of the Jagiellonian University in Katowice. Following a later merger with the Higher School of Pedagogy, this has been called 'the Silesian University' since 1968. In 1965, under the direction of Ryszard Sołtyński, a plan was drawn up for the development of Śródmiejska Dzielnica Uniwersytecka (the City-Centre University District), which occupied the area bounded by today's Bankowa, Moniuszki, and Uniwersytecka streets. The team of urban planners needed to include in their plan the building at 12 Bankowa Street which had been adapted in 1963 for use as the first university building. Originally, this was a school (1959; arch.: W. Lipiński); today it houses the rector's office. Until the end of the 1970s new developments for individual faculties and institutes were realised based on the concept adopted in 1965. The functional programme of the City-Centre University District was supplemented by residential buildings erected in the 1960s at the northern edge of the area (055).

Functionalist apartment block at the corner of today's St John and Dworcowa streets; photo by K. Boronowski, 1941

National Digital Archive (NAC)

KATTOWITZ
Bahnhof mit Bahnhofstrasse

Railway station on today's Dworcowa Street after its extension; photo by J. L. R., 1916

Spatial development since 1990

In the 1990s a decision was taken to continue spatial development of the Silesian University campus in an eastward direction. In 1996 an architectural competition was held for the design of a new building for the Faculty of Law and Administration (057), which was commissioned in 2003. Its completion coincided with preparations for another modern academic construction project – the Scientific Information Centre and Academic Library (065). In the immediate vicinity of the Silesian University campus the tallest building in Katowice and southern Poland (054) was completed in 2003. This was also when the headquarters of the National Bank of Poland was built on the corner of Bankowa and Warszawska streets (059). Meanwhile, substantial spatial changes were made in this part of the city centre in order to revitalise public spaces; this involved minimising vehicular traffic in favour of pedestrians and greening Mariacka Street (2008), Dworcowa Street (2018–2020), and Warszawska Street (2024).

View looking from Warszawska Street towards Market Square in 2024. In the distance we can see Skarbek Department Store.

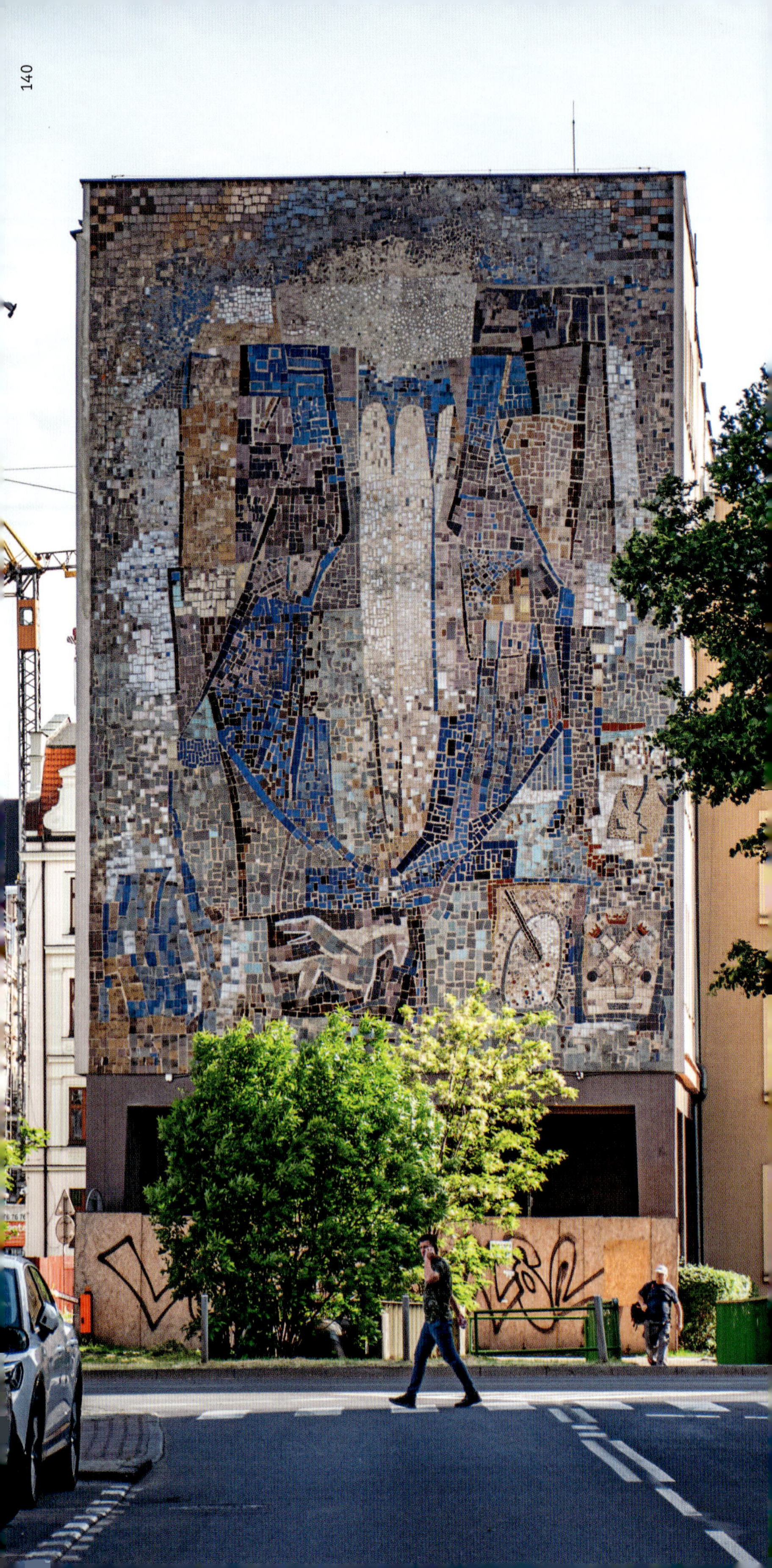

Mieczysław Karłowicz Music School

051 B

ul. Teatralna 16
Wacław Lipiński
1965–1968

Situated on a corner plot, the music school building was the first musical monument to the millennium of the Polish State in what was then Katowice Province. The relatively small space allocated to the new building posed a design challenge, given the extensive functional programme that was required. This comprised, among other things, the following rooms: a concert hall for 200, a chamber music hall for 70, 29 rooms for individual teaching, and seven rooms for collective teaching. The programme also included catering facilities, a group of offices, and several storage rooms for sheet music and instruments. When it was completed in 1968, the five-storey building was finished with high-quality materials and equipped with a state-of-the-art sound-recording system, allowing works performed in all the school's halls to be recorded. The double-layered ceilings and walls were fitted with sound-absorbent chipboard and glass wool in the gaps between the layers of brick. The reinforced-concrete structure is exposed externally at the building's north and south edges in the form of massive pillars. The challenge for the architects was to design a spacious concert hall in a building that is less than 12 metres wide. The concert hall occupies the entire width of the building on the second and third storeys. Abutting it is a spacious foyer connected by a staircase that terminates in the entrance hall. The second staircase is located at the opposite end of the block and serves classrooms and offices. A chamber music hall with facilities is located above the concert hall. A corridor connecting the two staircases runs through the top floor; adjacent to it are individual practice rooms. When looking at the building from the outside, it is worth noting two artistic compositions: a mosaic with bas-reliefs at the entrance and an abstract mosaic occupying the entire north wall, made in 1967 by Magdalena Kurek, Jan Stasiniewicz, and Henryk Kobyliński, artists from the Visual Arts Studio of the city of Katowice.

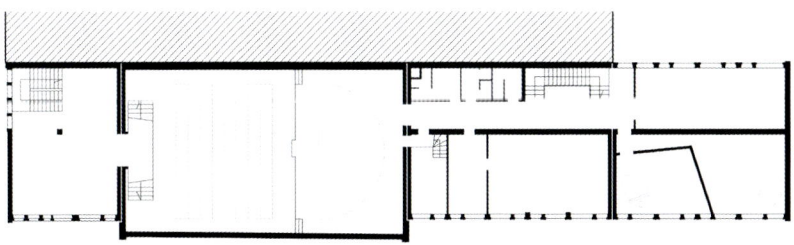

Residential and commercial building

ul. Teatralna 17, 17A, 17B
Henryk Buszko,
Aleksander Franta
1959–1962

052 B

Enclosing a block bordered by Szkolna and Teatralna streets, this mixed-use residential and service development commissioned by the Agricultural Bank is an intriguing example of a building with a diverse functional programme resolved within a challenging spatial context. Comprising two residential segments connected by what used to be a bank office, it fits well into the surrounding urban fabric. The lower, five-storey, residential block abuts a small apartment house built at the turn of the 1940s on today's Szkolna Street. Originally, it housed 12 one-, two-, and three-room apartments, along with two guest rooms with separate bathrooms. The second residential block has seven storeys and accommodates 30 apartments arranged in a split-level layout. Situated on the opposite side of the inner courtyard, this block abuts Teatralna Street. At ground level, facing the courtyard, it has garages and storage rooms for tenants. Each of the two residential blocks is served by one elevator and one stairwell. Connecting them

is a two-storey pavilion, which originally housed the bank's banking hall for clients on the ground floor and office spaces with a spacious conference room on the first floor. On the first floor the bank's employees could enter their office directly from the stairwells serving the residential units. At the present time the former bank space is occupied by the Rawa.Ink Municipal Entrepreneurship Incubator.

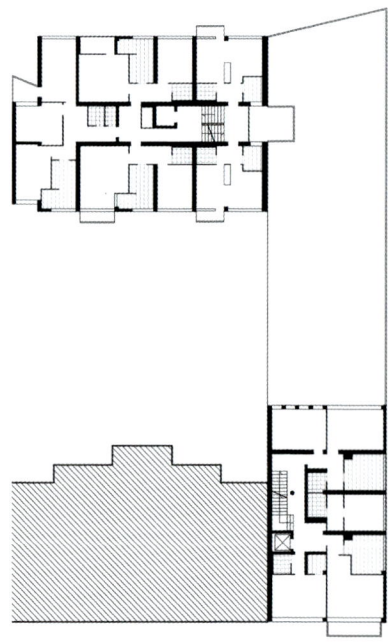

Qubus Hotel

ul. Stanisława Moniuszki 9
Czora & Czora
2019–2023

053 B

restaurant, and a cafe and evening bar. The hotel also has two conference rooms, a gym, and a rooftop terrace for use by guests.

An unusually difficult to develop triangular plot of land located between Moniuszki Street and a bend in the course of the Rawa River was chosen for the new headquarters of this hotel belonging to the Qubus chain. The architects implemented the hotel programme in a seven-storey building which tapers towards the east corner of the plot. Despite the proximity of the Rawa River, it was possible to realise an underground garage for the building. The four-star hotel has 97 single and double rooms. In addition to a spacious lobby, the ground floor contains a three-zone catering area with a breakfast restaurant, an afternoon

Altus office and commercial building

ul. Uniwersytecka 13
Dieter Paleta (Arkat),
Dieter Reichel (Reichel&Stauth)
1996–2003

054 B

One of the most distinctive buildings in the centre of Katowice is undoubtedly the office and service skyscraper known as 'Altus'. Its original name was 'UNI-CENTRUM', which is also how it was referred to in the design documentation. Until the of KTW. II, the neighbouring skyscraper, this was the tallest building not just in Katowice but in the whole of the south of Poland too. It occupies the entire city block bounded by Uniwersytecka and Piastowska streets, a site previously occupied, until the middle of the nineteenth century, by the Tiele-Winckler grange and park. The project's beginnings were complicated by numerous changes in the ownership of the land and buildings, which led to a halt being called on construction not long after it had started. These initial complications led to abandonment of the idea of purchasing Hotel Katowice in order to demolish it and build in its place a forecourt with a square on Korfantego Avenue. The general architectural concept for the complex was developed by a team from the German architects Reichel & Stauth. The detailed design is by a team from the Arkat Architectural Office under the direction of Dieter Paleta. The completed complex consists of four interlocking segments, the tallest of which has 30 floors above ground and is 114 metres high without its mast. The load-bearing structure is a reinforced-concrete frame and monolithic reinforced concrete. Due to the risk of damage caused by mining operations, the structure was reinforced with automated stiffeners to minimise the effects of shaking in the event of subsidence. This was one of the first buildings in Katowice to have such sophisticated systems for the monitoring and management of electricity, ventilation, and air conditioning. The garages in the complex's three-storey basement can accommodate 568 cars. The design approach is based on the idea of uniting zones with different functions in the building. The lowest segment houses, in addition to a commercial area with an open central space and services premises, cinema halls and a gym. The segments higher up contain hotel rooms (formerly the Qubus Hotel; now a hotel in the Courtyard hotel chain) and office spaces housing the headquarters of the companies renting them. Internal communication in the building is designed so that the different parts of the building are separately served by their own staircases and high-speed elevators. The complex is finished with high-quality materials, including aluminium joinery and façade panels of granite.

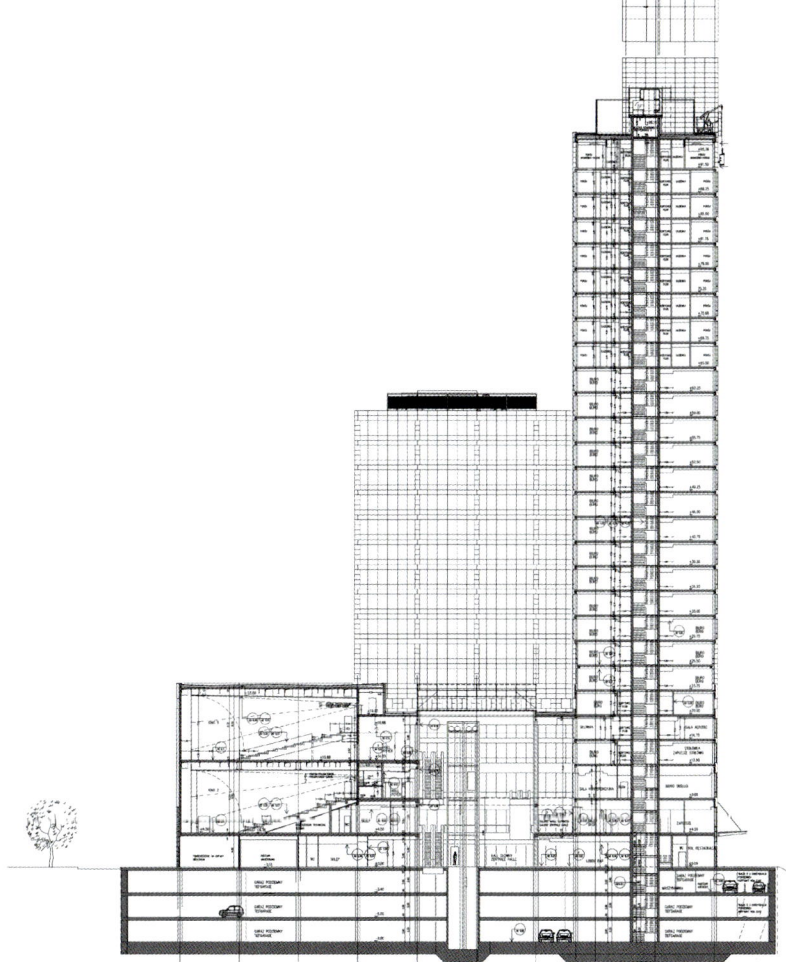

ARKAT Dieter Paleta

Residential complex
ul. Uniwersytecka 21, 25, 29
Stanisław Kwaśniewicz
1960–1966

`055` B

A complex of four identical 15-storey buildings located between to-day's Roździeńskiego Avenue and Uniwersytecka Street. The detailed lay-outs for the buildings were based on a pre-design study necessitated by this site's immediate proximity to what was then Katowice Coal Mine (now: the Silesian Museum complex; 024). Each building consists of two residential sections with apartments arranged along corridors; the two sections are linked by a seg-ment housing a staircase and elevators.

In three of the four buildings all the apartments are two-room. The end/corner apartments have a larger floor area (44 square metres) and a kitchen with abundant light provided by a large window overlooking a loggia that is accessible from the larger room. The other apartments have a floor area of 37 square metres with only porte-fenêtre windows. The entrances to the individual buildings are emphasised by pyramid-shaped pavilions that originally housed a porter's room and a trolley room. There are garages on the ground floors of the buildings and in the area between them. The buildings' roofs have small, glazed pavilions which were originally intended for use by officers of the citizen's militia as observation points from which to survey the surrounding streets. The design of the façades of three of the buildings is an avant-garde composition consisting of a juxtaposition of seemingly irregularly spaced window openings with vertical strips accentuating variations in texture and colour. This approach was, however, not used in the fourth building, which stands on the opposite side of today's University Street. Here the structural module and external dimensions are the same, but the façade design and interior layouts are different, including the addition of three-room apartments. This building has a higher standard of finish than the three others. It was commissioned by PKO Bank.

Scientific Information Centre and Academic Library 056 D

ul. Bankowa 11A
HS99 Herman i Śmierzewski
2003–2012

The string of buildings on the University of Silesia campus contains the only academic library to be shared by two universities in Poland – the University of Silesia and the University of Economics. The competition for the commission to design this building was held in 2002, but almost a decade passed before the library entered use. The competition organisers had envisioned a single target user and investor: the University of Silesia. However, in 2008 the two

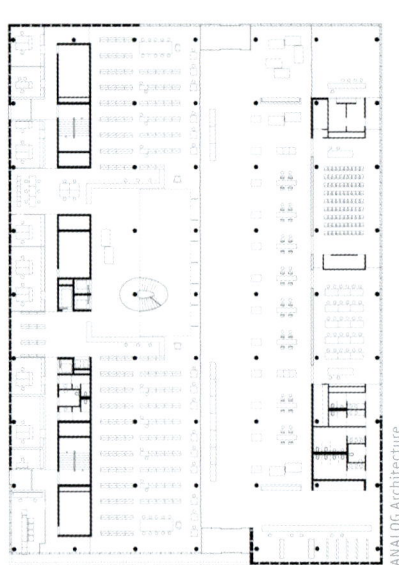

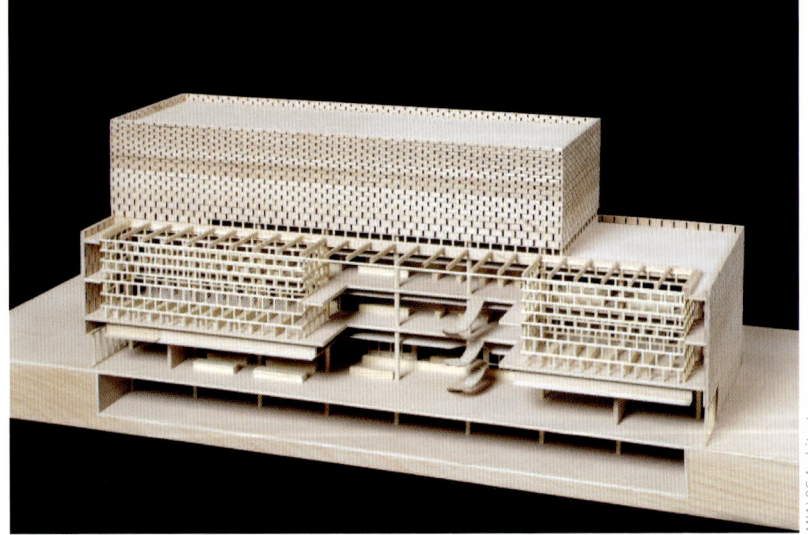

universities became partners in a consortium, which made it possible to obtain additional funds from the pool allocated by the Silesian Voivodeship Board. A year later, the final contract for the building was signed. The contractor selected was Mostostal Warsaw. The library consists of two blocks. The lower, three-storey, block with floors arranged in the form of mezzanines houses public areas, including reading rooms, a conference room, a teaching room, and a spacious hall. The taller, six-storey, block which abuts it to the east, contains rooms for staircases staff and specialised storage areas. The library's total projected capacity is approximately 1.8 million books. The façade design draws the eye with some interesting variation: slabs of rough red sandstone of different heights have the visual effect of elevating the edifice. Gaps between the slabs provide light for the building's interiors.

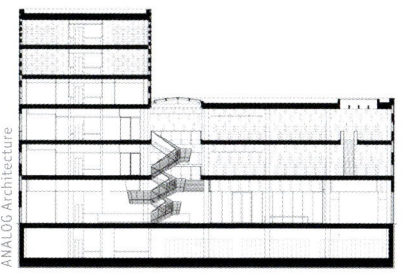

ANALOG Architecture

Faculty of Law and Administration, University of Silesia

057 D

ul. Bankowa 11B
Stabil sp.zoo.
1996–2003

On its east side the axis of the Silesian University campus is closed off by a distinctive semi-circular building housing the Faculty of Law and Administration. With four above-ground floors, this building has groups of rooms with different functions arranged in a ring formation. Around the glazed cylinder of the main hall are auditoriums and classrooms accessible from galleries leading off the hall. Another ring, preceded by an interior corridor, consists of offices for teaching and administrative staff and a library with thematic reading rooms. All floors are linked to one another by a glass elevator, from which the main hall and galleries may be observed. This building also has an underground floor containing a garage for 150 cars and a complex of rooms for technical equipment.

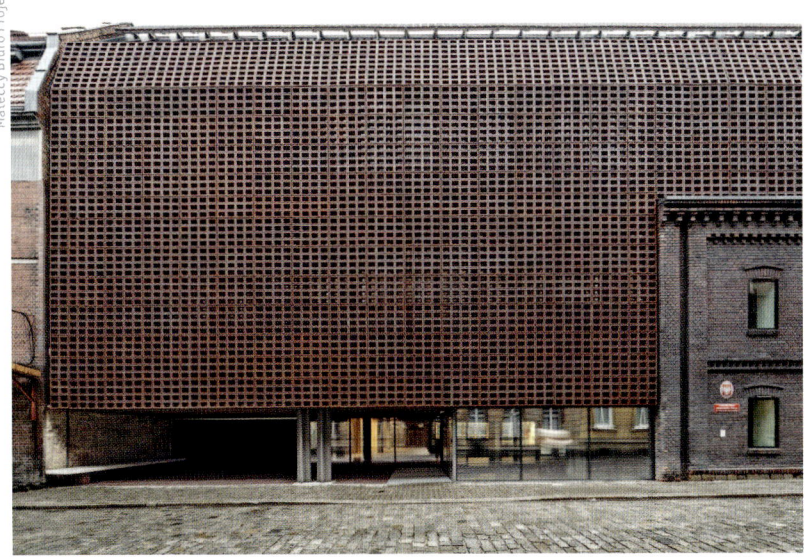

Krzysztof Kieślowski Film School, University of Silesia

 058 D

ul. Świętego Pawła 3
Małeccy Biuro Projektowe, BAAS arquitectura, Grupa 5 Architekci
2011–2017

Under a resolution passed by the Senate of the University of Silesia in 2019, the university's Faculty of Radio and Television, which had been operating in its original premises on Bytkowska Street in Katowice since the 1970s, was renamed 'the K. Kieslowski Film School'. The concept for the new teaching complex, selected in an architectural competition in 2011, included the then surprising solution of preserving a number of the old *familoks* (turn-of the century brick houses – see p. 26) on St Paul's Street and incorporating them in the main body of the new building. Assigned to use as the faculty library, the revitalised red-brick building is a two-storey space with a mezzanine floor. The main entrance area, located to the left of the library, leads into a hall that gives access to a spacious courtyard. The building's various wings are clustered

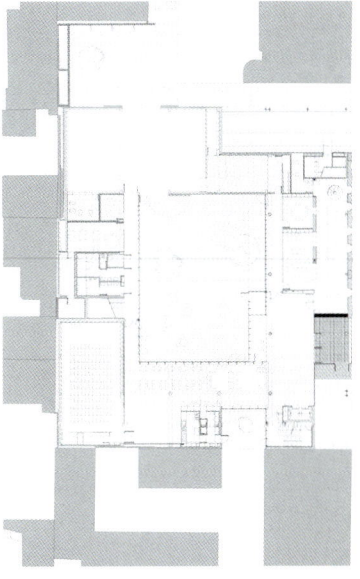

around this courtyard. They house an auditorium, a cinema room, a film studio, workshops, and staff rooms. The complex's masses have been arranged in such a way as to fit into the dimensions of the neighbouring buildings in this street block, while the internal development around the courtyard is lower, being limited to two above-ground floors. The main cinema hall and film studio are partially dug into the ground, which allows them to be connected to the underground garage and facilitates the unloading of equipment from cars. In addition, there is an internal manoeuvring area at the plot's southern border; this is accessed through an arcade. The street side elevation is finished with ceramic mouldings that form an exterior curtain wall attached to a steel frame. A mesh stretched inside the wall prevents birds from entering the gap between the wall layers.

Mateccy Biuro Projektowe

Headquarters of the National Bank of Poland

059 D

ul. Bankowa 1
Dieter Paleta, Teodor Badora,
Wojciech Wojciechowski, Mikołaj Machulik
2003–2006

The headquarters of the national bank stands on an exposed plot of land at the junction of Bankowa and Warszawska streets, on the site of a villa once owned by Friedrich Grundmann, one of the city's builders. Its north side borders the original, pre-war headquarters of the National Bank of Poland. Due to the vicinity of historical church buildings and bourgeois apartment houses, the dimensions of the new building were limited by restrictive conservation guidelines: the height of the new headquarters could not exceed the level of the cornice of the neighbouring former bank headquarters, and its layout had to permit an unobstructed view of the silhouette of the church from the east part of Warszawska Street. The main entrance was placed in the southwest corner of the plot, and the entrance for employees, together with the entrance to the ramp leading to the underground floors, in the northeast corner. The underground floors house a garage and vaults. The above-ground sections of the building have a functional layout that is composed of separate strips. The strip located in the innermost part of the plot houses administrative rooms. The middle strip was designed as a public services area with a spacious operations room. The core directly adjacent to Warszawska Street, on the other hand, is occupied by rooms for managers of this bank branch, as well as by staff apartments and guest rooms.

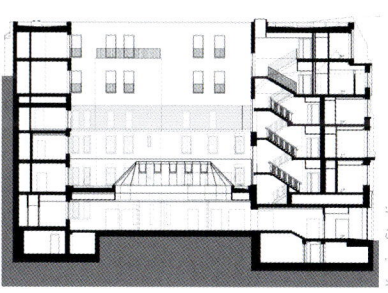

Hotel Diament Plaza

ul. Dworcowa 11
Konior Studio
2017–2020

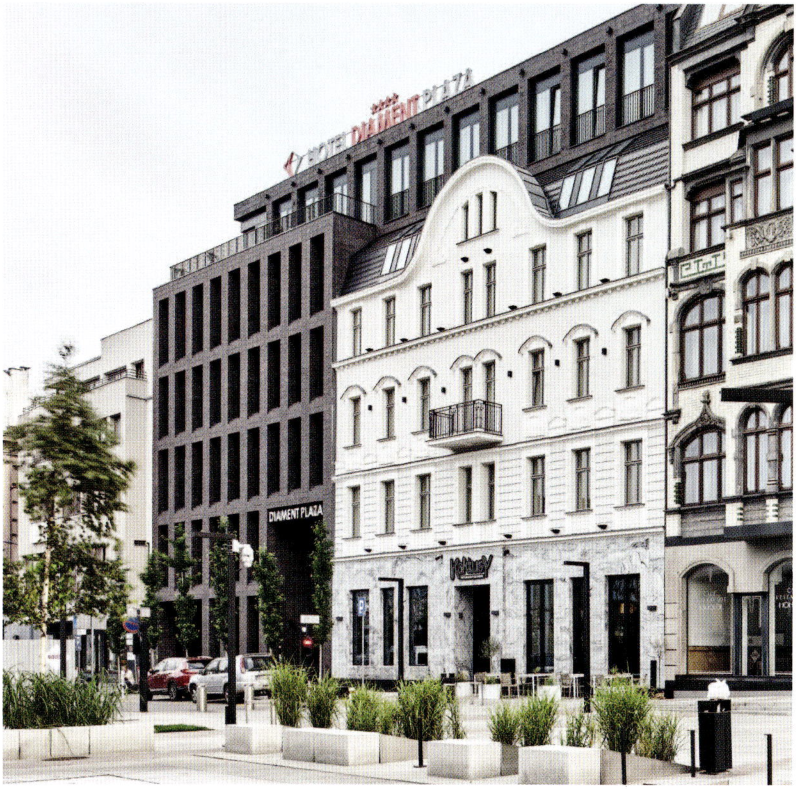

060 B

This hotel building is the result of the fusion of the first building on this site (a nineteenth-century apartment house) with an addition on a vacant adjacent parcel of land. The resulting four-star hotel has 135 rooms of various sizes. The top floor of the extension has apartments with access to roof terraces. This storey runs partially over the historical part of the hotel, thus creating the visual effect of absorbing the existing building into its structure. The extension has also resulted in a green courtyard, overlooked by the balconies of some of the rooms. In addition, the underground floor houses a spa area and a garage. The façades of the new part are finished with hand-formed bricks from Patok, fired in a historical brickyard that has been in operation for more than 120 years. This kind of brick is characteristic of the region. Here it has been used to create a regular grid accentuating the arcade of the main entrance and the arcade of the entrance gate to the underground storey.

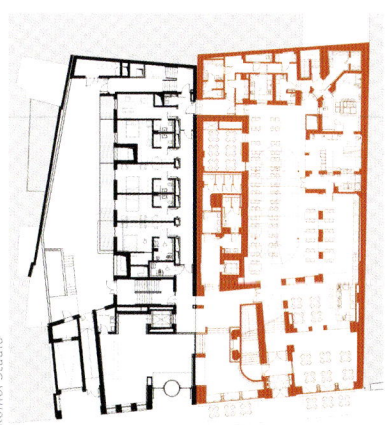

The Centre:
the Southeast and
Paderewskiego Housing Estate

The Centre:
the Southeast and Paderewskiego Housing Estate

For the purposes of this guide this relatively large notional area has been defined as including the Paderewski housing estate. The reason for this is mainly spatial: Osiedle Paderewskiego (the initial project for which in the 1960s was called 'Śródmiejska Dzielnica Mieszkaniowa – Wschód [City Centre District East]') is based on an urban-design approach which connects and interacts closely with the inner city fabric. This area is bounded to the west by Plebiscytowa Street, to the south by Upper Silesian Avenue, and to the east by Three Ponds Valley.

In the nineteenth century the development of buildings in this part of the inner city was mainly concentrated around today's Voivodship Street (Holteistraße) and Plebiscytowa Street (Heinzelstraße). Most of the bourgeois houses still standing today were built in the 1880s and 1890s. In 1899 the impressive Neo-Gothic building of the Royal School of Building Crafts was completed; this is now home to the Karol Szymanowski Academy of Music at 33 Wojewódzka Street. Bordering this building on its east side is today's Damrota Street (originally: Letochastraße), adjoining which are two historical cemeteries: the Catholic Cemetery (1860) and the Evangelical Cemetery (1882) . To the north, a complex of hospital buildings from the 1870s and 1880s adjoins

School of Construction Crafts on today's Wojewódzka Street, photographer unknown, 1921

Private collection, postcard

Part of a plan of the city of Katowice, 1900

the Catholic Cemetery. One of the first inner-city headquarters of the professional fire brigade was also established in this area; its building (substantially unchanged since the 1920s) is located at 11 Wojewódzka Street. After the transition of the city to Polish administration in 1922, a significant development was the construction of a very modern and extensive complex of Functionalist buildings for the Silesian Technical Scientific Establishments (1928–1932; archs.: J. Dobrzańska, Z. Łoboda) in the spot where Krasińskiego Street was laid out as an extension of Wojewódzka Street. Since 1972 this building has served as a teaching building of the Silesian University of Technology. In parallel with the construction of the Silesian Technical Academic Institutes building at 23 Voivodship Street, an eight-storey residential building for professors was erected, using a steel-skeleton construction that was innovative for the time (1929–1931; arch.: E. Chmielewski). At the same time, in the late 1920s and early 1930s, the road system between Francuska and Plebiscytowa streets was extended. As well as luxurious private apartment buildings, prestigious public buildings began to be erected here too. One of the most important examples of these is the Silesian Parliament Building (1929; archs.: L. Wojtyczko, P. Jurkiewicz, K. Wyczyński), built in a historicist Modernist style on the plot of land bounded by Jagiellońska, Reymonta, Ligonia, and Lompa streets. The largest public building in interwar Poland, it retains its original function to this day. Before the outbreak of World War Two, two other buildings were erected in its vicinity: the Functionalist edifice of the Offices of Non-Assembly (1937; arch.: W. Kłębkowski) on the opposite side of Sejmu Śląskiego Square and, in close proximity to Chrobry Square, the ultramodern Silesian Museum building (1939–1941; arch.: K. Schayer), which, as a symbol of modern Polishness, was demolished during the German occupation.

National Digital Archive (NAC)

Silesian Parliament Building; photographer unknown, 1930–1935

Spatial development between 1945 and 1989

The post-war spatial development of the southeast part of the city centre proceeded mainly through the construction of individual buildings complementing the historical development. At the end of the 1940s and the beginning of the 1950s, in order to emphasise the official character of the space around the Provincial Government Office and the Silesian Parliament, the planners decided to develop the area around the demolished Silesian Museum through construction of a new imposing building. Originally housing the District Council of Trade Unions, this is one of the most interesting examples of the Socialist Realist aesthetic in Katowice (061). Sejmu Śląskiego Square also received new buildings more than two decades later, when, at the initiative of the city's party activists, a multifunctional building was constructed to fill the city block between Sienkiewicza, Ligonia, and Lompa streets (072). The turn of the 1960s and 1970s brought the beginning of work on improving transit traffic in the south of the city centre, including the start of construction of Górnośląska Avenue, which is now part of the A4 motorway. The aim of this new thoroughfare was not only to relieve the traffic load on the inner city streets, but also to provide transport services for the emerging 'City-Centre

Private collection, postcard

The Silesian Technical Scientific Schools building on Wojewódzka Street; photo by K. Boronowski, 1941

Documentation of the Silesian Library in Katowice

Photograph of the planned Paderewskiego housing estate; photo by J. Badner, 1965

Residential District – East' (known today as 'Osiedle Paderewskiego'; 067), which was originally intended for 20,000 residents. On Upper Silesian Avenue several well-presented buildings were constructed in the 1970s and 1980s, including the distinctive complex of buildings of the former Provincial Civic Militia Headquarters, now the Police (071), and the so-called 'Provincial Office Building' at 31 Wita Stwosza Street, which entered use in 1985.

Spatial development since 1990

The first decade of the country's political and economic transformation resulted in a number of public investment projects in this part of the city. A flagship project was the construction of the new Silesian Library building (068) between Graniczna, Powstańców, and Damrota streets. At the same time a bank building was erected on the opposite side of Powstańców Street with an architectural form that was modern for the time, resembling a glass sail (069). The 1990s were also characterised by numerous modifications to buildings in line with the then fashionable aesthetic of Postmodernism. An example is the corner building in the city centre which was rebuilt for the Wojewódzki Fundusz Ochrony Środowiska i Gospodarki Wodnej (073). The beginning of the 2000s and Poland's accession to the European Union in 2004 led to projects that occupied a border area between renovation, revitalisation, and extension of existing buildings for science and education. A good example is the renovated and extended premises of

the Academy of Music (062). It is worth noting that the development of this institution in the Zacisze and Wojewódzka streets area has continued with a new teaching building (063). Together with the existing buildings, this will form an intimate inner-city academic campus. The last two decades have also seen the development of housing stock. The complexes of the Katowice Social Housing Association in the Krasińskiego Street area (065) offer over 300 residential units for rent. Meanwhile, the eastern strip of Osiedle Paderewskiego, directly adjacent to Dolina Trzech Stawów Park, became, at the beginning of the second decade of the twenty-first century, an area abundant in new housing projects in both the cooperative and private sectors (066).

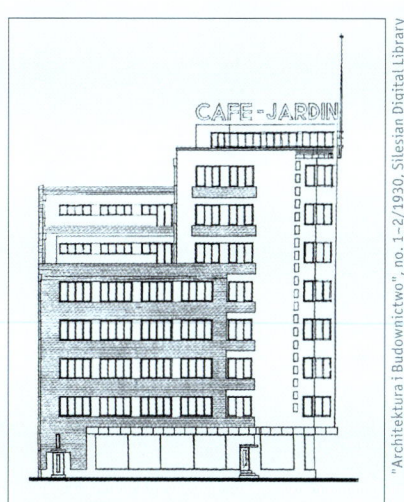

"Architektura i Budownictwo", no. 1–2/1930, Silesian Digital Library

Drawing of the north elevation of the House of Professors of Silesian Technical Scientific Schools on Wojewódzka Street, E. Chmielewski, 1930

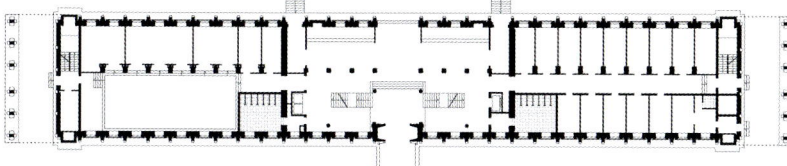

Public administrative building

061 C

ul. Dąbrowskiego 23
Henryk Buszko, Aleksander Franta, Jerzy Gottfried
1950–1955

Between Dąbrowskiego Street and Chrobry Square an impressive administrative building was completed in the mid-1950s, originally designed as the headquarters of the District Council of Trade Unions. The plot of land earmarked for this building was the plot previously occupied by the Modernist structure designed by Karol Schayer before the war for the Silesian Museum, which had been demolished by the Nazis when they occupied the city. A nationwide architectural competition resulted in the selection of a design by a team of young architects comprising Henryk Buszko, Aleksander Franta, and Jerzy Gottfried. As they later recalled, this was their first serious commission, and, in their opinion, had a significant impact on their subsequent careers. It is worth mentioning at this point that the team known as 'the green horses' soon became nationally recognised and respected for their interesting designs. The seven-storey building they proposed here is distinguished by its elegant monumentalism. Influenced by the era in which it was built (the period of Socialist Realism), it exhibits a typical monumentalism, but no direct historical citations or sculptural works can be seen on its façades or in its interiors. Due to the massive exposed pillars of its symmetrical end arcades, its compositional design brings to mind associations with Modernism. The building has a three-strip layout: a central corridor with staff rooms and conference rooms arranged on either side of it. The eye is drawn to the original position of the imposing main staircase, located at the focal point of the building. The staircase is open to a two-storey hall space with a mezzanine gallery. The building has a basement, whose layout was determined by the need to manage the difference in level between Chrobry Square and Dabrowski Street, which is five metres lower than the entrance from the square.

Katowice City Hall archives, prepared by Marek Peczak

Centre for Music Learning and Education, Academy of Music

062 E

ul. Zacisze 3
Barysz-Konior Architekci;
Konior Studio
2003–2007

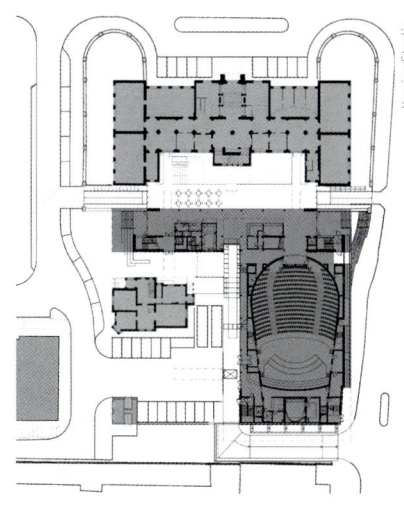

The headquarters of the Karol Szymanowski Academy of Music has a long history. The original Neo-Gothic edifice was designed in 1899 by Albert Weiss for the Royal School of Building Crafts, which operated here until 1922, when Katowice became part of Poland. In the 1920s the building housed the Silesian Provincial Office until a new edifice was assigned to the latter on Sejma Śląskie Square. In 1929 the building on Zacisze Street became the headquarters of the Music Conservatory. The tradition of teaching generations of musicians continues here to this day. In 2003 the university authorities began a fundraising campaign in a bid to expand the original building with, among other things, a large concert hall, a library, and space for staff and students. Following an architectural competition held in 2004, an architectural concept by Krzysztof Barysz and Tomasz Konior was greenlighted for implementation. From 2005 forwards, this was independently developed by a team from Konior Studio. The concept envisaged arranging the library, administrative offices, and concert hall in two perpendicularly juxtaposed blocks, with the longer side of the concert hall facing Damrota Street. The administrative rooms and the library open onto an inner space covered by a glass canopy, which not only provides a meeting place for the academic community but also links the new part of the academy to the original Neo-Gothic building. On the second floor there are, additionally, two pedestrian passageways providing a view of the foyer space. Construction began in 2005, and the combined complex entered use two years later. Budimex was the general contractor. The glazed hall connecting the historical part with the new Centre for Science and Music Education has two axially aligned entrances – from Zacisze Street and from Damrota Street. Following the closure of the historical main entrance from Provincial Street, these entrances now serve as the main entrance area to the Academy of Music. An important element of the complex is the 470-seat concert hall. This is lined with pear wood, which ensures excellent acoustics. The hall has a rich programme of auxiliary rooms, including a recording studio, rooms for instrument storage, and a complex of dressing rooms. The beginning of 2024 saw completion of a concert organ built by the Slovenian company Škrabl. The extension of the Academy building has a basement and a garage for 70 cars.

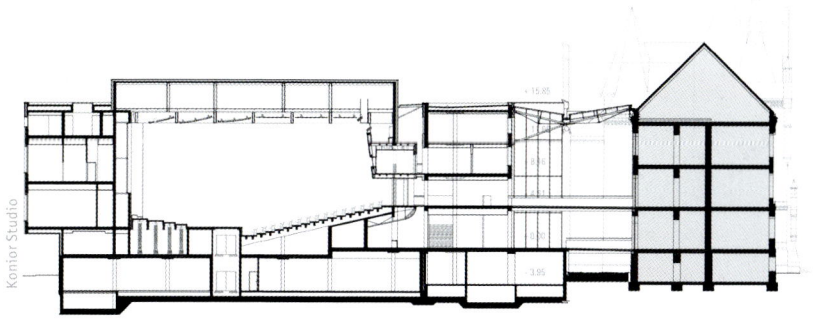

Academic Performing Arts Zone, Academy of Music

063 E

ul. Zacisze 3
SLAS Architekci
2019–2025

More than a decade after the Centre for Music Learning and Education (062) entered use, the board of the Academy of Music started pursuing the idea of building a new teaching facility to serve students and employees of the dance department at the Faculty of Voice and Acting. These efforts bore fruit in the acquisition of financing for the holding of an architectural competition, as a result of which the concept proposed by SLAS Architekci was selected in 2019. The design brief called for a teaching building with an audiovisual hall and a stage located on a plot of land exactly opposite the Neo-Gothic façade of the Academy of Music. The concept by SLAS Architekci involved arranging the functional programme around a centrally located double-height atrium on the second and third floors. Leading to it from the main entrance on Wojewódzka Street is a wide staircase, which additionally functions as seating. The hall for stage shows occupies the entire left

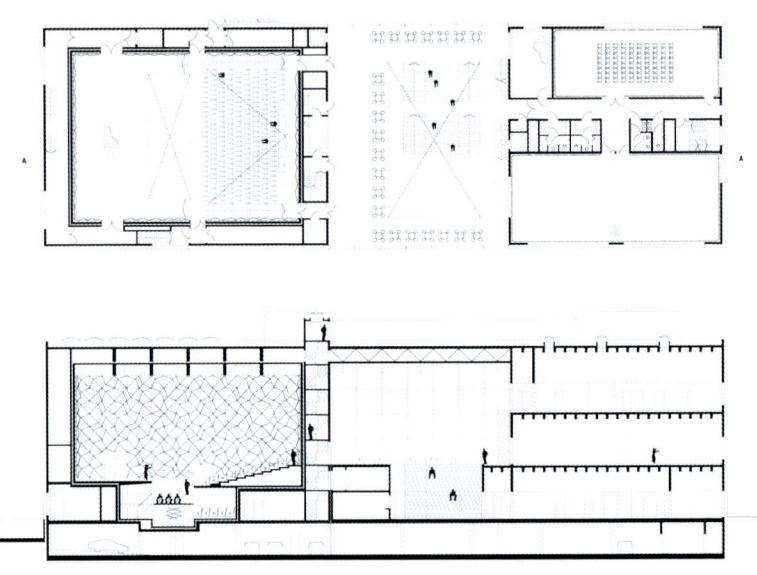

SLAS Architekci

part of the building (as you look from the street). An interesting device has been employed to visually unite the space on the axis of the Neo-Gothic Academy building and the likewise Neo-Gothic St Mary's Church, which stands on the opposite side of the railway tracks. This consists of providing a view of these two buildings in two directions through the two-sided glazing of the main hall. An observer standing on the Provincial Street side should be able to see the silhouette of the church's tower, while travellers passing behind the new building on a train should be rewarded with a glimpse of the Neo-Gothic façade of the Academy of Music.

Parish church

064 E

ul. Graniczna 26
Stanisław Kwaśniewicz
1978–1987

Conspicuous thanks to its soaring belfry with a cross-shape perforation at its top, this church was built for the residents of the nearby Paderewski Estate. Its longer side adjoins Graniczna Street. The site posed a considerable challenge for the design of the layout: together with the parish house, the church building needed to fit into a narrow strip that was 24 metres wide and 62 metres long. In addition, the new structure was to be adjacent to an existing pre-war monastery building on its north side. The project was designed in 1978 and received a building permit in the same year. It was built under the so-called 'self-managed construction system' with considerable financial participation from parishioners. In 1983 the main body of the church was ready. By the end of 1987 the tower was complete, and the gradual fitting out of the building began. This parish church is notable for its layout: the amphitheatrical hexagonal nave with, opposite the chancel, a two-flight staircase serving as an entrance to the gallery has a longitudinal axis (the axis leading to the altar) that is shorter than its transverse axis. This unusual design was adopted both because of the width of this plot of land and to ensure that all the faithful have a good view of the altar area. The church is oriented, which means that worshippers pray facing east. Directly behind the chancel runs busy Border Street. In order to insulate the interior acoustically, the architect designed the church's east elevation in the form of a sequence of risalites with window openings turned perpendicular to the road. Visually, in its use of sloping surfaces and undercuts, the body of the building evokes associations with the headquarters of the Silesian Institute of Science, also designed by Stanislaw Kwaśniewicz in the Brutalist style and demolished in 2022.

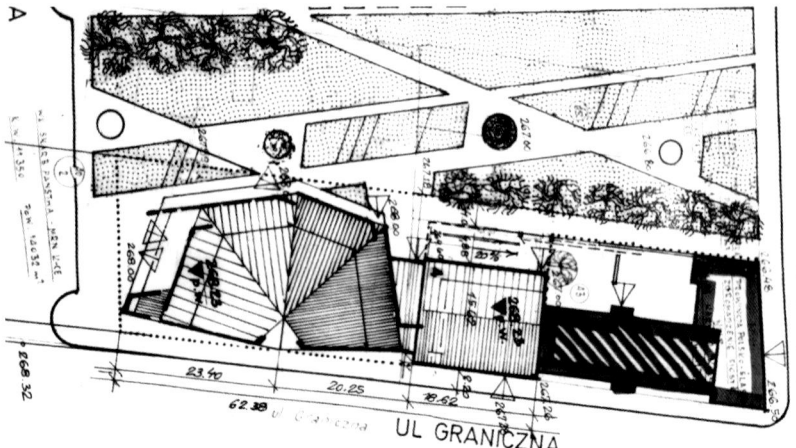

KTBS residential and commercial complex

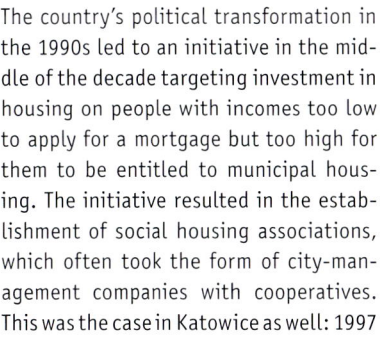

ul. Zygmunta Krasińskiego
14–14K, ul. Skowrońskiego 2, 4,
ul. Równoległa 7, 8.
Gronner & Rączka Architekci
2002–2004, 2007–2008

The country's political transformation in the 1990s led to an initiative in the middle of the decade targeting investment in housing on people with incomes too low to apply for a mortgage but too high for them to be entitled to municipal housing. The initiative resulted in the establishment of social housing associations, which often took the form of city-management companies with cooperatives. This was the case in Katowice as well: 1997 saw the registration of KTBS sp. z o. o, which included the boards of Katowice Municipality and the Katowice Housing Cooperative. The first decade of the twenty-first century resulted in the construction of numerous housing estates with a high standard of housing for their time. Projects for residential buildings were selected through nationwide architectural competitions; the resulting housing estates were comfortable to live in and had functional architecture. One example of such development is three residential buildings in the area of Krasińskiego, Skowrońskiego, and Równoległa streets. The project was divided into two stages. The first stage involved construction of a quadrangular, four-part building with an inner courtyard adjacent to Krasinskiego

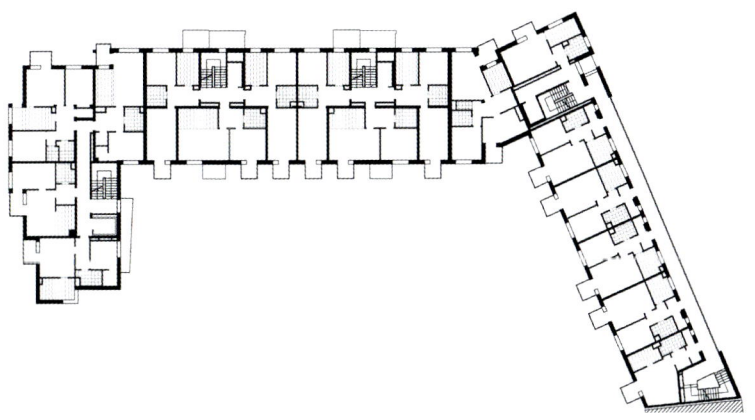

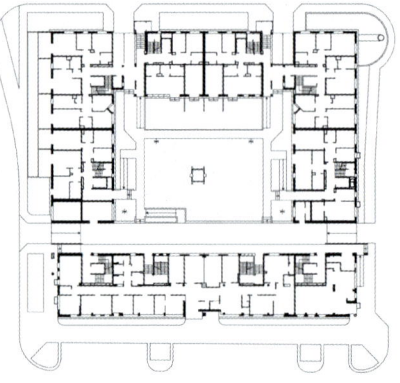

7

Street. The south-facing parts of the building have four floors, while the remaining parts have seven – which allows a more favourable supply of natural light for the apartments facing the courtyard. The ground floors of the sections of the house facing Krasińskiego Street contain services and administrative and management offices for Katowickie Towarzystwo Budownictwa Społecznego, the buildings' investor. On the underground floor is a garage for the use of residents with capacity for 100 cars. If we now turn and head into Skowrońskiego Street, we come across two more buildings completed during the second stage of the project. On the left is an intimate, five-storey house consisting of two sections with one staircase in each section. A little farther to the right is a larger building that fills a development site at the intersection of Skowrońskiego and Równoległa streets. This consists of three sections with different layouts based on the stairwell, corridor, and gallery principles of layout formation (see floor plan on previous page). It is worth looking at the gallery-based section with north elevation facing Równoległa Street. The architects opted for this design solution in order to acoustically protect the apartments from the sounds of trains arriving and departing on the opposite side of the street.

Residential complex

ul. gen. Kazimierza Pułaskiego 24–38

Jan Pallado, Aleksander Skupin

2008–2013

066 E

This territory's location directly adjacent to Three Ponds Valley, a favourite park and forest area for residents of Katowice looking for opportunities for recreation, has encouraged investment in construction of new housing complexes here over the last more than two decades. Nine new housing complexes have been built on former degraded plots of land located between the Paderewskiego Estate complex (067) and the park, and more developments are in the pipeline. In this case the land was owned by the Katowice Housing Cooperative, which held an architecture competition in 2008. The winning design by the team of Jan Pallado and Aleksander Skupin was implemented; the residential complex entered use in 2013. The complex consists of four two-storey buildings containing a total of 128 apartments with a variety of layouts ranging from two-room (with a floor area of 56 square metres) to four-room (with a floor area of 85 square metres). The rooms are arranged in a striking cascading layout and are sheltered by spacious loggias fitted with a system of sliding glass panels that contribute to the buildings' curved façades. This original design solution both ensures good ventilation and reduces energy losses, especially in winter. The ground floors of the buildings contain a series of garages and technical rooms. The complex is distinguished by the use of high-quality finishing materials and the thoughtful arrangement of groups of greenery in façade pots and in the inner garden.

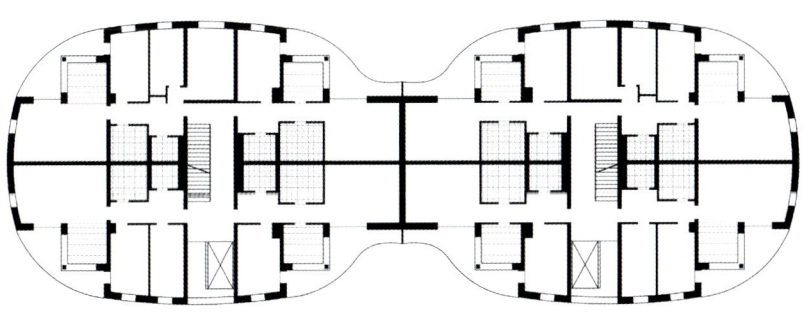

Paderewskiego Housing Estate

067 E

ul. Graniczna, Sikorskiego, Paderewskiego, Sowińskiego
Jurand Jarecki, Stanisław Kwaśniewicz, Ryszard Ćwikliński (Miastoprojekt)
1965–1980

Paderewskiego Housing Estate is a large residential complex intended for nearly 18,000 residents. Occupying an area of about 24 hectares, it borders the city centre in the west and the park and forest of Three Ponds Valley in the east. Its history

goes back to the mid-sixties when, at the initiative of the Katowice Housing Cooperative, a competition was held to devise a spatial concept for this housing estate, which was described in the documentation as 'City-Centre Housing District East'. The winning proposal was the jury's unanimous choice. The concept involved the use of a wedge-shaped layout and the introduction of greenery in such a way that the green recreational areas would seem to continue the course of the park in a westward direction – towards the city centre. Wind management was also an important consideration in the project: the estate needed to serve as 'lungs for the eastern part of the city centre'. The original design envisaged the estate as consisting of three groups of offset two-section buildings, with the number of floors decreasing in each successive row: from eleven-storey buildings on the western edge of the estate to four-storey buildings that blend into the greenery of the park. Unfortunately,

shortly after the winner of the competition was announced, the authorities were swayed by economic considerations and the shortage of public housing in deciding to abandon the principle of different heights for the buildings: accordingly, all the buildings were designed with 11 storeys. The idea of erecting a major residential services centre on Graniczna Street, in the northwest corner of the complex, also went unrealised. The role of the services centre was instead assumed by a large square, near which, in accordance with decisions taken at a higher level of authority, the monumental Monument of the Polish Soldier was placed on an elevation. It is worth noting the well-thought-out traffic system inside the estate. This has been arranged in such a way that pedestrians are prioritised – and can pass through the entire estate without ever having to come into contact with car traffic. Particularly convenient are the two pedestrian thoroughfares surrounding the centrally located green strip, where the school complex and service pavilions are located. Today, the residential buildings have mostly lost their original aesthetic qualities as a result of reconstruction to incorporate improved thermal insulation. The original design had used vertical stripes in vivid colours to visually break up the perpendicular building blocks and impart to them the impression of lightness; the stripes have now been covered with a layer of insulation and pastel-coloured plaster.

Silesian Library

pl. Rady Europy 1
Jurand Jarecki,
Stanisław Kwaśniewicz,
Marek Gierlotka (ARAR)
1990–1997

068 **E**

The Silesian Library is an important provincial institution with the status of an academic library, a large collection of books, and an innovative book-delivery system. The library's history goes back to the 1920s, when its first dedicated building was established at 12 Francuska Street. The collection grew at a rapid pace, and by the end of World War Two a new home for it was needed. A dozen or so architectural concepts were developed over a period of 30 years, but none were built. The situation changed only in the second half of the 1980s, when a site for the new headquarters of the Silesian Library at the intersection of Damrota and Powstańców streets was finally assigned. In 1989 an invited architectural competition was held, involving two teams (the second team, whose project was not implemented, was Marian Skałkowski and Aleksander Czora). The detailed design was approved in 1990. Construction began shortly afterwards, arousing great interest among residents. This distinctive building was officially opened in 1997. There is a gradual increase in the height of the individual blocks of which the library building is made up. The outer sequence of lower floors consists of administrative rooms and specialised studios; the middle sequence contains spacious reading rooms; the highest part of the building, its core and landmark feature, houses book storage. The compositional principle used here is notable: the

Documentation at the Silesian Library

sides of the nine-storey core are not parallel to the street edge but diagonal to it. This has the effect of preserving the continuity of the structure of the surrounding park, without dividing it into separate parts. In addition, the use of green roofs over the administrative part of the building and the artificially mounded green slopes reinforce the visual impression that the building's blocks gradually grow out of the green surroundings. The library has two underground floors and seven above-ground floors. It also exhibits many technical solutions that were innovative for its time and allow it to be operated economically and ecologically. The library has modern conservation and other specialised laboratories, but the innovative system that is most important for its functioning is located in the central core of the building: the system for storing and distributing books. The system adopted is 'high storage', based on a computer-controlled set of robots and telelifts that ensures the continuous transfer of books from and to the storage area. Thanks to this solution, innovative for the 1990s, the waiting time for ordered collections was significantly reduced. Today the Silesian Library building is one of the most interesting examples of Polish Postmodernist architecture from the 1990s.

Documentation at the Silesian Library

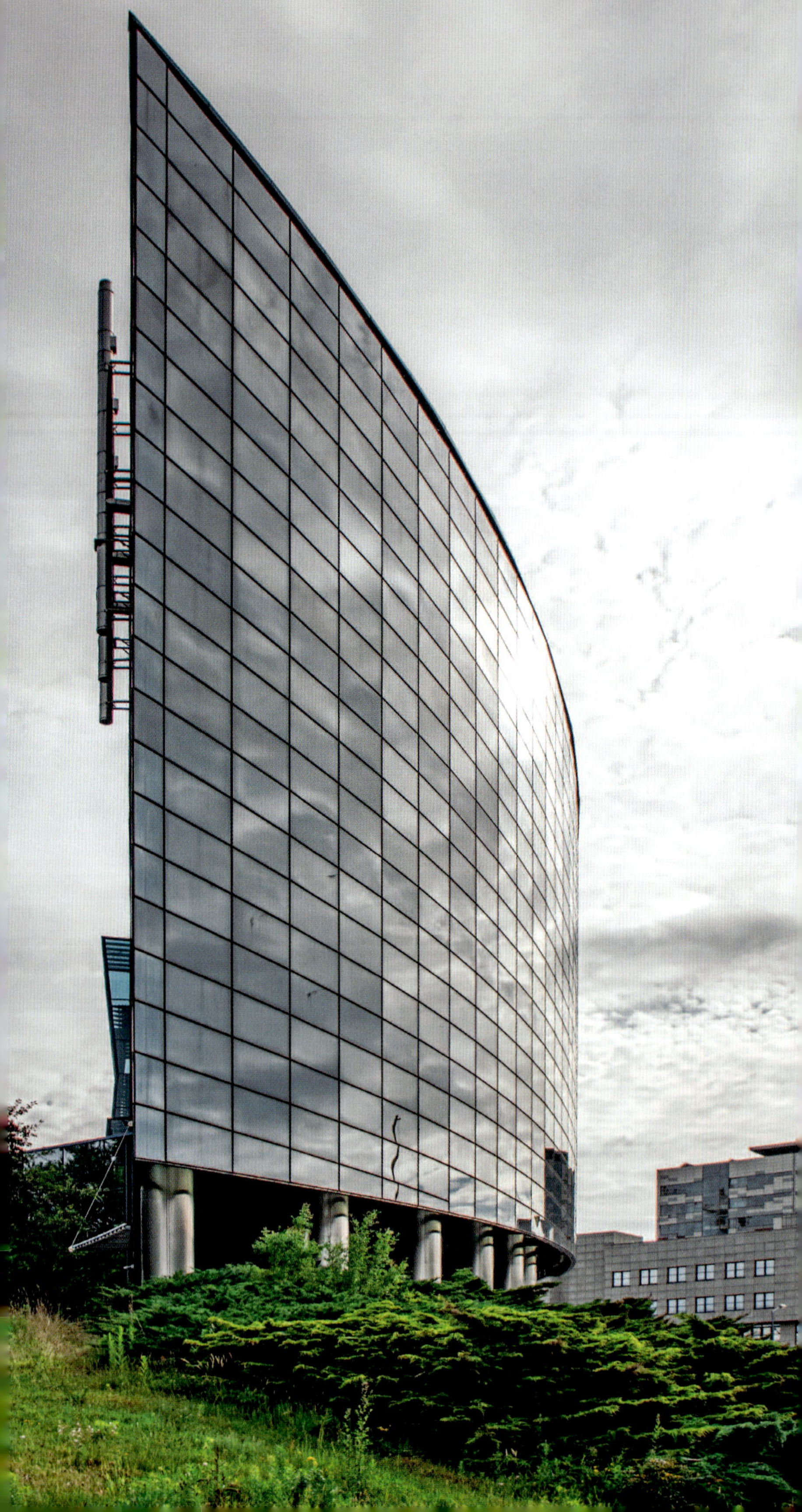

Former BRE-Bank headquarters ←

ul. Powstańców 43
Jan Lelątko, Piotr Pawłowski,
Zdzisław Stanik, Jakub Czarnecki,
Antoni Pietras
1997–1999

Headquarters of the Regional Court ↓

ul. Francuska 38
Archistudio
Studniarek+Pilinkiewicz
2003–2009

On the corner plot opposite the Silesian Library building (068) is another large building with a distinctive shape constructed in the late 1990s: what was originally the BRE-Bank building (it has since changed hands) was designed to look like a sail. At the time of its completion, this was a very modern building both visually and in terms of its interior layout. It consists of two segments. The six-storey part, with an impressive curved glass curtain wall that is visible from the street, contains office space and conference rooms centred around a multi-height main hall with semi-open, glazed lift shafts. Abutting this is a lower, two-storey, fully glazed volume. It is worth noting the sharp corner of the building's taller section, which is, additionally, visually undercut at ground-floor level, creating an interesting, dynamic frame and an illusion that the building is more slender than it actually is. A ramp leading to the underground garage with 130 parking spaces is located on the building's south side.

The building housing the Regional Court on a site between Francuska and Damrota streets opened in 2009. The court's various departments and management had previously been dispersed throughout the city; this new building brought them together in a single location. The design concept was selected in 2003 in an architectural competition. The detailed architectural drawings were completed a year later. The location chosen determined the building's orientation on an east-west axis while allowing a hierarchy of entrances: the main entrance is from Francuska Street; the entrance for employees, together with the exit from the underground garage, is on Damrota Street. Each of the two entrance areas is designed as a recessed portal with an arcade extending upwards over all six above-ground floors. The monumental main entrance is emphasised by a diagonal wall which guides those approaching the building towards the glass doors. The building is a compact, cuboid

Archistudio Studniarek+Pilinkiewicz

block with internal courtyards. There are two strings of rooms – on the north and south sides – connected at ground level by the main hall and on the upper floors by internal open courtyards, communication structures, and sanitary areas. One of the largest court buildings built from scratch in Poland after 1989, Katowice's Regional Court contains 51 courtrooms and over 600 rooms. Its internal communication divides into communication for the use of the public and communication for the use of court personnel. The latter takes the form of eight separate communication hubs located in the wings of the building and consisting of staircases leading from the judicial area through meeting rooms to the courtrooms of individual departments. The judges' area and the judges' communication hubs are inaccessible to other users of the building.

Archistudio Studniarek+Pilinkiewicz

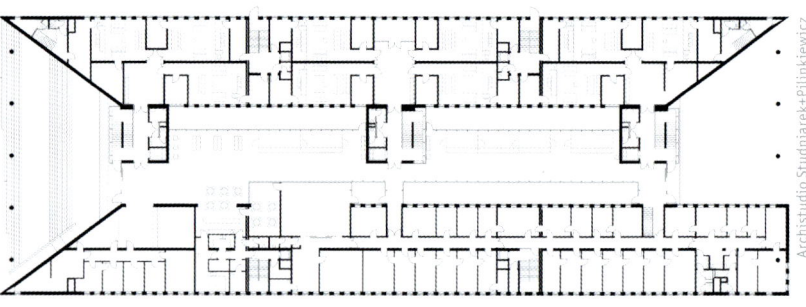

Archistudio Studniarek+Pilinkiewicz

Archistudio Studniarek+Pilinkiewicz

Provincial Police Headquarters

ul. Józefa Lompy 19
Marian Kruszyński
(Miastoprojekt – Częstochowa)
1972–1979

Due to the nature of its function, the Provincial Police (originally, during the communist period, Militia) Headquarters complex still evokes negative associations for many Katowice residents. It remains an object shrouded in mystery and legend, fuelled by the fact that information about it is restricted for security reasons. At the same time this is an interesting example of a composite architectural complex designed in the style of late Modernism. An architectural competition held for the design of the headquarters complex in 1972 was won by Marian Kruszyński, an architect active in Częstochowa. He proposed a complex of six interconnected buildings, the two tallest of which, as mirror images of one another, are best seen from the nearby A4 motorway (formerly: Górnośląska Avenue). These two 135-metre-long buildings each consist of three sections; their layouts have rooms of identical dimensions arranged along a corridor. The other buildings are cuboid structures with different numbers of storeys. Among them the two-storey casino pavilion plugging the gap between the complex's main buildings on the north side stands out for its internal green atrium. On the south side the rotunda located between the two high-rise buildings and housing an auditorium attracts attention when you look in this direction from the motorway. The façades of the complex's buildings require comment. The complex was intended to have a defensive capability. Accordingly, its façades needed to be able to repel an

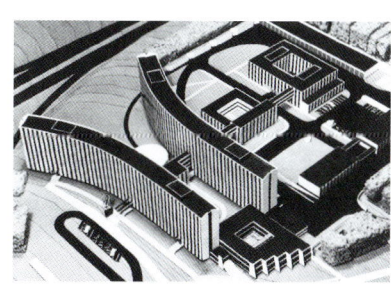

attack with machine guns. The architect opted for a vertical arrangement of concave, reinforced-concrete strips that could be used as shields. Eventually, however, due to a change in the regulations and against the wishes of their author, the strips were covered with glass façade panels in navy, blue, and orange. A further, recent, modernisation project, dictated by the need for more efficient insulation for the building, has partly distorted the proportions of the façade stripes.

**Dezember Palast
multifunctional building**

`072` `C`

pl. Sejmu Śląskiego 2
Zdzisław Stanik, Wiktor Jackiewicz
1976–1979

In the immediate vicinity of the pre-war Provincial Office building is an intriguing and massive structure whose original function was defined by the Provincial Committee of the Polish United Communist Party as 'a centre for ideological and educational training'. In practice, the building served for a number of years as a venue for party rallies and conferences before in 1982 becoming the headquarters of Polish Radio's Grand Symphony Orchestra, which adapted the auditorium for use as its concert hall. The orchestra was housed here until 2014, when a special building was built for it in the Culture Zone (023). To form a plot of land for building on in a prestigious location, a pre-war villa and the adjacent tobacco warehouse were demolished in the mid-1970s. The plot presented a challenge to the architects working under the direction of Zdzisław Stanik. As the functional programme drawn up by the party committee significantly exceeded what

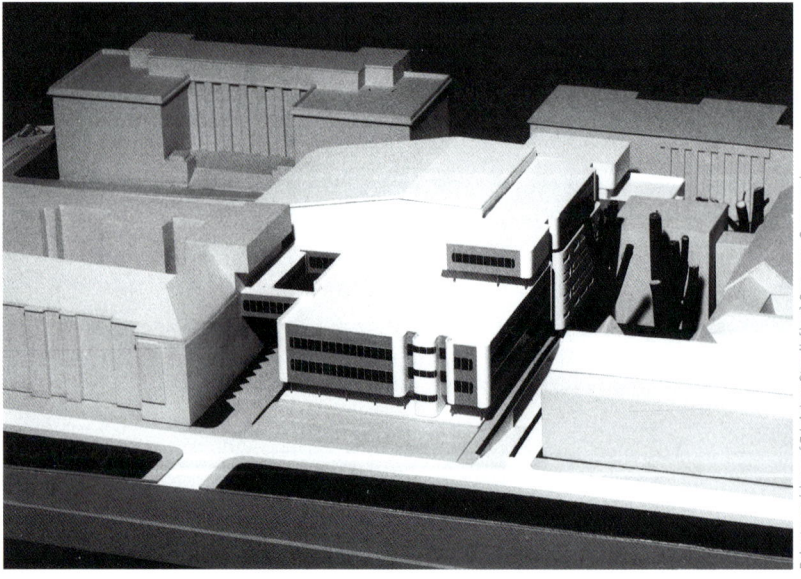

was possible on the plot, the initial design concept was based on the assumption that part of the building would overhang in the direction of Sejmu Śląski Square. It is this section that contained the auditorium, which later became the concert hall. The space below serves as foreground for the main entrance, which leads to a spacious hall with a wide single-flight staircase to the level above. Interestingly, the hall in question is overlooked by the end part of Ligonia Street. Despite the subordination of the entrance area to pedestrians, it is possible to drive underneath it by car if necessary. In addition to the formal spaces centred around the auditorium, the complex was originally planned to contain a hotel with 80 beds, a conference and banqueting hall, and a medical centre. While costs were kept under control (for propaganda reasons), the building was equipped with modern facilities, including air-conditioning throughout, low-noise lifts imported from abroad, and high-quality seating, which is still used today for cultural events in the concert hall. The building currently houses numerous cultural initiatives and organisations, including Korez Theatre and Katowice City of Gardens Cultural Institution.

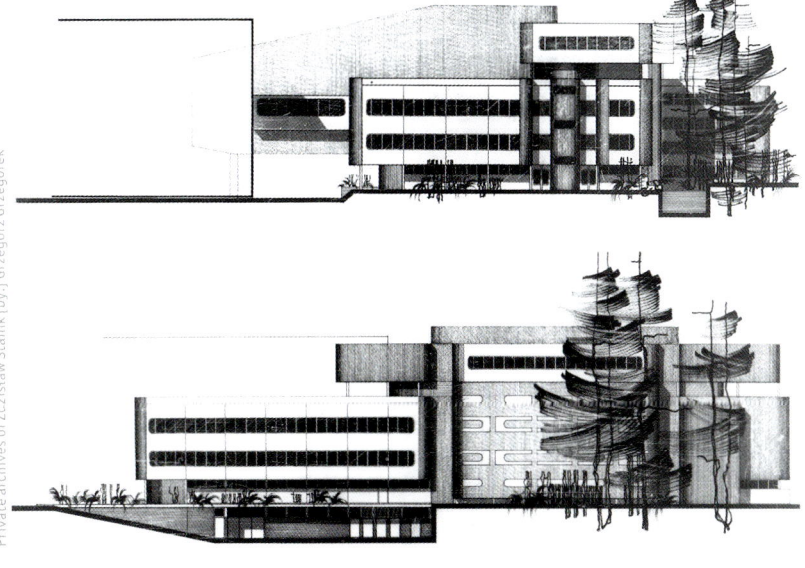

Private archives of Zczisław Stanik [by:] Grzegorz Grzegorek

Headquarters of the Provincial Environmental Protection and Water Management Fund

073 C

ul. Plebiscytowa 19
Henryk Buszko, Aleksander Franta
1967 (Rzemieślnik department store))
Jan Pallado, Aleksander Skupin
1998 (redevelopment)

Archives of the Institute of Architecture Documentation at the Silesian Library

As one's eye travels along Jagiellońska Street, which is lined with apartment blocks dating to the turn of the twentieth century, it is inevitably drawn to this corner office building, which has a markedly different character. The building's present form is the result of its conversion in 1998 to house the Provincial Environmental Protection Fund. Originally, this was home to the Rzemieślnik department store and offices. It was designed by an esteemed team of architects, Henryk Buszko and Aleksander Franta. Selected in an architectural competition, the project to adapt the building for new purposes was by Jan Pallado and Aleksander Skupin. An important requirement for the concept was that the building's usable floor area should be enlarged. Accordingly, the plan was to build an extra storey along Plebiscytowa Street. To respect the surrounding historical apartment buildings, the building's height on Jagiellońska Street was left equal to that of its neighbour. In an allusion to design devices typically used in corner apartment buildings, the architects marked the corner of the plot with a superstructure evoking a corner bay window. The double façade, innovative for its time, is also notable for its practical functionality: air extracted by mechanical ventilation from the rooms to between the two layers is cooled in summer and heated in winter. This solution improves the energy balance and makes it easier to maintain a constant indoor temperature. The additional storey has a roof lined with photovoltaic cells; at the end of the 1990s these were not yet widely known or used in Poland.

The Centre:
the Southwest

8

Central Katowice: the Southwest

At the end of the nineteenth century construction of apartment buildings in the southwest part of the city centre proceeded most intensively in the area around today's Kościuszko Street (originally: Beatestraße). The history of this imposing urban artery dates to the 1820s, when it was an unpaved route used to transport coal from the Beata Mine, which operated until 1880 in what is now the city's Brynów District. Adjacent to Kosciuszko Street is Miarki Square (originally: Blücherplatz), which became a city square back in the 1890s. Slightly to the west, at today's 32 Mikołowska Street (formerly: Nicolaistraße), a Neo-Gothic church with a square (today's Hlonda Square) was completed in 1902 to serve the inhabitants of the southern part of the city centre. At the beginning of the twentieth century, Andrew Square (formerly: Andreasplatz) was also a newly formed city square; its east and south frontages were completed with buildings in the Functionalist style in the interwar period, when Katowice became a Polish city. One notable building is the garrison church of the Polish Army (1930–1933; arch.: L. Dietz d'Arma), which was designed on a plot of land unfavourable to this building's function at the junction of Kopernika and Skłodowska-Curie streets. From the early 1930s until the German occupation, southwards along Skłodowska-Curie Street (also PCK and Juranda streets), there was dynamic construction

Buildings on Blücherplatz (now Miarki Square); photographer unknown, 1916

Apartment house owned by the Wędlikowski family at the corner of today's Skłodowska-Curie and PCK streets; photographer unknown, 1943

Part of a plan of the city of Katowice, 1900

The Silesian Tax Chamber building (the so-called 'Cloudscraper'); photo by K. Boronowski, 1934

of private apartment buildings, whose architecture today constitutes valuable Functionalist heritage. Also of interest in this part of the city centre is an intimate complex of residential buildings stretching along Zajączka Street; this is a colony of Neo-Baroque and Eclectic villas built by the Katowice Housing Estate Building Society for high officials, executives, and business owners (1924–1927). One of the most spectacular residential buildings of this period is the so-called 'Silesian Cloud Drapacz [Silesian Cloudscraper]' at 15–17 Żwirki i Wigury Street (1929–1934; archs.: S. Bryła, T. Kozłowski). Built using a steel skeleton construction for employees of the Tax Office, this has 17 storeys, making it one of the tallest buildings in pre-war Poland. As late as the 1920s, construction of another important edifice began between Wita Stwosza, Powstańców, and Plebiscytowa streets: the Cathedral of Christ the King and the Metropolitan Curia building (1927–1955; arch.: Z. Gawlik).

Spatial development between 1945 and 1989

The southwestern part of the city centre is the area that was subject to the fewest interventions in the second half of the twentieth century, in terms of both street layout and development. New buildings complemented the pre-war neighbourhoods. Particularly noteworthy is the early post-war development of the site for the Palace of Youth on Mikołowska Street (082), which was designed in the late 1940s and early 1950s. On the same street, at the intersection with Poniatowskiego Street, two detached residential buildings were completed in 1962 with an architectural design that refers to the most interesting patterns of Western post-war Modernism (080).

Garrison Church, view from today's Kopernika Street; photo: S. M. P., 1938

Silesian library in Katowice, postcard

Drawing for the 'Children's Palace' (subsequently renamed 'the Palace of Youth') in Katowice; author unknown, 1949

Meanwhile, an interesting example of a building sensitively fitted into a frontage formed by buildings from the 1930s is the Healthcare Building on PCK Street (074).

Spatial development since 1990

The period since the 1990s has likewise brought scattered new development that complements the fabric of the city centre – most notably, projects initiated by the Katowice Metropolitan Curia. Two buildings that were modern for the time of their construction were built in the close vicinity of the Archcathedral of Christ the King in the 1990s and 2000s. These are the archdiocesan nursing home (077), which borders the Curia's gardens to the south, and a teaching and research building designed to serve the needs of the newly established Faculty of Theology at the University of Silesia (075). The latter abuts another archdiocesan project – a publishing house headquarters, a printing house, and a museum housed in a building from the 1980s with a façade design characteristic of Postmodernism (076). This part of the centre of Katowice has also gained several new buildings and housing complexes: on Koszarowa Street (081) and Skłodowska-Curie Street (079) two multi-family buildings have been completed, complementing existing buildings from the 1930s. Meanwhile, on Raciborska and Strzelecka streets, the first phase of a residential complex in a coherent street-block development was completed in 2022.

8

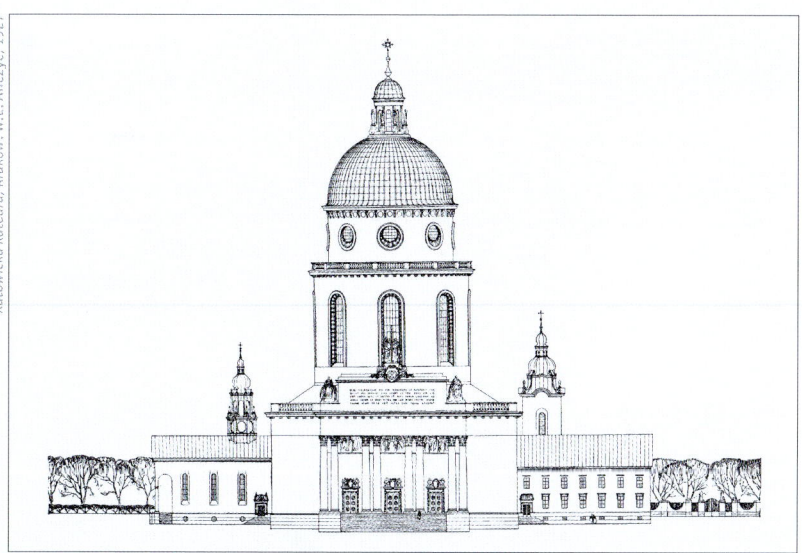

Katowicka Katedra, Kraków: W. L. Anczyc, 1927

Drawing of the front (north) elevation of the archcathedral in Katowice; Z. Gawlik, 1927

Healthcare Building ↓
ul. PCK 1
Henryk Buszko,
Aleksander Franta (PPBO)
1965–1966

Faculty of Theology,
University of Silesia →
ul. Henryka Jordana 18
Henryk Wilkosz, Jerzy Stysiał
(Stabil sp.zoo.)
2000–2004

The only post-war building inscribed into the block of inter-war apartment houses on PCK Street is the Healthcare Building. Originally erected for the Guild of Building Craftsmen of Katowice and constructed at great speed, this seven-storey building makes a good fit with the architecture of the apartment house on the opposite side of the street designed by Karol Schayer. With the exception of a curved, glazed pavilion containing a pharmacy and the latter's office and storage facilities and a slender volume protruding towards the street and housing the staircase, lift shaft, and sanitary facilities, the two bottom storeys are almost unenclosed. The entrance to the pharmacy is separate from the main entrance, which is in the aforementioned protruding block housing the communication riser. The remaining floors are identical: a wide corridor with waiting rooms and windows facing PCK Street leads to doctors' offices overlooking the inner courtyard.

A modern teaching building for the Faculty of Theology is located in the immediate vicinity of the Silesian Theological Seminary and the cathedral. The idea of establishing this faculty as part of the University of Silesia was conceived in the second half of the 1990s; it led to the need to acquire a site that would be suitable for this function. A large plot of land extending from existing buildings in Podchorążych Street to the site of the seminary was allocated for this purpose. It should be noted, though, that the completed building occupies slightly less than half the area assigned for construction of academic facilities, being merely the first stage in a larger development project that was intended to extend further to the south and also involve construction of a library for the same faculty. The library was to be built next to the seminary building. Completed in 2004, the Faculty of Theology building consists of two interpenetrating volumes: a U-shaped volume with five above-ground

storeys and an elliptical block partially sunk into the ground and housing an auditorium for nearly 240 people. On the east side, the faculty building adjoins the Archdiocesan Printing and Museum building (076), which was built in the 1980s. In order to satisfy the demands of the conservation authority and ensure the availability of wider views of the cathedral, the building's body was moved back from the axis of the Jordan Street pedestrian zone, leaving only the dynamic volume of the auditorium protruding. The main entrance area was accentuated by cutting it into the inclined façade of the taller of the two volumes and placing it under an arched canopy. The part of the building facing Podchorążych Street is more static in character, being integrated with the neighbouring residential building from the late 1930s. The entrance to the faculty's underground garage is on the same street. The faculty building is classified as 'smart' since it is fitted with electronic devices and other equipment that improves management of electricity, ventilation, and air conditioning.

Archdiocese Printing House and Museum

 076 C

ul. Wita Stwosza 11
Dieter Paleta
1983–1987

On the opposite side of Wit Stwosza Street, facing the western elevation of the Cathedral of Christ the King, is an elongated building of interesting architectural design. It occupies the corner of the street block bounded by the pedestrianised Jordana Street, on which stands the Faculty of Theology building (075). Designed for the use of the archdiocese, it has for many years contained a printing house, headquarters of publishing houses, a warehouse, and a bookshop. It also houses the exhibition rooms of the archdiocesan museum and a conference room, as well as the headquarters of the Catholic newspaper and radio station. The land on which it was built slopes markedly towards the north, which made it possible to fit in an additional ground floor. The building's most interesting exterior elements are undoubtedly the semi-circular bay providing light to the staircase through windows of an original shape (reminiscent of the playful geometry of Postmodernist architecture) and the slender window of the south staircase, which has a horizontal intersection on the top storey to give the impression of an asymmetrical cross. Between the administration and office area and the Faculty of Theology building is a volume containing warehouses and a printing house.

8

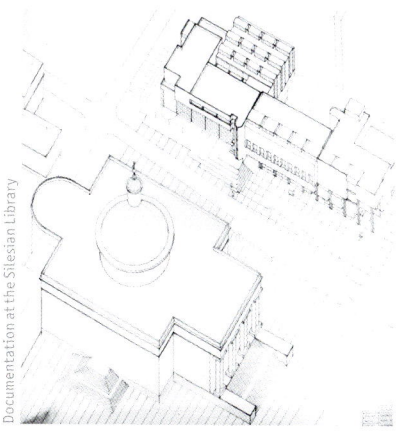

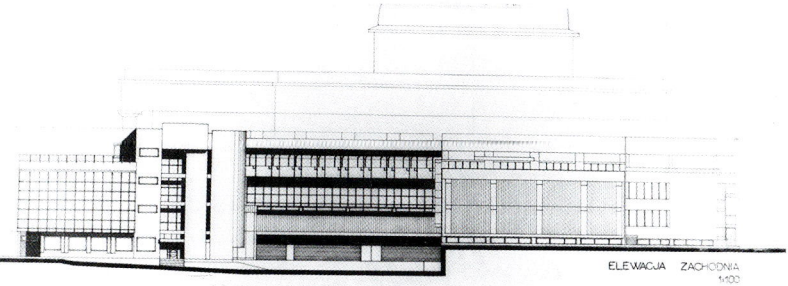

ELEWACJA ZACHODNIA

Archdiocesan retirement home

ul. Czempiela 1
Dieter Paleta,
Maciej Laskowski
1992–1997

077 C

The beginning of the 1990s brought an initiative to build modern facilities for the elderly and those in need of care, following the example of countries in the West. One of the first such facilities in Katowice was a nursing home built by the Katowice Archdiocese, intended for retired priests in particular. For this purpose the Curia allocated a large plot of land just to the south of its gardens. The headquarters of the Curia is a building in the style of historical Modernism, with clear Neoclassical and Neo-Baroque elements, and symmetrical in plan. The design of the nursing home was clearly strongly influenced by the layout of the Curia complex. The main entrance, on Czempiel Street, is located on an axis of symmetry extending from the entrance to the Curia

and its semi-circular apse overlooking the gardens. The three-storey building consists of an elongated segment of similar length to the Curia building, which is visible in the distance, and a second segment adjoining it on the southwest side, parallel to Wita Stwosza Street. The east end of the building is closed off by a cuboid section whose ground floor contains a swimming pool used for rehabilitation, a chapel with well thought-out indirect lighting, a library, and a dining room with kitchen facilities. On the floors above are small apartments consisting of a living room with access to a balcony or conservatory, a sleeping annex, and a bathroom. The apartments are accessible from the corridors, which are abundantly illuminated by large windows and overlook the archcathedral and Curia buildings. The underground storey abutting the inner courtyard and garden has a row of individual garages, which are accessed by a ramp from a street which runs inside this complex and is reached from Wita Stwosza and Plebiscytowa streets.

8

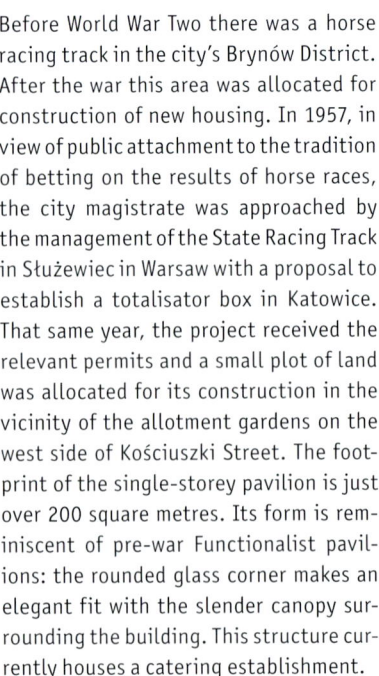

Former racecourse ticket office ↑

078 **C**

ul. Kościuszki 81
Roman Rudniewski
1957–1958

Before World War Two there was a horse racing track in the city's Brynów District. After the war this area was allocated for construction of new housing. In 1957, in view of public attachment to the tradition of betting on the results of horse races, the city magistrate was approached by the management of the State Racing Track in Służewiec in Warsaw with a proposal to establish a totalisator box in Katowice. That same year, the project received the relevant permits and a small plot of land was allocated for its construction in the vicinity of the allotment gardens on the west side of Kościuszki Street. The footprint of the single-storey pavilion is just over 200 square metres. Its form is reminiscent of pre-war Functionalist pavilions: the rounded glass corner makes an elegant fit with the slender canopy surrounding the building. This structure currently houses a catering establishment.

Residential infill building ↓→

079 **C**

ul. Marii Skłodowskiej-Curie 44
Dieter Paleta (Arcat)
2016–2018

2018 saw the completion of a multi-family building that filled one of the few gaps in the line of apartment blocks from the interwar period stretching along Skłodowska-Curie Street. The private developer had to meet the city's conditions relating to the nature of the project and provide enough parking spaces for 1.5 cars per apartment. With 14 flats planned for the building, a total of 21 parking spaces

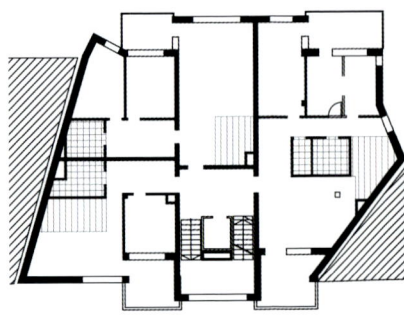

were required. It was decided to arrange them on two levels – in the underground storey and in a large part of the ground floor. This means that the building does not have a services unit facing the street. The small size of the plot prevented construction of a ramp connecting the two parking levels; here the natural slope of the terrain came to the rescue – by making it possible to create an independent entrance to the underground storey from the street. The layouts of the flats vary, comprising two- and three-room units with kitchenettes, ranging in size from 57 to 86 square metres, served from a single staircase with a lift. An interesting element that refers to nearby housing is the glazed conservatories on the street-facing side of the house.

8

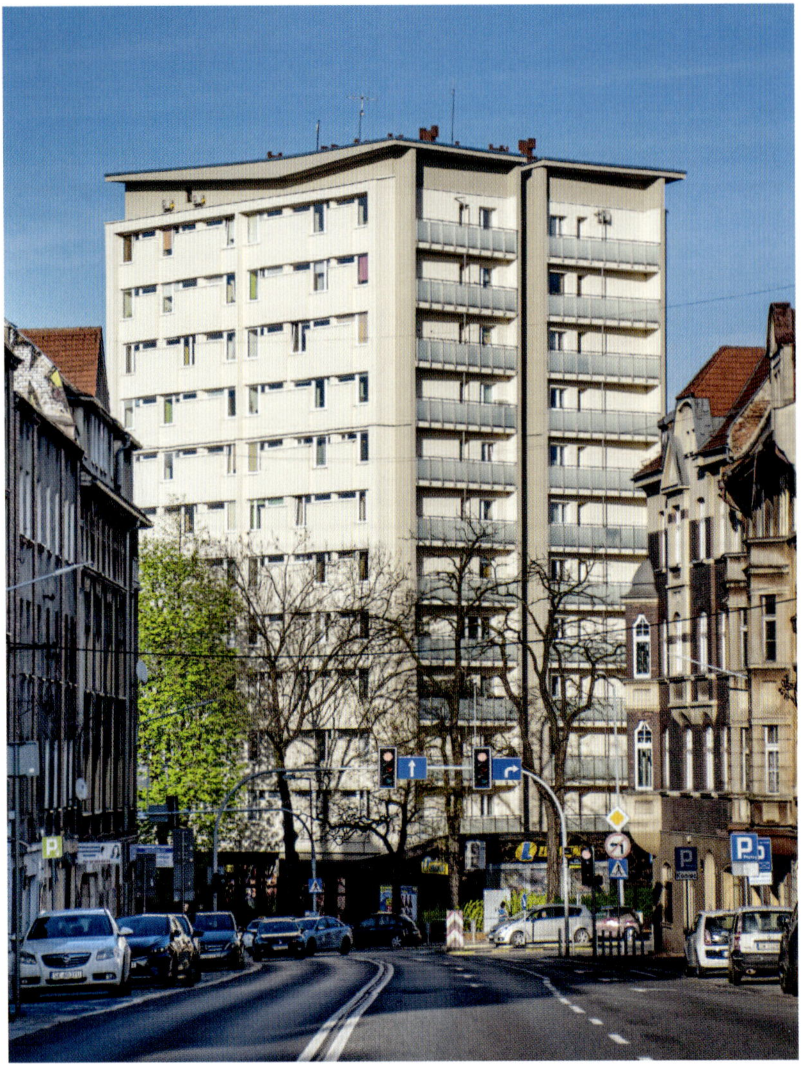

Archives of the Institute of Architecture Documentation at the Silesian Library

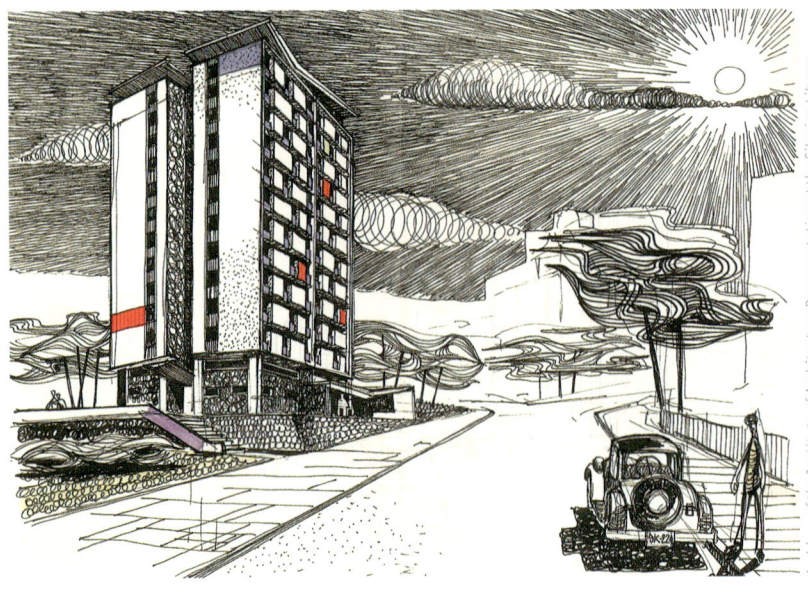

Residential complex

080 C

ul. Mikołowska, 40,
ul. Poniatowskiego 14A–B
Jurand Jarecki
1960–1962

At the end of the 1950s the Katowice Housing Cooperative held an architectural competition for a concept for a residential development on the plot at the corner of Mikolowska and Poniatowskiego streets. The winning entry by the architect Jurand Jarecki was for a complex of two buildings. The first of the two buildings, a five-storey block, is an oblong cuboid stretching along Poniatowskiego Street. Its ground floor contains small commercial premises and ancillary spaces, while the storeys above have identical arrangements of one- and three-room flats, with three flats accessed on each floor from each staircase. Here it is worth noting the composition of the rhythm of loggias and windows. Under the original concept, the loggias were to be accentuated with vivid colours. To the west of the oblong building, a 13-storey block intended as a local stand-out feature is made even more conspicuous by the fact that it is located on the axis of Mikolowska Street in that part of it which leads to the entrance to the city from the motorway. Variety has been introduced into the cuboidal massing through the use of a number of compositional devices. The first is the layout of the window openings: strings of full-length windows juxtaposed with horizontal louvres have been disrupted every two storeys using a mirror effect. The second compositional intervention involves making the building visually more dynamic by giving the top floor the shape of a canopy; this is a pavilion housing the shared loft and drying room. Thirdly, the use of a clear vertical indentation in the north and south elevations has the effect of breaking up the massive mass. This building contains only two-room flats with kitchens that are indirectly lit through an adjacent room (the exception being the outermost flats, where the kitchen has a window). It is interesting to note that the lines of flats on each side of the corridor are slightly slanted towards the north; this has the benefit of giving the flats light from the southeast and southwest. The complex has been thermomodernised, causing loss of its original character. The taller building has been painted a uniform white – in contrast with the original design, whereby the rhythms of the façade were additionally emphasised using colour and texture. Among other things, the finishing of the inter-window strips with fine ceramic tiles in an orange colour has been obscured.

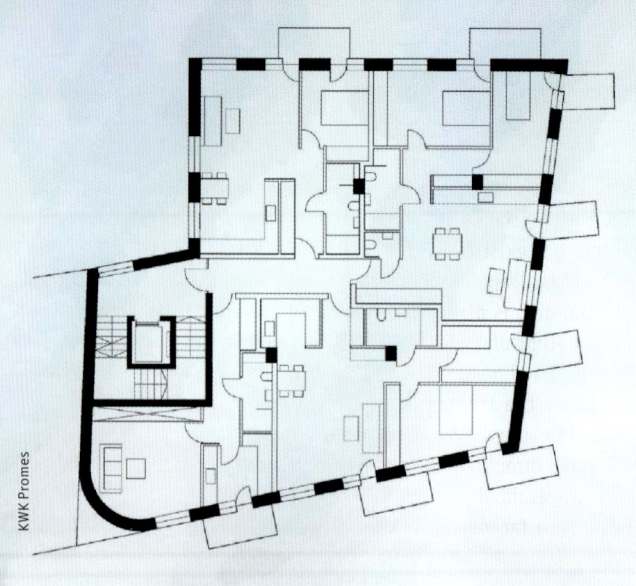

Unikato
residential building

ul. Koszarowa 1
KWK Promes
2013–2018

081 C

An interesting example of residential development complementing an existing street block is Unikato. Clad in graphite render, this seven-storey building is distinguished by the offset rhythm of the lines of balconies on its south and north façades, but even more so by the form given them by the architects: the balconies are elongated in one direction, and this direction has been retained in the balconies on the other two façades.

This means that, looking from Koszarowa Street, you get the impression that the balconies on the east façade extend eastwards from the block. On the top floor the corner at the junction with the neighbouring building has been rounded off. The white window joinery is not the only colour accent on this dark-coloured block: the ground floor containing the 10-car garage is clad in steel panels. Unusually, the main entrance to the staircase with its central lift is located in the courtyard: to reach it, you have to walk around the building to its north side. Each of the residential floors contains four flats with different layouts (from one to five rooms), making a total of 24 flats in the building.

KWK Promes

The Palace of Youth

ul. Mikołowska 26
Julian Duchowicz,
Zygmunt Majerski
1948–1951

082 C

Filling almost the entire street block bounded by Żwirki i Wigury, Mikołowska, and Stalmacha streets, the Palace of Youth is a very important educational and cultural institution in the history of post-war Katowice. The idea for its construction came to Aleksander Zawadzki, the governor of Silesia, in 1947. That same year, he headed the committee responsible for building what was then still known as 'the Children's Palace'. In 1948 an architectural competition was held. Among the 12 entries submitted, the winning proposal was from Zygmunt Majerski and Julian Duchowicz; the jury noted that it allowed the widest range of uses. Although the foundation stone was laid as early as 1948, the design documentation, functional programme, and architectural form for the palace were still being updated two years later, while the palace was still under construction. The opening ceremony took place in 1951, although all the finishing work was not completed until a year later. The complex consists of six interconnected segments: administration, teaching rooms, indoor swimming pool, gymnasium, theatre with accompanying facilities, and a residential segment with a separate entrance from Żwirki i Wigury Street. These segments form four interpenetrating wings centred around an inner courtyard with a fountain, which is accessed through a monumental gate from Mikołowska Street. The total usable area of all rooms (excluding technical rooms) is almost 13,500 square metres. According to some sources, there are 365 rooms in the building, which, together with the number of wings it has, may evoke symbolic associations with the number of seasons and days in a year. A highly interesting feature is the theatre hall, which regrettably no longer has all its original furnishings. In this project the authorities placed particular emphasis on providing showcase conditions for the promotion of culture. The stage was equipped with a revolving section, trapdoors, and cranes, and three types of curtains were used for overshadowing. High-quality spotlights and cooling and humidification systems were an added convenience for the performers. The auditorium was designed for 700 spectators. The balcony is connected to the ground floor by a staircase housing additional seating. Above the stage is a decorative relief depicting a folk dance motif.

East Katowice: Roździeńskiego Housing Estate

9

East Katowice:
Roździeńskiego Housing Estate

This complex of distinctive residential buildings with unobstructed views was erected on the site of an industrial waste dump which had belonged to nearby Katowice Mine since the first half of the nineteenth century. A large part of this area consisted of ponds and wash water reservoirs, which did not make it an attractive spot on which to build. The situation was exacerbated by the fact that illegal mining pits, known as 'borings', had become widespread at the beginning of the twentieth century; this significantly weakened the bearing capacity of the land.

Spatial development since 1945

The delineation of the course of W. Roździeński Avenue in the 1950s triggered discussions on the development of this degraded area. Early concepts, developed by a team of designers from Warsaw, assumed low-rise linear development limited to five storeys. However, these found no favour with the decision-makers, who argued that what was needed in this location was a showcase development that would serve as a showpiece at the east entrance to the city on the route leading from Warsaw. In 1966 the architects Henryk Buszko and Aleksander Franta presented Jerzy Ziętek, the then chairman of the board of the Provincial National Council in Katowice, with an innovative concept for residential tower blocks with a footprint resembling an eight-pointed star. The architects' arguments that their proposal would provide good living conditions, boost the construction economy, and have a favourable spatial impact on the skyline of the developing city met with approval. Later that year, land surveys were commissioned with a view to using the latest technology for the foundations of tall buildings. The following year, the plan was centrally approved by the ministries responsible for housing resources and construction. In the late 1960s and early 1970s seven buildings (083) with 23 residential floors were completed (the target was to build as many as 12, with various numbers of floors). The seemingly haphazard way in which these blocks are positioned conceals a number of deliberate urban-planning measures aimed at achieving aesthetic sequences of views of individual buildings from different directions. Particularly interesting is the deliberate effort to expose the dome of the archcathedral, which can be seen between the 'stars' by those entering Katowice by vehicle from the direction of Warsaw (this is now the S86 road). In the 1970s, in the vicinity of the Rawa River, along which the architects envisaged a pedestrian promenade, two further buildings referring to the shape of a star entered use: a school (084) and a commercial pavilion (085). The above-ground multi-storey parking lots designed for the complex were never realised: parking spaces are located on the internal road fringing the estate on its north side. At the end of the 1970s part of the land at the east end of Osiedle W. Roździeńskiego (Roździeńskiego Housing Estate) was handed over to the Academy of Economics (now: the University of Economics), which built two academic and teaching buildings on it. Although the estate is today administratively assigned to the city's Zawodzie District (discussed in the next chapter), its location, surrounded by busy roads on three sides and separated from the dense urban fabric in the south by the River Rawa, means that it is spatially perceived as an independent urban unit.

View of the dome of the archcathedral between two 'stars', seen from the east entrance to the city, 2024

Photograph of a model of the planned Roździeńskiego housing estate, 1966

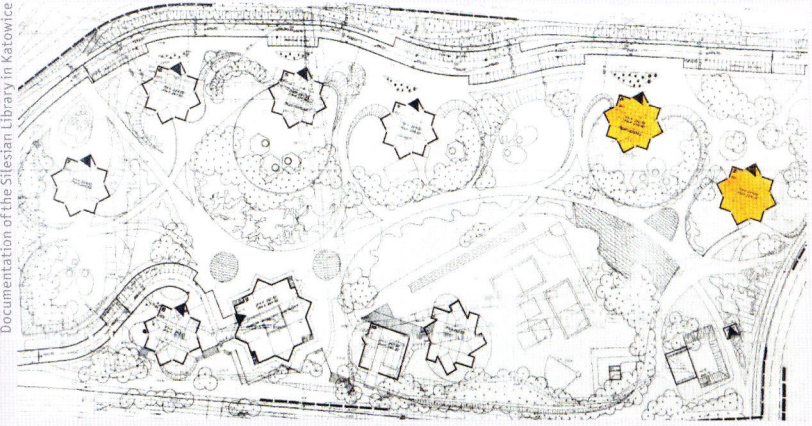

Drawing of the site development plan for the Roździeńskiego housing estate; H. Buszko, A. Franta, T. Szewczyk, 1967

'Stars', residential buildings 083 D

al. Walentego Roździeńskiego
86, 88, 90, 96, 98, 100
Henryk Buszko,
Aleksander Franta (PPBO)
1967–1979

The residential development of Osiedle Walentego Roździeńskiego consists of seven 25-storey buildings with a footprint in the form of an eight-pointed star. As explained by the buildings' architects, the layout derived from the desire to give all the flats on each storey the advantages usually enjoyed only by corner units. Each floor has eight flats of a single type: three-room apartments with a kitchen on a polygonal plan with a total floor area of approximately 65 square metres. Each building has a total of 192 flats surrounding a core containing a staircase, three lifts, and storerooms. Retail and service units are located on the ground floor. The Roździeńskiego estate stands on land that was not ideal for development, having been left over from mine tailings ponds. In the course of erecting these tall buildings, an even greater problem proved to be the remnants of unofficial coal mining, the so-called 'biedaszyby'. In the end, thorough geological surveys permitted the completion of all the buildings whose construction was underway to their planned full height. The towers were prefabricated using custom-made slabs of pumice

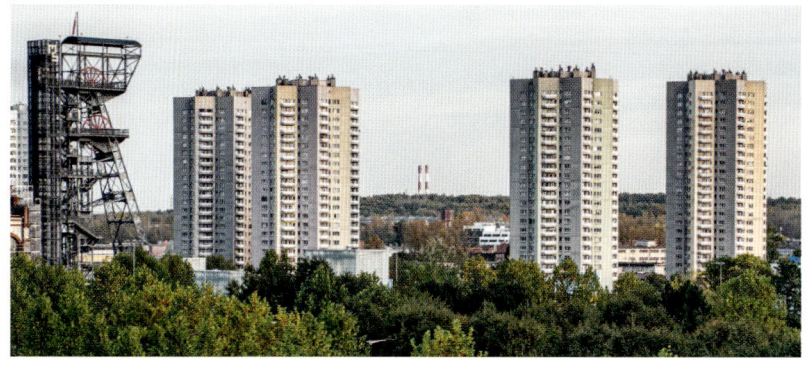

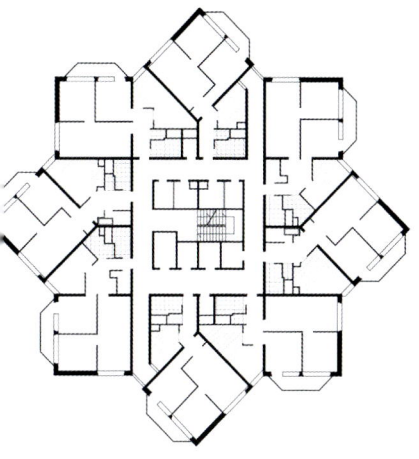

concrete. This material, however, led to technical problems in the late 1980s and early 1990s, when numerous leaks occurred due to differences in the shrinkage of walls and gas pipes. To address such risks, the managers decided in 2001 to completely decommission the gas installations in all the buildings. Given the complications described above, the structurally similar buildings in the 'Kukurydzy' (Corncobs) on Millennium Housing Estate (106), construction of which began almost a decade after the 'Stars' had entered service, were built entirely without gas installations.

Archives of the Institute of Architecture Documentation of the Silesian Library in Katowice

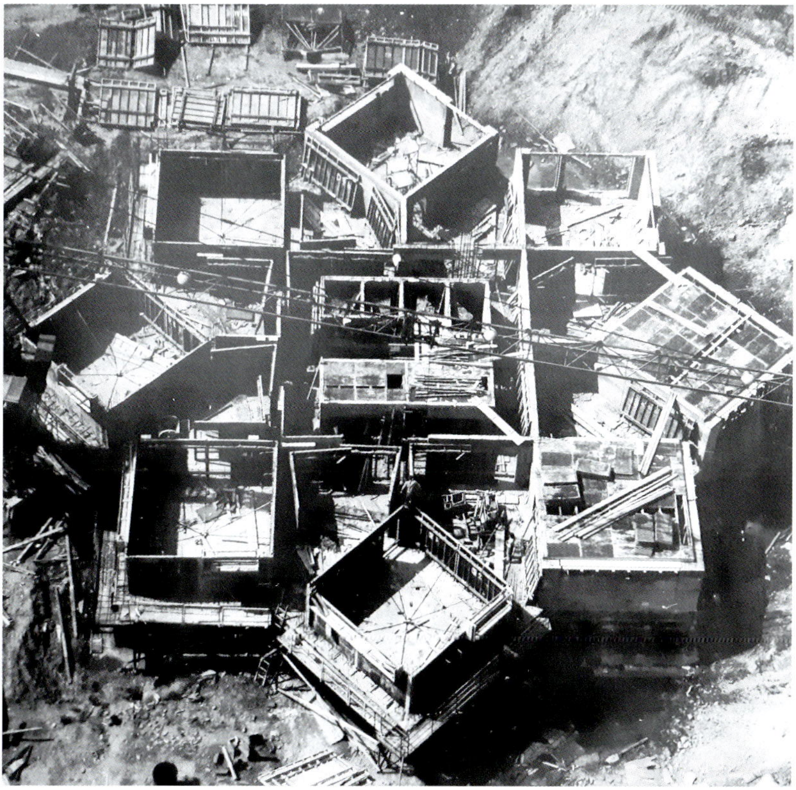

083

Primary school 084 D

al. Walentego Roździeńskiego 82
Henryk Buszko,
Aleksander Franta (PPBO)
1973–1979

The functional programme of the housing estate is completed by a primary school with sports and recreational facilities on the banks of the Rawa River. Of the building's three interconnected segments, the four-storey irregularly shaped block, whose main entrance is covered with a triangular canopy and faces the riverside pedestrian promenade, houses a gym and a swimming pool. The middle section, originally overhanging (its ground floor has since been filled in with built structure), houses administrative offices and the teachers' room, under which is a second entrance to the school, facing the residential buildings. This is integrated into the third segment, the teaching block, which contains classrooms arranged in a similar way to the apartments in the Stars complex, with an eight-pointed star footprint, except that the rectangular classrooms slightly protrude in such a way as to provide additional light for the internal communication between them. This in turn is lit from above by a skylight. The extension towards the outside of the classrooms enables the classrooms to receive light from as many as three sides.

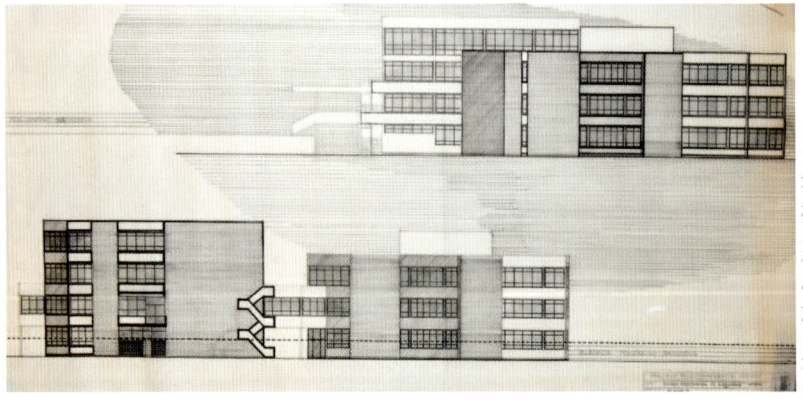

Archives of the Institute of Architecture

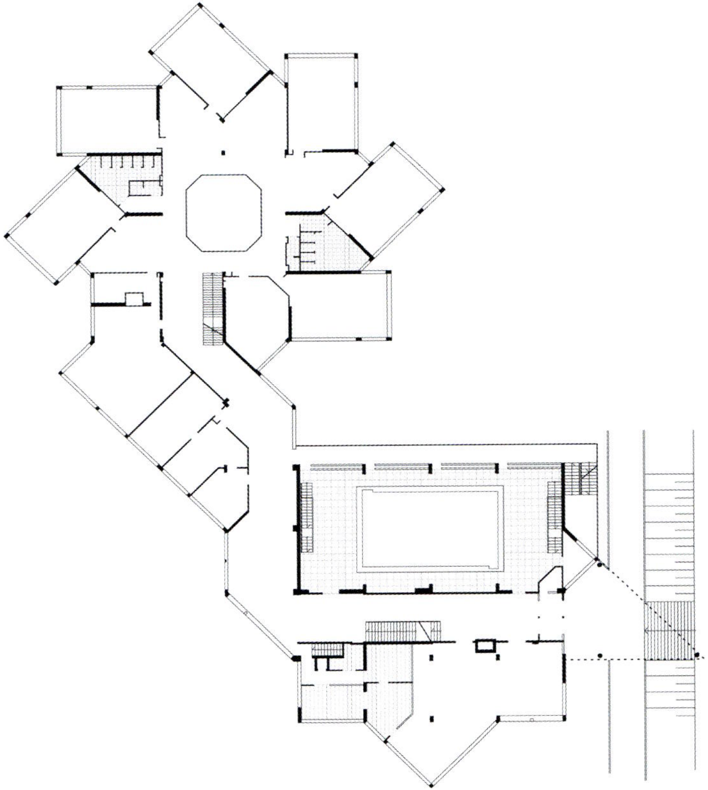

9

Commercial pavilion

085 D

al. Walentego Roździeńskiego
88A
Henryk Buszko,
Aleksander Franta (PPBO)
1967–1972

Before construction of the primary school (084) began, a star-shaped commercial and retail pavilion was completed and entered use. Viewed from the outside, the pavilion appears to be an enlarged copy of the plan of the residential building, but instead of an inner core, it has an atrium in the middle to illuminate the office and administrative facilities of the units inside. The six units on each of the three floors are fringed by covered, open galleries which are connected between floors by four open staircases, each consisting of a single flight of stairs. The lowest level of the atrium serves as an unloading courtyard and can be accessed through a gate on the west side.

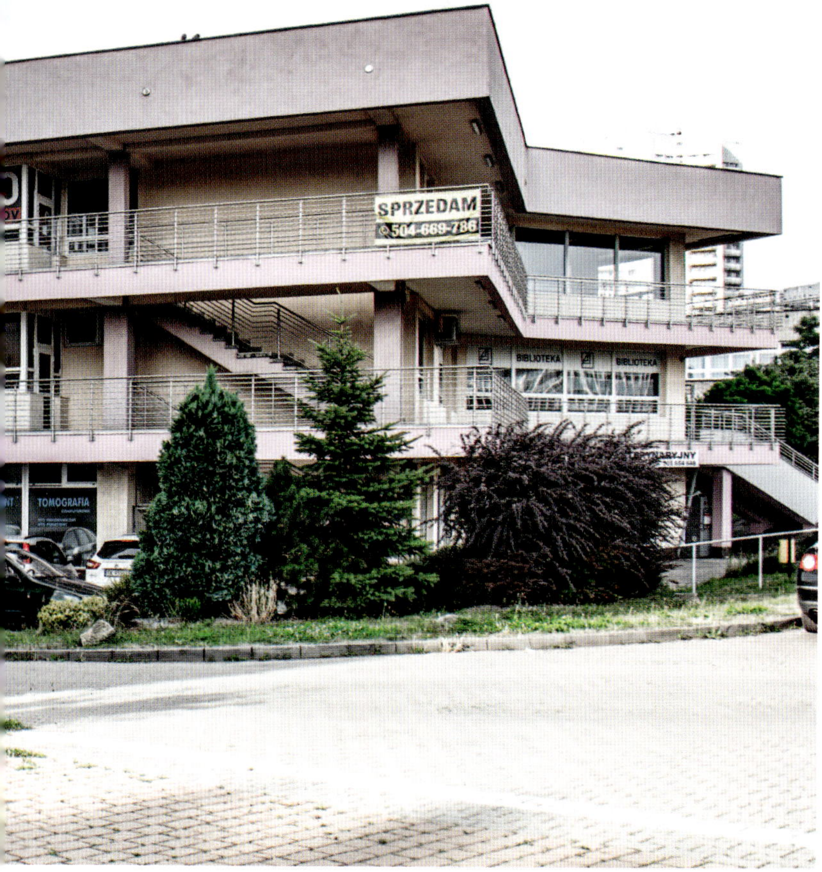
SPRZEDAM
504-669-786
BIBLIOTEKA
BIBLIOTEKA
TOMOGRAFIA

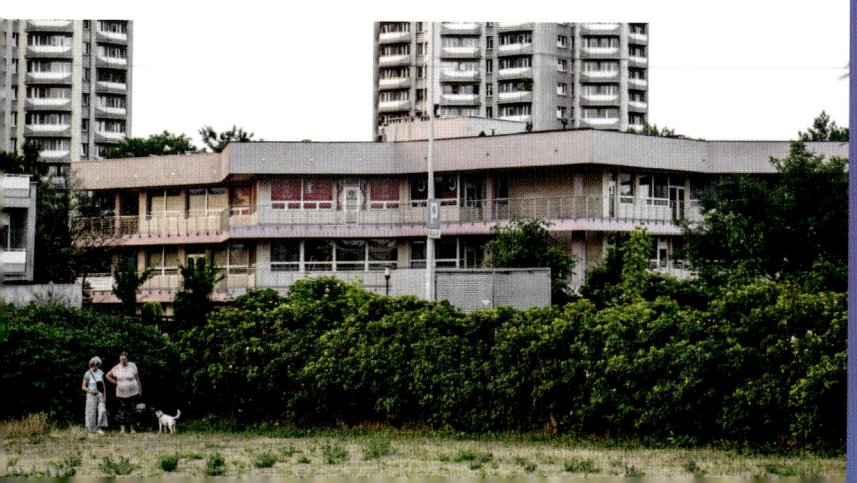

East Katowice:
Zawodzie District

10

East Katowice: Zawodzie District

The origins of today's Zawodzie District date to the late seventeenth century, when this area was a residential colony belonging to nearby Bogucice. In the mid-nineteenth century the settlement's character began to change to industrial. In addition to the forges on the Rawa River – to which the colony and, later, the district owes their name – there was the Kunegunda zinc smelter, which operated until the 1950s. Other factories active at the turn of the twentieth century were iron foundries, including Ferrum, which was set up as a result of a merger with the Jacob Ironworks. In the 1920s this enterprise specialised in the production of pipelines.

At the end of the nineteenth century Zawodzie was an independent municipality. The beginning of the twentieth brought rapid development and construction following the creation of the joint Bogucice-Zawodzie municipality. Today's 1 Maja Street was built up with Neoclassical and Art Nouveau apartment blocks, and in 1912 the community's monumental town hall (arch.: A. Hartmann), now the seat of the Rector's Office of the University of Economics, entered use. After Zawodzie, which already had the status of urban district, was incorporated into the city of Katowice in 1924, development of the area progressed. At this time a start was made on erecting

Private collection, postcard

Church of Divine Providence and the Municipality Hall building; photo by K. Boronowski, 1940

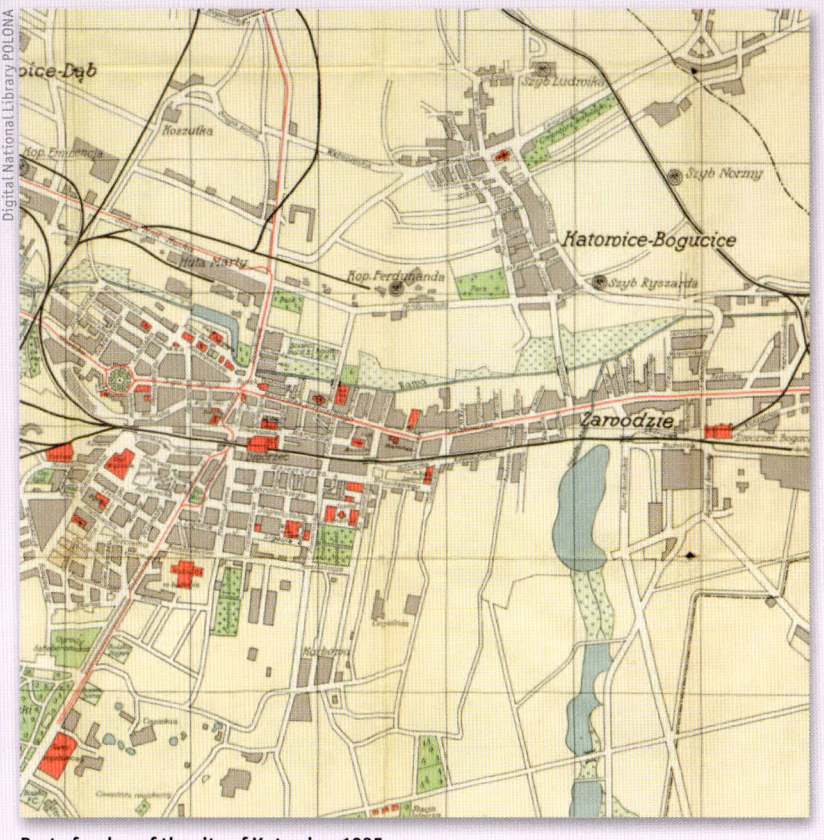

Part of a plan of the city of Katowice, 1935

10

several interesting buildings in the Functionalist style, including the Church of Divine Providence (1929–1950; arch.: T. Lobos) and the Queen Jadwiga Public School complex on Bogucicka Street (1929–1936; arch.: L. Dietz d'Arma).

Spatial development between 1945 and 1989

The post-war years in this part of Katowice were not rich in new construction projects: the main activity was reconstruction or expansion of existing buildings. Such was the fate of the aforementioned school complex, designed by Leon Dietz d'Arma, which was handed over to the State Higher School of Business Administration (today: the University of Economics) in 1946. Changes were made to the building's interior layout. A year later, in the line of buildings fronting today's 1 Maja Street (at number 47) construction began of a five-storey academic building

in the style of pre-war Functionalism (1947–1952; arch.: E. Tatarczyk). This building has two wings; the inner wing, not visible from the street, originally contained 36 rooms intended for a total of about 100 people. In the 1960s the west, north, and staircase wings of the 1930s building were extended by one storey (arch.: M. Sramkiewicz), and in the 1970s two new buildings were erected on the inner side of the headquarters complex to house teaching rooms and a swimming pool with a gymnasium. On the opposite side of Bogucicka Street a prefabricated 'Leipzig'-type building housing staff offices and small teaching rooms (demolished in 2019) entered use in 1979.

Residential development in this district in the 1970s included the construction of standardised, prefabricated blocks of flats in the vicinity of today's Bohaterów Monte Cassino and Łączna streets. These, however, cannot be considered architecturally of value.

The public school in Zawodzie (now Building A of the University of Economics), 1937

Spatial development since 1990

Since the mid-1990s Zawodzie District has gradually been built up with modern housing. A significant contribution to this process has been made by a company established by the city in co-operation with the Katowice Housing Cooperative: Katowickie Towarzystwo Budownictwa Społecznego (KTBS) in 1994. The company's goal is not only to meet housing needs but also to undertake revitalisation activities and provide spaces for social use that improve the district's image. Following a number of architectural competitions held in the period 1999–2007 in the area of Saint Etienne and Marcinkowskiego streets, the Bulwary Rawy residential complex (86–88), notable for its high-quality layouts, was created. Slightly to the east, on Szeroka Street, a modern multi-family building with rental apartments was realised in 2019–2020.

In addition to residential developments, it is also worth mentioning the modern research and teaching building of the University of Economics, which was completed in Zawodzie District in 2014 (089). Particularly interesting are the distinctive entrance façade (west façade) and the north and east façades with their rhythmic division of brick-finished curtain walls overlooking a busy dual carriageway. A notable investment project aimed at improving the city's public transportation is the interchange centre with distinctive corrugated roof which opened next to the tram terminus in Zawodzie in 2019.

Building D of the University of Economics, 2018

KTBS multi-family residential building in
the Bulwary Rawy II complex

Bulwary Rawy I, KTBS residential complex

086 D

ul. St Etienne 2–7a
Jan Pallado,
Aleksander Skupin
1999–2001

The first stage of Katowickie Towarzystwo Budownictwa Społecznego's project to develop a large section of Zawodzie District for housing was the construction of six two-storey buildings. The design project for the buildings was selected in an architectural competition

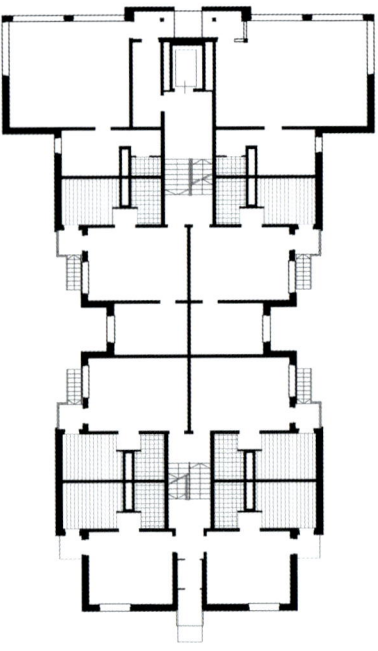

organised by KTBS. The two groups of buildings have different numbers of storeys. The three buildings located closest to the Rawa River are the tallest with six storeys, while the three others, located to the south of them, have four storeys. The lower segments have a staggered floor plan, which, combined with the stepped arrangement of the rooms in the flats, enhances the cascading effect of the buildings. All apartments have a separate kitchen with a window. Two-room flats predominate, with three-room flats only in the highest part of the buildings (facing the River Rawa). The first phase of the project contains a total of 205 flats. Between the buildings are green open spaces and gardens assigned to apartments located on the ground floors. Completing the programme for this phase is a two-storey car park for residents; this is located adjacent to the residential buildings and has a total of 145 parking spaces. Its lower storey is half embedded in the ground.

Bulwary Rawy II, KTBS residential building

087 D

ul. St Etienne 9–15a
Jan Pallado, Aleksander Skupin
2001–2003

The large building constructed at the bend of St Etienne Street for the second phase of the KTBS project offers a spatial contrast with the dispersed layout of Bulwary Rawy I. It has seven above-ground storeys and eight staircases. Planned as a half-ring, this house is immediately noticeable from the street due to the curved façade on its upper two storeys – something that is not visible from the inner courtyard with its greenery and playground. The eye is drawn to the distinctive circular windows between the sixth and seventh storeys; these 'portholes' provide illumination for the stairwells. On each level of each stairwell there are three flats; the two outermost staircases on opposite sides of the building, however, give access to only two flats. A major advantage of the layout of the flats is that most are double-aspect, with windows facing both St Etienne Street and the inner courtyard. This arrangement provides optimal conditions for natural ventilation in the flats. There are a total of 154 one-, two- and three-room flats in the building.

10

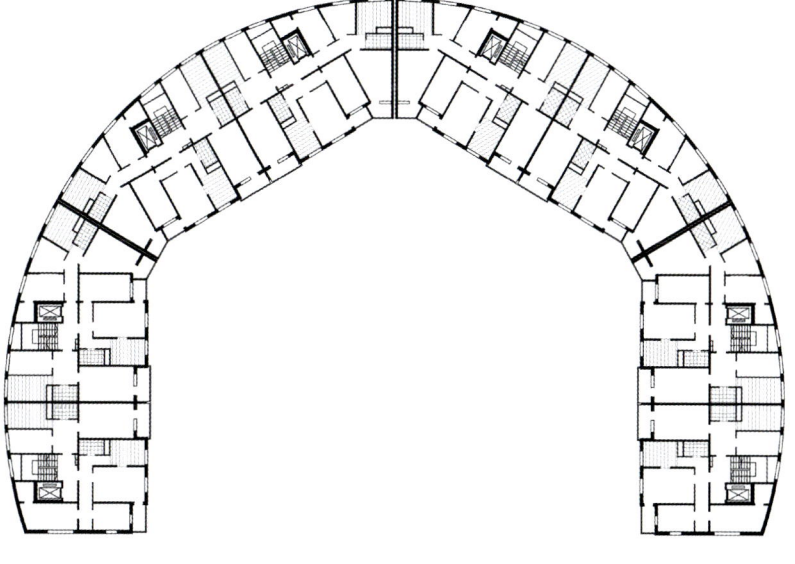

Bulwary Rawy III,
KTBS residential complex

ul. Marcinkowskiego 2A–6C
Jan Pallado,
Aleksander Skupin
2004–2005

The third stage of Bulwary Rawy (Boulevards of the Rawa) is situated at a distance from the first two stages, on a plot bounded by Morcinka and Braci Stawowe streets. It consists of three identical six-storey buildings in which each staircase leads on each floor to four flats served by two lifts. In all, there are 198 apartments in the three buildings. The ground floor of each building contains 14 individually lockable garage spaces and one spacious commercial unit. An original design solution imparts visual lightness to the massive buildings. The flats are arranged in a composition of interpenetrating, recessed, and overhanging cuboids. The latter are further differentiated by being painted different pastel colours (pastel colours were popular at the time this complex was built). Slender reinforced-concrete roofs cover the terraces of the flats on the top floor.

Centre for Modern Information Technologies, University of Economics

089 D

ul. Bogucicka 5
Pracownia Projektowa Wojciech Podleski
2011–2014

The Centre for Modern Information Technologies building is the first new investment project by the University of Economics in Katowice since the 1970s. To build it, the university's Building D was demolished. The new building has six storeys. Pedestrians approach the main entrance via a footbridge passing over a lower piece of ground on which an external car park is located. The entrance to the garage is beneath the main part of the building. Groups of rooms are arranged in the two parts of the building. The tallest, slender part is finished in dark brown brick and has an L-shaped footprint with its inner sides facing south and west. Sandwiched between the wings of this taller section is a glazed block whose intricate form is shaped by a variety of risalites and roof terraces. The computer labs housed in the taller section are located on the north and northeast sides of the building, which reduces the risk of overheating in the summer. The orientation of the windows was dictated by the desire to create acoustic protection from the impact of the dual carriageway which passes nearby. There are meeting rooms, staff offices, and a server room. The main space in the middle of the building is an auditorium for 200 people. According to the architect's calculations, more than 800 students can use the educational facilities in the building at the same time.

10

East Katowice: Giszowiec and Nikiszowiec Districts

11

East Katowice:
Giszowiec and Nikiszowiec Districts

Giszowiec and Nikiszowiec are two of the most distinctive worker settlements of the early twentieth century in Silesia. Although built almost simultaneously and designed by the same architects, they represent completely different types of development. Giszowiec (formerly: Gieschewald) is a complex of low-rise two-family or single-family houses with individual gardens. It has a centre in the form of a market square and a community garden. Nikiszowiec (formerly: Nickischschacht), on the other hand, has an urban character, consisting of nine blocks of multi-family housing, with green courtyards inside each block and a centre in the form of a marketplace on which there is a church. The two neighbourhoods are two kilometres apart.

Giszowiec: history and spatial development in the twentieth and twenty-first centuries

Gieschewald housing estate was built on forested land in the municipality of Janow that belonged to Count Franz Tiele-Winckler. When the Georg von Giesches Erben company decided to start coal mining in the area, its management set about building a housing estate to attract future workers. The design for the estate was conceived by two brothers from Charlottenburg, Emil and Georg Zillmann, who were chosen by Anthon Uthemann, the then director of the Giesche factory. The concept involved provision of housing for more than 600 families ranging from blue-collar workers employed in the

Miners' houses roofed with wooden shingles; photo by R. Bombik, 1919

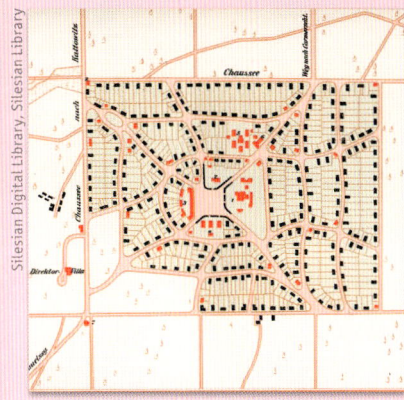

Silesian Digital Library, Silesian Library

Part of a plan of the Giszowiec housing estate; compiled by. H.von Reuffurth, 1910

mines and clerks to teachers. Giszowiec's spatial layout differed from those of workers' housing estates built in the region so far: here the architects applied the idea of a garden city, a concept which had been invented and promoted by the English urban planner Ebenezer Howard. As well as building double- and single-family houses (the floor area of most of the dwellings did not exceed 60 square metres) for employees to live in, the developer and architects provided residents in the central part of the settlement with a number of amenities, including a bathhouse with a laundry, a mangle, a post office, an inn with accommodation, and two schools (Catholic and Evangelical). The project did not include the construction of a church: residents went to the nearest church, located in Nikiszowiec, for services. In the interwar period, when Giszowiec became part

of the Republic of Poland, the Giesches Erben company began suffering financial difficulties. As a result, in 1926 it decided to join forces with American investors from Anaconda Cooper Mining Co and Averell Harriman. At this time the company's board of directors changed, filling with US citizens. This necessitated that board members be present on site, hence the decision to build a villa colony for them and their families on the edge of the Giszowiec estate. The six villas were served by an independent water tower. A modern golf course was established south of the complex. The spatial structure of the Giszowiec estate remained almost unchanged until the post-war period and the establishment of the People's Republic of Poland.

After Poland was occupied by the Red Army in 1945, mining resumed almost immediately, in the same year, at the Giesche mine (renamed 'Wieczorek' in 1946). In the first half of the 1960s mining began at a new plant – Staszic Mine. In order to provide housing for the ever-growing number of employees, in 1969 a decision was made to demolish the low-rise buildings designed by the Zillmanns and replace them with a complex of ten-storey prefabricated residential buildings. Demolition of the miners' cottages began in the early 1970s and was not halted until 1978, following the intervention of the province's conservation authority. Roughly one-third of Giszowiec's historical low-rise housing complex has survived to the present day, contrasting with the blocks

11

Private collection, postcard

Buildings on Market Square; photo by R. Bombik, 1919

Post-war Staszic Coal Mine building; photographer unknown, 1966

polska-org.pl

of flats built from large panels that entered service in the 1970s. The 1980s and the initial period of the country's political and economic transition brought discussion about perception of Giszowiec's buildings as an important cultural heritage for the city and the region. The new buildings introduced at this time were already being designed so that their scale would fit in with the intimate character of the original workers' estate. Examples include the rehabilitation and education centre on Guest Street (090) and the school complex on Friendly Street (091). In the twenty-first century projects realised by the Katowice Housing Cooperative (Katowickie Towarzystwo Budownictwa

National Digital Archive (NAC)

St Anne's Church; photographer unknown, 1937

Pprivate collection, postcard

Guest house at the community garden, photo by R. Bombik, 1919

Demolition of miners' houses on Wojciecha Street; photographer unknown, 1977

Społecznego) have likewise been tailored to the spatial and cultural context of their locations on the estate (092, 093).

Nikiszowiec: history and spatial development in the twentieth and twenty-first centuries

The housing estate originally named 'Nickischschacht' has the same genesis as the Giszowiec estate described above. Its name derives from one of the mining shafts that belonged to Giesche. After the Giszowiec workers' housing estate, built nearby, was settled, it soon became apparent that the number of housing units provided was insufficient to cope with the constant influx of workers. The company's board of directors accordingly decided to build a second housing estate with a development structure that would allow for denser construction of housing units on the available area of 20 hectares. After Anthon Uthemann, the company's director, had approved the architectural concept submitted by the brothers Emil and Georg Zillmann in 1908, construction began of four-storey, red-brick, multi-family buildings that formed closed blocks around green inner courtyards. The last of these was completed in 1919, at which time the number of residents in the housing development was approximately 5500. The apartments (mostly two-room with

11

Nikiszowiec housing estate, view towards today's Wyzwolenia Square; photo: M. Steckel, 1912

separate kitchens) were served by shared staircases, on which there were toilets accessible from the floors above and below. On the central square construction of the Neo-Baroque St Anne's Church began in 1914; its consecration took place in 1927. Opposite it, in the buildings fronting the square, were a bathhouse, a mangle, an inn, and a post office. Behind the church, school buildings were built.

After World War Two the structure of the Nikiszowiec neighbourhood remained virtually unchanged. Some outbuildings (including those used before the war for animal husbandry) were demolished. In the 1960s the Jantor sports hall and ice rink (1962–1964; arch.: Z. Fagas) was built on today's Nalkowska Street. This was replaced in 1982 by a new hall (Jantor II). The Nikiszowiec housing estate has been listed in the register of monuments since 1978 and has had the status of a monument of history since 2011.

An architecturally interesting contemporary development referring to the history of Nikiszowiec is the New Nikiszowiec Housing Estate (94), built under a government programme in 2018–2021. The design for this was selected in a nationwide architectural competition.

Nikiszowiec Housing Estate with the industrial buildings of the Wieczorek Coal Mine, 2020

National Digital Archive (NAC)

Drawing of the development plan for Nikiszowiec Housing
Estate; E. and G. Zillmann, 1908

(iStockphoto/peeterv_paul)

11

Rehabilitation and education centre

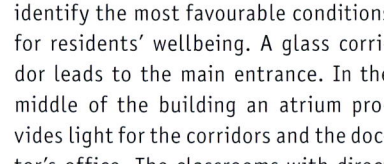

ul. Gościnna 8
Wacław Raubiszko,
Wojciech Bojemski
1984–1986

The rehabilitation centre is integrated into the old-growth forest of the Giszowiec garden, in the immediate vicinity of a villa from the early twentieth century, which originally housed a forester's lodge and is now a municipal kindergarten. Formally, the investor was the management of Staszic Coal Mine, but the real initiative for establishing a modern rehabilitation centre for children and young people came from Maria Trzcińska-Fajfrowska, a doctor specialising in children's diseases and a member of parliament. The first of its kind realised in Poland, the centre now bears her name. The architectural design was commissioned from Wacław Raubiszka, head of the Health Service Design Office in Katowice. The detailed design was completed in 1985, and the centre's pavilion entered use the very next year. The architects' decision to divide the building into sections that are offset in relation to one another and separated by patios and terraces was not only dictated by the need to integrate the composition into its green surroundings. The design team carried out pre-design studies and consultations in order to

identify the most favourable conditions for residents' wellbeing. A glass corridor leads to the main entrance. In the middle of the building an atrium provides light for the corridors and the doctor's office. The classrooms with direct

access to the terraces and garden are arranged in three spacious pavilions on the west side. The building gives the impression of being on one level due to the ground floor being visually masked by the slopes. It is interesting to note that this project's architectural design has been so highly appreciated by specialists that it has been replicated in several other locations in the country, including in Katowice itself – on Ułańska Street in Osiedle Tysiąclecia.

prepared by Marek Pęczak

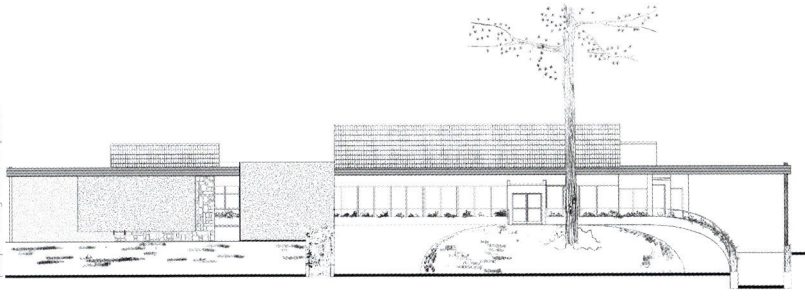

11

Primary school
ul. Przyjazna 7A
Stanisław Niemczyk,
Marek Kuszewski
1991–1993

091 **G**

The previous school building on this spot was cramped and had been badly damaged by mining subsidence, hence the urgent need for a new building. A competition for a concept to revitalise the district, held on the eve of the country's transformation, provided an opportunity to design a new school. Stanisław Niemczyk and Marek Kuszewski, the authors of the winning study, included in their proposal an extensive complex inscribed into the structure of the Giszowiec development. The completed school building occupies a large area of approximately 1.8 hectares bounded by Przyjazna, Radosna, Kwiatowa, and Działkowa streets. Taking advantage of the possibilities offered by the large plot of land, it was decided to adopt an extensive functional programme for the new building, which, in addition to a complex of teaching and administrative rooms, includes an indoor swimming pool, two gymnasiums, an auditorium, and a small library. The complex is also the headquarters of the Municipal Public Library.

Giszowiec Kasztany,
KTBS residential complex ↓
ul. Pod Kasztanami 41–83
Jan Pallado,
Aleksander Skupin
2002–2004

`092` G

In 2002 Katowickie Towarzystwo Budownictwa Społecznego undertook to build new modern housing in the historical Giszowiec district. The aim was to skilfully and sensitively insert the new buildings into the structure of the existing

development by means of creative elaboration of the architectural threads that have been present in Giszowiec since the beginning of the twentieth century. In order to generate a concept to realise this approach, the board of Katowickie Towarzystwo Budownictwa Społecznego in Katowice initiated a nationwide architectural competition, in which victory went to a proposal submitted by Jan Pallado and Aleksander Skupin. Completed two years later, the complex consists of seven groups of multi-staircase, three-storey buildings. The stairwells give access to three or four apartments on each level. All buildings have partial basements containing personal garages for the residents. The complex has a total of 200 flats with different layouts and sizes of floor area. Additionally, there are two small commercial units on the ground floor of the longest building line. In the middle, stretching all the way between the two strips of buildings, a green recreational area with a playground is planned. The complex is an example of good integration into the existing urban layout: from the perspective of Kosmiczna Street, it is difficult to make out where the sequence of pre-war buildings ends and where the contemporary residential development begins.

Pod Kasztanami, KTBS residential complex ↓

093 **G**

ul. Górniczego Stanu 79–85
Jan Pallado,
Aleksander Skupin
2017–2019

Katowickie Towarzystwo Budownictwa Społecznego (KTBS) also acquired a plot of land on Górniczegoust Stanu Street, to the east of a residential complex (092) that was completed in 2004. The aim was to launch a housing project of a new kind for Katowice: apartments for rent with the possibility of subsequent ownership. The idea is that the purchase price of an apartment can be systematically repaid as part of the rent, enabling tenants to become owners of their apartments within five to 20 years of joining the programme. The architectural design of the four buildings was entrusted to the same team of authors that had designed the neighbouring complex in 2002. The buildings contain 24 flats with a variety of layouts, including two-storey flats. There are no shared common areas: each apartment has its own separate entrance from the outside, and each unit is assigned a private garden (to which ground-floor apartments have direct access from their living room).

11

Nowy Nikiszowiec, PFR residential complex

094 A

ul. Gospodarcza 24–84
22Architekci
2017–2021

Nowy Nikiszowiec is a development of rental flats which was created as one of a dozen or so investment projects by the Housing for Development Fund. Its uniqueness lies in the way it alludes to the historical workers' housing estate in this neighbourhood (1908–1919; archs.: G. and E. Zillmann). This can be seen, among other things, in the way the buildings have been positioned and in the brick colour of their façades, which are clad with plaster mixed with quartz and mica. The architectural concept for the development was selected in a nationwide competition. Three-quarters of the buildings along ul. Gospodarcza

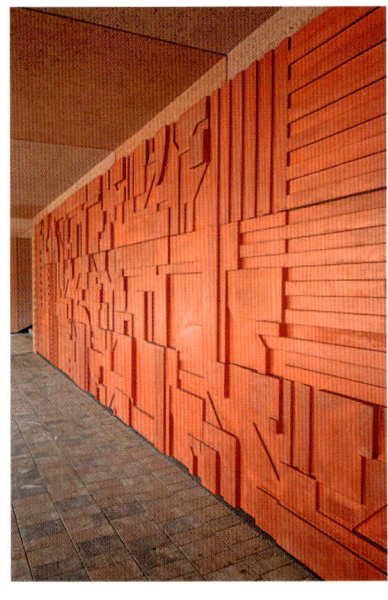

have a varying number of storeys – from three to eight. The development provides 513 flats for rent and 11 ground-floor commercial premises accessed from the development's central square. The flats vary in size and layout to suit residents' needs: from 36 square metres in two-room flats with a kitchenette to 95 square metres in four-room flats with a separate kitchen. The courtyards inside the blocks of housing are accessed through arcades, where a notable feature is the detailing of the wall finishes in the form of geometric reliefs.

South Katowice: Brynów District

12

South Katowice: Brynów District

The history of documented settlement in the area of modern Brynów dates to the late fifteenth century. At the end of the nineteenth century this area became the property of the Tiele-Winckler family and was part of the Katowice municipality until Katowice was granted the status of city, when an independent, autonomous municipality of Brynów was created. In 1899 Oheim Coal Mine, now known as 'Wujek Mine', opened in the northwestern part of the municipality. Replacing Beate Mine, which had been in operation since the beginning of the nineteenth century and closed in 1880, this was the second mine in the immediate area. In the case of both mines, an important role was played by the paved road (following the course traced by today's Kosciuszko Street, formerly Beatestraße) connecting them to the developing city of Katowice. The character of this road began to change when in 1894 a start was made on laying out Südpark (South Park), which is now part of Kosciuszko Park.

Bismarck Tower in Südpark (now: Kosciuszko Park); photo by O. Ziemer, 1908

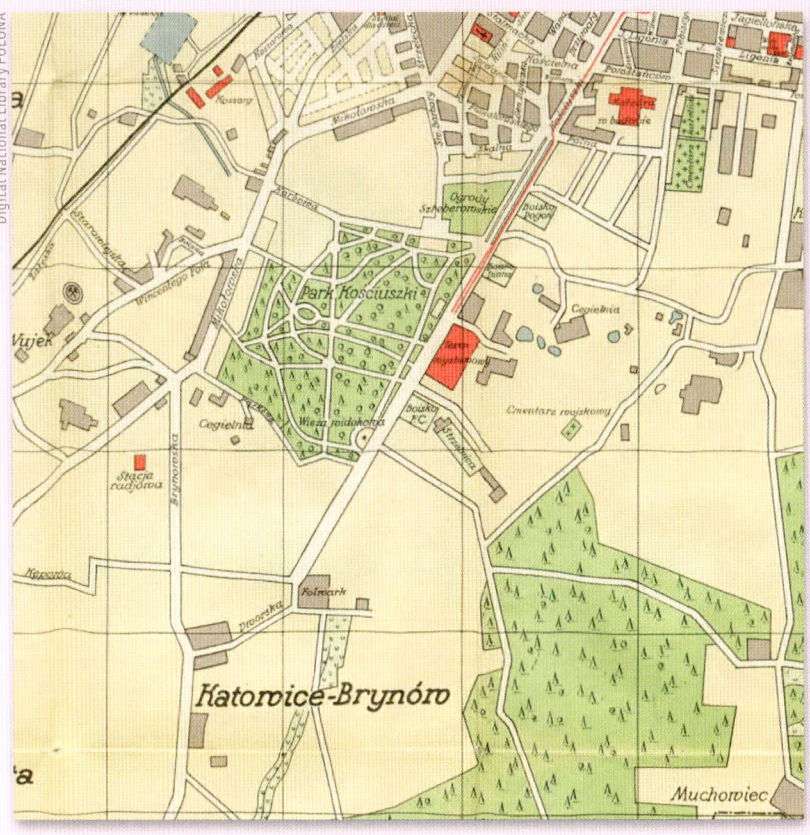

Part of a plan of the city of Katowice, 1935

An interesting structure erected in the park in 1903 was Bismarck Tower, which was built on the site now occupied by the wooden St Michael's Church and demolished in the early 1930s; stone recovered from the tower was used in the foundations of the city's archcathedral. The wooden church was brought to this spot and installed on the foundations of the Bismarck Tower as the nucleus for an open-air museum of Silesian wooden buildings and an ethnographic park. The church dates to the sixteenth century and originally stood in the village of Syrynia. It should be noted that the future Kosciuszko Park enjoyed good links with the centre of Katowice from 1914: a tram route was extended here at this time, and a tram depot opened between today's Ceglana and Gierek-Lapicka streets (the depot was upgraded under the Polish administration in the 1920s). On the west side of Südpark (later: Kosciuszko Park), on today's Mikolowska Street, a colony of eight clerics' houses

containing two or four apartments each was built between 1910 and 1912.

Spatial development between 1945 and 1989

After World War Two Brynow was gradually built up with residential buildings. The 1950s brought the construction of Osiedle A (Estate A), an estate of single-family houses south of Kosciuszko Park, between Brynowska and Kosciuszko streets. At the same time, parallel to Mikolowska Street, in the immediate vicinity of the park, Piękna Street was laid out and built up with single-family and two-family houses. Both in Osiedle A and on Piękna Street the design of most of the buildings was based on stylised solutions. These houses may be described as belonging to the so-called 'Polish cube' type. A different situation is found on Estate B, which was delineated in 1957 on the opposite side of Kosciuszko Street, within the borders marked by Drozdow,

12

Lower Silesia Digital Library (DBC)

Buildings in the clerical colony of Oheim (later Wujek) Mine on today's Mikołowska Street; photo: K. Seidl, 1913

Kukułek, Przepiórek, and Kosów streets (these are all streets named after birds, which explains why this housing estate is popularly known as 'Bird Estate'). In the early 1960s interesting single-family houses began to be built here, in most cases individually commissioned by private investors (098). The owners were most often doctors, engineers, managers of state enterprises, and privileged members of the party apparatus. The streets of this neighbourhood are a good place to explore: you often come across examples of houses in the late Modernist style. In addition to individual houses, a number of terraced housing complexes, an advanced phenomenon for the time of their construction, were also built. At the aforementioned Piękna Street a cozy complex of low-rise multi-family buildings with expressive risalites housing staircases (100) entered use in the mid-1960s. High-rise residential buildings were also built in Brynow: between Wozniczki and Brynowska streets, four prefabricated, twelve-storey apartment blocks were erected in the 1970s. Later, in the late 1970s and early 1980s, an interesting complex of terraced housing (095) was built between Zgrzebnioka, Gawronów, and Kościuszki streets.

Spatial development since 1990

Since the country's political and economic renewal, the low-rise housing estates (estates A and B) have been undergoing a process of transformation and overdevelopment. Many buildings have lost their original, unique, architectural design as a result of being insulated with modern materials or due to a deliberate change of style to suit the tastes of new owners. The turn of the 1990s and 2000s brought construction of new residential buildings on Kawek, Sparrow, and Czajek streets. At the same time a church on Gawrons Street (096) opened in the neighbourhood. The part of this neighbourhood in close proximity to Kosciuszko Park is now an attractive location for private investors building residential development: in 2011–2014 a cozy complex of low-rise multi-family buildings was built at the park's west edge (099), while in the area of Brick and Meteorologists' streets there has been an increase in new high-density residential development.

Silesian Digital Library, Silesian Library

A 16th-century church moved to Kościuszki Park from Syrynia; photo by A. Stelmach, 1973

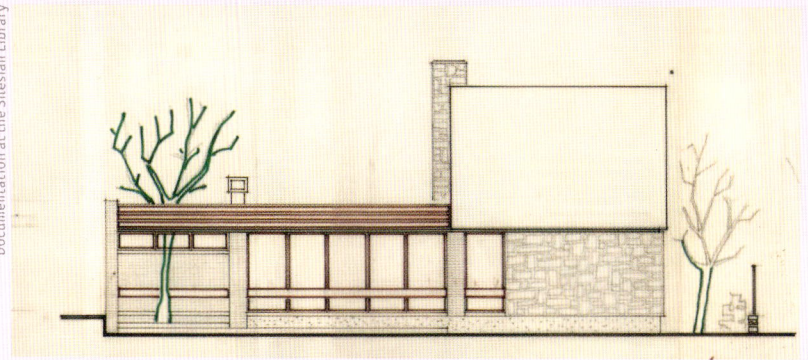

Elevation of a single-family house in Ptasie Osiedle, designed by the architect W. Lipowczan, 1972

A complex of terraced housing in Ptasie Osiedle; photograph by H. Buszko, 1969

Perspective drawing of a single-family house in Ptasie Osiedle, designed by the architect J. Jarecki, 1968

12

Perspective drawing of a single-family house in Ptasie Osiedle, designed by the architect J. Gottfried, 1959

Zgrzebnioka
residential complex

095 C

ul. Alfonsa Zgrzebnioka,
ul. Bocianów, ul. Pelikanów,
ul. Kormoranów

Dieter Paleta, Andrzej Gałkowski,
Tadeusz Czerwiński

1977–1982

This is a complex of single-family and multi-family residential buildings on the Alfons Zgrzebnioka Housing Estate, which was formerly the XXXV-lecia PRL Housing Estate. The spatial and architectural concept for the complex was selected in a competition held by the Association of Polish Architects and commissioned by the Katowice Housing Cooperative in 1977. The winning team was from Katowice-based Inwestprojekt, a state-owned architectural office specialising in the design of cooperative housing. In places the project implementation departed from the competition proposal – in the positioning of the internal streets and the locations and layouts of the buildings, although the buildings' structure remained unchanged. The residential complex consists of four types of buildings: single-family single-storey buildings in an L shape, arranged around an atrium; single-family two-storey buildings linked together in terraces;

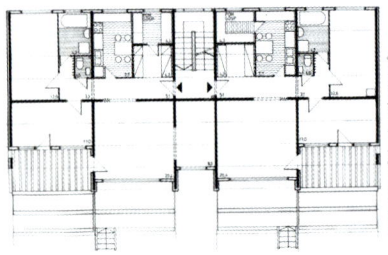

Archives of the Institute of

Archives of the Institute of Architecture

terraces of multi-family three-storey buildings; and cuboidal volumes containing multi-family four-storey buildings. Despite the use of full prefabrication (based on the W-70 large slab) for the multi-family buildings, the architects succeeded in providing them with individualised features, such as façade solutions and lighting in the common areas. The flats in the terrace-type buildings were designed to a higher standard, which is reflected not only in increased usable floor space but also in well-thought-out layouts, which contribute to comfort of living by means of, for example, separate wardrobes and pantries. The two-storey detached houses are notable for the impressive way in which the living space is shaped, opening up to the upper storey with a mezzanine floor and a skylight under the sloping roof.

12

Parish church

ul. Gawronów 20
Andrzej Gałkowski
1990–2001

096 C

From the early 1990s efforts were made by the Archdiocesan Curia to complete the Zgrzebnioka Housing Estate programme with a church for its inhabitants. In 1992 a plot of land adjacent to Gawronów Street was purchased, for which a team under the direction of Andrzej Gałkowski drew up a design for the future church. Construction work began the same year. Implementation proceeded in stages: first, the circular chapel was erected; then, the parish house with its amphi-theatre and meeting place. Construction of the main body of the church began in 1996, and its official opening and conse-cration took place five years later. This project would not have happened without the support of the parishioners: for ex-ample, the purchase of the bells and the completion of the bell tower were funded by the world-famous composer Wojciech Kilar. It is worth walking around the body of the main church and exploring the space between the individual segments. The brick façade and individual details are a picturesque addition to this space dedicated to quietude.

12

[Full-width photograph of a red-brick residential building with balconies, surrounded by greenery and a wooden fence]

Residential complex ↑

ul. Lelków 10–14,
ul. Cyranek 1–9
Tadeusz Czerwiński
1996–1999

097 C

An example of a cozy housing complex from the 1990s is this complex of three sequences of buildings with a multi-segment layout built by the Katowice Housing Cooperative between Leków and Cyranek streets. After decades of communism in Poland, the 1990s brought the opportunity to invest in flats with spacious floor areas as well as unusual layouts. In the buildings on Cyranek Street variation in the size of the flats is reflected in floor areas that range from 55 to 135 square metres. In Western European countries such a combination would probably not be surprising, but the reader should bear in mind that such apartments were not yet common in Poland during the years of construction. The shape of the blocks and the composition of the loggias, balconies, and terraces were also something new in residential architecture.

Ptasie Osiedle, single-family housing development ↗ ↘

ul. Drozdów, ul. Słowików,
ul. Kukułek
Various architects
1958–1990

098 A

Fringed by Katowice Forest Park in the south and east and by Kościuszki Street and the tram line in the west, this low-rise housing estate is considered one of the most prestigious residential locations in Katowice. Located in Brynów District, it is better known under its nickname 'the Bird Estate' – which it owes to the fact that the surrounding streets are named after different species of birds. The single-family housing here is mainly houses built in the late 1950s, 1960s, and 1980s. In addition to terraced housing, an example of which is the so-called 'professors' houses', built for academics, on Drozdów Street (1968; archs.: H. Buszko, A. Franta), there are some very interesting examples of luxurious custom-designed villas from the communist period, often the work of leading architects working in the post-war Modernist style, such

as H. Buszko, A. Franta, J. Gottfried, J. Jarecki, M. Król, and S. Kwaśniewicz. These houses were usually built by managers of state-owned enterprises, party activists, and government employees, but also by highly qualified specialists, such as doctors or architects. Today many of these buildings are hidden behind lush green gardens. On the Bird Estate one can also observe contemporary private residences designed by living architects who have made a name for themselves in the region (e.g. T. Konior, J. W. Małeccy, and R. Konieczny).

12

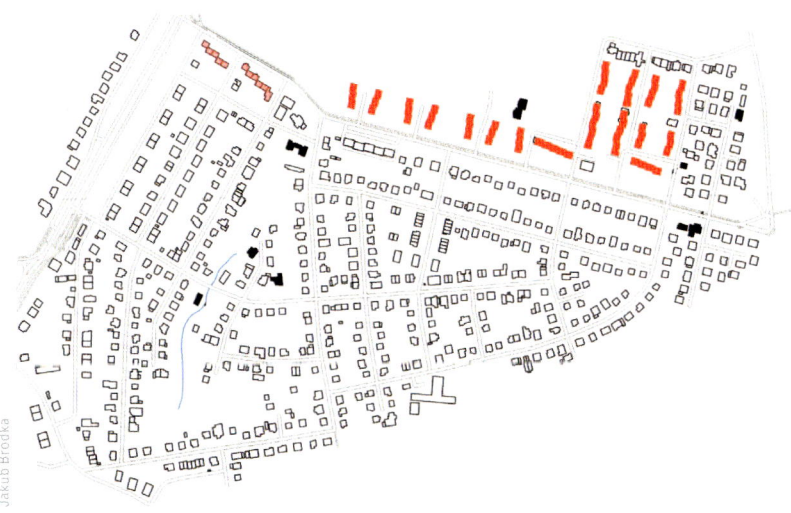

Jakub Bródka

Konior Studio

Wille Parkowa residential complex

099 C

ul. Parkowa 6–14
Konior Studio
2011–2014

On the west side of Kosciuszki Park, on a plot adjacent to a church from the 1980s (archs.: J. Kubica, J. Machnikowski), allotment gardens, and single-family buildings from the 1960s, a complex of five four-storey multi-family buildings was completed in 2014. The buildings are connected by a shared basement garage, an arrangement which eliminated

Konior Studio

Konior Studio

the necessity to insert parking spaces for cars between the buildings. The entrances to the houses have been accentuated by recessing them deep into the rectangular volumes; they are lined with high wooden cladding. The same material has been used for the window frames, which combine favourably with the brick façades. Each building's staircase serves two apartments on each level. In the two outermost buildings the top two storeys house duplexes, whose top floors have access to a spacious roof terrace. Most of the apartments are three-room apartments with floor areas of approximately 90 square metres. There are deeply recessed, heavily glazed loggias.

Residential complex

ul. Mikołowska 104–116,
ul. Piękna 49–59
Jerzy Gottfried (Miasoprojekt)
1964–1968

Looking from the direction of Mikołowska Street, you see a complex of four-storey residential buildings which intrigues the eye with the dynamic form of its risalites and the rhythm of its arrangement of windows. In each of the juxtaposed two-, three- and four-storey segments of the building, the risalite houses a side-lit staircase giving access to two flats on each level. The two-room flats come in two variants (with floor areas of 39 and 49 square metres), while the three-room flats have a floor area of 58 square metres. In all flats the kitchens are separate and well illuminated and can be completely opened up to the living room by means of sliding and folding doors. Between the two parts of the building is an attractive public green

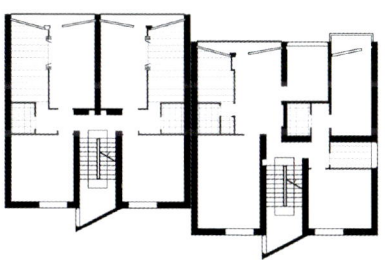

space. The fact that the buildings are more than 50 metres apart guarantees the residents good views from their flats and an optimal feeling of privacy. Also noteworthy is the composition of the slightly sloping walls with windows leading to the loggias; this gives the buildings a visual dynamism.

12

West Katowice:
Tysiąclecia Housing Estate

13

West Katowice:
Tysiąclecia Housing Estate

Chorzowska Street, which separates to-day's Osiedle Tysiąclecia (Millennium Housing Estate) from Park Śląski, was already a clearly formed thoroughfare in the 1820s. It connected industrial plants, including the Marta Steelworks, located on the site of what is today the northwestern part of downtown Katowice, with Königshütte (now: Chorzow). In 1820 or thereabouts Father Joseph Beder created a small hamlet, called 'Dąb', which was subsequently renamed 'Bederowiec' in honour of its founder. Over the next 100 years, the hamlet developed into a workers' colony inhabited by dozens of families. A carpenter's shop and a steam-powered mill were built here. At the beginning of the twentieth century Bederovets had more than 300 residents. Its character began to change in the 1920s, when, after this area was incorporated into the city of Katowice, the authorities decided to create barracks settlements for the unemployed and homeless in the area. Bederowiec acquired an increasingly poor reputation: the unsanitised and unelectrified district was called, among other things, 'Morocco' (hence the name of the recreational pond in the south of today's Tysiąclecia neighbourhood). In addition to low-standard wooden buildings, this part of town still had areas of sprawling farmland in the 1930s.

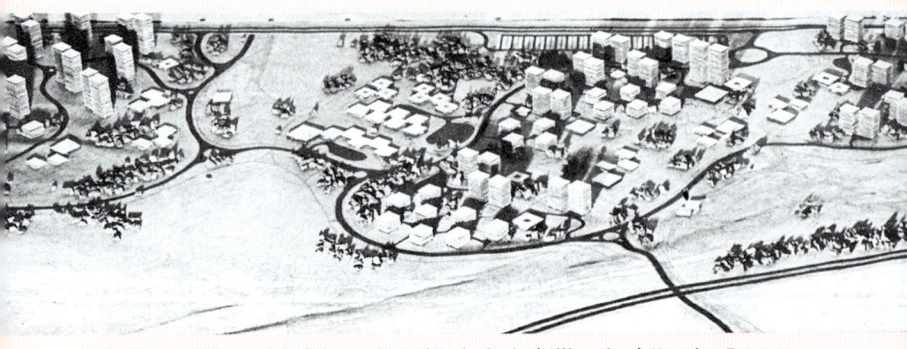

Photograph of a model of the projected Tysiąclecia (Millennium) Housing Estate; photographer unknown, 1959

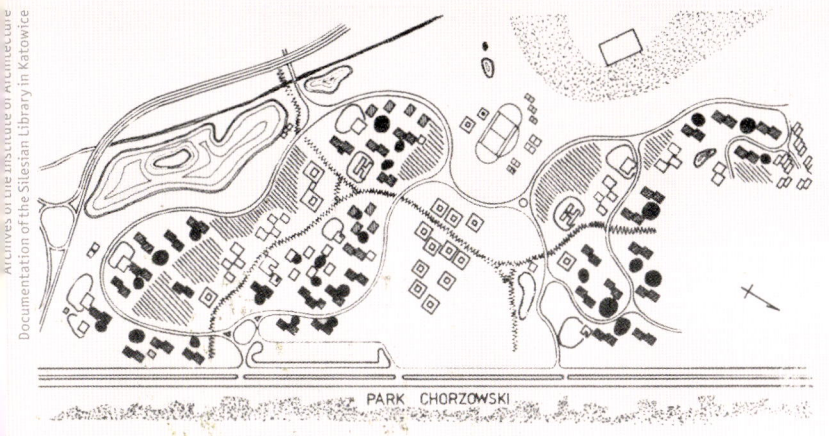

Drawing of the general layout of the Tysiąclecia Housing Estate; A. Franta, 1960

Spatial development between 1945 and 1989

After World War Two, in the late 1940s and early 1950s, a complex of dozens of wooden houses, each 70 square metres in size, was built for employees of the Chorzow President Mine in the area alongside today's Ulanska Street. Commonly called 'Finnish houses', these structures were imported by the communist government as part of a barter transaction in exchange for exported coal. Today they no longer stand: they were demolished in the mid-1960s to make way for work on the next phases of the Millennium Estate.

On the opposite side of Chorzowska Street, the largest investment project for recreation in post-war Poland got underway in the early 1950s. This was the Provincial Park of Culture and Recreation in Katowice (since 2012 known by the shorter name 'Silesian Park' and now officially part of the city of Chorzow). In a short period of time the park became a reference point for new park complexes in the country. The initial concept for the development of over 600 hectares of land (mostly devastated post-industrial wasteland) was developed as early as 1950 under the direction of Kazimierz Wejchert, Tadeusz Baum, and Krystian Olszewski. In 1952

General Jerzy Ziętek studying a model of Tysiąclecia Housing Estate, 1959

High-rise buildings beside 'Morocco Pond'; photo by A. Stelmach, 1967

'Corncob' buildings under construction; photograph unknown, 1988

A group of 'corncobs' above the greenery of the residential complex, 2024

a team under the direction of Wladyslaw Niemirski completed the detailed design documentation for the first stage of development of the park and the general design of the entire amenity, which was divided into functional-thematic sectors, such as political, cultural-physical, defence and national heroism, children, youth, botanical, and zoological. In 1953 the Provincial Park of Culture and Recreation became a state-owned enterprise, a change in status which improved the course of implementation of its gradually updated projects. The late 1950s and early 1960s saw the implementation of the largest number of elements in the park: the stadium, planetarium, amusement park, zoo, exhibition hall, tourist centre, swimming area with restaurant, and narrow-gauge passenger railway. In 1967 a cable car (chairlift), the so-called 'Elka' (Little L), was launched, taking its name from the doglegged course of its route.

Simultaneously with the implementation of the early stages of the Silesian Park, in 1958 it was decided to earmark the Bederowiec area and the colony of wooden 'Finnish houses' for the development of a modern residential complex with the functional programme of an independent residential district for 25,000 residents (over the next ten years the number of planned residents grew to as many as 45,000). The design of

Tysiąclecia (Millennium) Housing Estate, developed by a team led by Henryk Buszko, Aleksander Franta, and Tadeusz Szewczyk, was selected in an architectural competition in 1958. The very next year, it was approved and greenlighted for implementation by the Presidium of the Provincial National Council. The programmatic and spatial concept for the new housing estate envisaged that the complex would have a close spatial and functional connection with the Provincial Park of Culture and Recreation, which is nearby, on the opposite side of Chorzowska Street. Construction work began in early 1961. First to go up in place of the demolished buildings of the Bederowiec colony were low five-storey buildings (101). They were followed by tall, twelve-storey, buildings (102). By 1964 (when the first tenants moved into their apartments), two elementary schools (104), four kindergartens, a nursery, a student house, and commercial pavilions had also entered service. The mid-1960s saw the completion of a services centre located in the central part of the Millennium Estate. The entire complex consists of two parts: the Lower Estate and the Upper Estate. The two parts are connected by roads arranged in a loop system; most of the residential buildings are located inside this loop. The locations of the individual high-rise buildings (12-, and, later 15-, 18- and

A group of high-rise buildings above the greenery of the residential complex, 2024

20-storey) were adjusted to take account of the belts of mining faults belts in the project area. The implementation plan from the early 1960s already envisaged inserting residential buildings between the Lower and Upper estates to serve as the complex's compositional main feature, but it was not until the late 1970s that the designers presented their design for the 'corncob' (106), a tower building which owes its unofficial name to the way in which its distinctive body is shaped by rounded balconies. The design was based on a modification of the design for the previously completed 'star' buildings at W. Roździeńskiego (083). In the late 1980s and early 1990s a total of five 'corncobs' were built: three taller towers with 25 residential floors and two lower towers with 15 residential floors. Complementing the programme for the Millennium Estate are two churches that were not included in the original 1960s implementation plan. Thanks to the efforts of the metropolitan Curia and the residents of the estate, construction of a large two-storey church (105) began on the Lower Millennium Estate in the late 1970s, but by the late 1980s it had already proved insufficient for the growing number of residents. As a result, a decision was made to build a second, smaller church on the Upper Millennium Estate (107), construction of which was completed in the early 1990s.

Spatial development since 1990

The turn of the 1990s and 2000s saw the overdevelopment of Osiedle Tysiąclecia, a process which continues to this day. Designs for new buildings, produced by both the cooperative and private investors, have taken no account of the overall urban and architectural concept for the Millennium Estate; this led to protracted discussions among architects and planners and to protests by the architects Henryk Buszko and Aleksander Franta. It has been alleged that the composition of the Millennium Estate as a whole has been violated and there has been disruption of the ventilation channels and of the observation lines that were established with such care when the project for the housing estate was initiated. A strong spatial accent is the Four Towers residential and commercial complex (109), whose location in close proximity to Chorzowska Street, together with the height of its buildings, has a significant impact on scenic views of the 'corncobs', among other things.

The second decade of the twenty-first century also brought the construction of new residential buildings on Zlota Street, adjacent to Silesian Park. Housing built by private investors (114, 115) offered original architecture and an attractive location near the park complex.

Low-rise residential buildings 101 F

ul. Mieszka I 1–11,
ul. Tysiąclecia 7–11 and 33–39
Henryk Buszko,
Aleksander Franta (PPBO)
1960–1964

The lowest of the buildings on the Tysiąclecia Estate belonged to the first phase of this large-scale development project. Their construction began as early as 1958, shortly after the concept for the entire housing complex was approved. The buildings, which have a rectangular plan and five identical storeys, were built in two parts of the Lower Millennium Estate: four along the western curve of Mieszka I Street and 11 in the central area of this part of the housing estate. They have no basement. The ground floor contains storage rooms, technical rooms, a garage for one car, and four flats (two two-room and two three-room) with southern exposure. The staircase is centrally positioned with a single-flight staircase, around which eight two- and three-room flats are grouped on each of the upper floors. All kitchens are separate and have no window, being illuminated by indirect light coming through the living room.

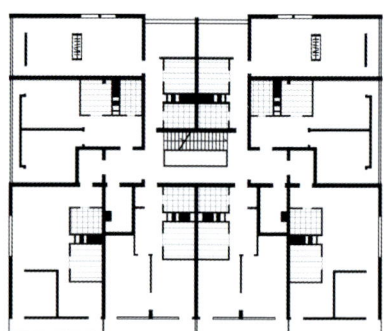

High-rise residential buildings

102 F

ul. Tysiąclecia, ul. Piastów,
ul. Bolesława Chrobrego
Henryk Buszko,
Aleksander Franta (PPBO)
1961–1979

The most common type of multi-family building on the Millennium Estate is a two-segment building with a central communication core. There are variants of this building with different heights: 12-, 15-, 18-, and 20-storey. The communication core (fully glazed in some buildings, which looks striking at night) contains two lift shafts and two staircases. A controversial point is the design of the lift exits leading to the landing, which entails having to climb half the height of a storey by stairs – a considerable inconvenience for disabled people and parents with small children. Internal exits on opposite sides of the communication shaft lead to two corridors: both are double-loaded, with each corridor leading to eight flats arranged on its two sides. Evacuation staircases are located at the end of each corridor. The two- and three-room flats have separate kitchens illuminated by indirect light coming through the flat's living room. Note the consistently shaped façades: the horizontal white strips of balconies contrast with vertical strips emphasising the lines of windows on the shorter walls. A curiosity is the visual identification system used on the façades; this takes the form of a chromatic accent on the balustrade of the second or third storey (depending on the height of the building).

13

Jakub Bródka

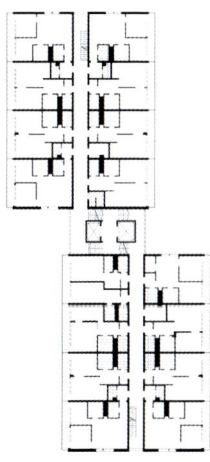

'Wypych', experimental residential building

ul. Tysiąclecia 41
Henryk Buszko,
Aleksander Franta (PPBO)
1964–1966

103 F

One of the two-segment buildings is immediately distinguishable thanks to its lines of balconies with a geometric composition of white panels on their balustrades. Additionally, this variant has no internal corridor; instead, access to the flats is via overhanging, open galleries in the form of bridges between the segments. The most important distinctive feature, however, that makes this building unique not only in the city but also in the country as a whole is its experimental use of 'push-up' floors (to which the building owes its nickname, 'wypych' or 'push up'). This method was developed by the engineer Konrad Korpys together with the architects Henryk Buszko and Aleksander Franta and was given official approval in 1965. Before construction began, a trial prototype was made on the site of the Technical Progress Centre (since demolished). The implementation involved placing actuators on the ground floor of the building. The actuators pushed the building's floors up, one by one. When the floors reached their target height, they were held in place by reinforced-concrete columns that are partially visible between the bands of windows. Stairwells with lifts are located centrally in each of the two segments. The building contains a total of 196 one-, two- and three-room flats ranging in size from 30 to 55 square metres.

13

Primary school

ul. Bolesława Krzywoustego 9
Henryk Buszko,
Aleksander Franta (PPBO)
1965–1966

104 **F**

The concept for the Tysiąclecia (Millennium) Estate envisaged supplementing the residential facilities with nurseries (kindergartens) and schools. The school located near Morocco Pond is an example of a school realised on the basis of a design developed in the early 1960s. A number of other schools have been built based on the same design (including in the complex neighbouring this school to the east). This is a two-storey building with a clear spatial layout: four segments of functional rooms are attached to an east-west communication passage. The first segment beside the main entrance area is larger than the others. It contains the administrative offices and the gymnasium with south-facing windows. The other segments contain classrooms arranged on two sides of a light-flooded corridor. Facing the inner courtyards are practical arcades located beneath the communication passageway. A notable feature is the window joinery, whose articulations create interesting avant-garde, geometric compositions. The joiner's original colours are contrasting (white and black).

Parish church with vicarage

105 F

ul. Mieszka I, 6
Henryk Buszko,
Aleksander Franta (PPBO)
1978–1981

Among Katowice's post-war churches, one of the most original was built for the residents of the Lower Millennium Estate on Mieszka I Street. Neither of the two churches (the other is no. 107 in this book) built on the estate was officially included in the project at any stage of its planning. When permission to build a church was obtained in the late 1970s with the support of the Katowice Curia, the authorities allocated for this purpose an inconspicuous plot of land in the south of the housing estate, outside the boundaries determined for the estate's development. Left over from a concrete-making factory, the site was a wasteland with soil of a quality that required considerable amelioration. The design of the church was commissioned from the team responsible for the Millennium Estate development project. The guidelines stipulated the provision of two independent levels containing two churches – a lower church and a main church. In shaping this building, the architects adopted the principle of contrast with the cuboidal masses of the nearby residential buildings, whose façades are distinguished by emphatic horizontal and vertical stripes. The individual walls of the church, which are sections of arches with different radii, were juxtaposed in an avant-garde composition, and glazing with geometric woodwork divisions was inserted between them. To construct a building with this layout was a challenge: each wall has its own foundation in the form of a footing that follows its course. Analysis of the church's layout shows that it does not contain a single right angle; this also applies to the building's ancillary rooms, such as the sacristy

13

and sanitary facilities. The same architectural principle has been adopted for the parish house building located at the southwest end of the plot. The church has several entrances, with the main entrance accentuated by its proximity to the spiralling bell tower, which is as tall as the 15-storey residential buildings opposite.

Krzysztof Nahlik | Dreamstime

'Corncobs', residential buildings

106 F

ul. Zawiszy Czarnego 2, 4, 6, 9, 10
Henryk Buszko,
Aleksander Franta (PPBO)
1978–1992

The central part of Millennium Housing Estate tangential to Chorzowska Street remained undeveloped until the end of the 1970s. The general plan of the housing estate produced in the 1960s already envisaged an alternative spatial solution for this part of the estate in the form of tower buildings – stand-out structures – but their form was not specified. Eventually, over the course of the 1970s and early 1990s, five buildings commonly referred to as 'kukurydzy' (corncobs) were erected; their aesthetic qualities have secured them a place among the icons of Polish post-war Modernism. Involving the use of solid balustrades to define rounded balconies adjoining all the tower's walls, this design approach ensured that these buildings would be perceived differently from their prototype – the 'stars' on the Walenty Roździeński Housing Estate (083). The architects added a number of improvements: the buildings are placed on octagonal plinths accommodating a multi-car garage and parking on the upper slab. The principle used for shaping the distribution of flats on each storey remained largely unchanged; however, in contrast to the 'stars', a greater variety of layouts was achieved: the flats range from one- to four-room. Due to the problems with gas leaks that had arisen in the 'stars', the 'corncob' was one of the first buildings in Poland where installation of gas equipment was banned.

13

Parish church

ul. Ułańska 13
Henryk Buszko,
Aleksander Franta (PPBO)
1985–1991

107 F

The second church on the Millennium Housing Estate is a much smaller building compared to the church on Mieszka I Street. Its construction was initiated later, in the mid-1980s, when it became clear that the first church would be insufficient for the large number of worshippers. Completed at the beginning of the 1990s, this building is based on a hexagonal ground plan, but the shaping of its mass is more complex due to the addition of soaring pylons and skylights, which allude to the form of the bell tower. Abutting the church is a lower structure, the catechist's house, which balances the composition of the massive structure of the canopy overhanging the main entrance to the church.

13

Arts and music school complex

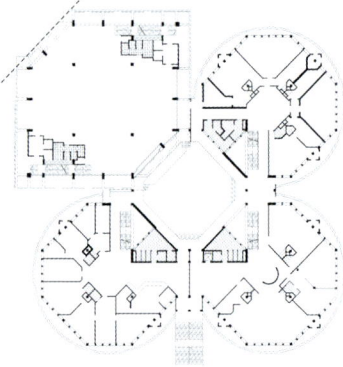

ul. Ułańska 7A
Henryk Buszko,
Aleksander Franta
1989–1998

The arts school complex consists of eight octagonal, four-storey composite volumes and a centrally located hexagonal structure. It houses facilities shared by two schools (the arts school and the music school); they include: a swimming

pool and attendant facilities, a gym, a socialising space, and staff rooms. The octagonal volumes are fringed by curved balconies, giving them a visual resemblance to cylinders. The north part of the complex houses the arts secondary school. In addition to three octagonal volumes containing classrooms with an auditorium placed between them, the functional programme includes an art workshop in a free-standing building connected by a glazed passageway. This building consists of two parts that are structurally twinned with the teaching buildings. The south part of the complex houses the music school. The layout here is identical to that of the secondary arts school, except that the part that corresponds to the arts school's auditorium is a concert hall. The two schools have separate entrances despite the fact that the central section connects them to one another. At present, one of the north volumes houses a dormitory.

Four Towers residential complex

109 F

ul. Chorzowska 210, 212, 214, 216
Activ Investment
2011–2018

An example of the contemporary over-development of the Millennium Estate is the Four Towers residential complex, which was built by a private development company. The complex consists of four 17-storey buildings placed on a shared three-storey plinth containing retail and catering units. The plinth abuts the strips of balconies of one of the 15-storey buildings forming part of the Millennium Estate's original layout – something which has caused dissatisfaction among long-standing residents of the estate. The four buildings contain a total of more than 300 flats, ranging in size from 25 to 85 square metres. The multi-storey car parks offer just over 600 parking spaces.

13

West Katowice:
Silesian Park and its Fringes

14

Administration building of Silesian Park

110 F

Chorzów, ul. Różana 2
Henryk Buszko,
Aleksander Franta (PPBO)
1963–1967

In the early 1960s a need arose to build a headquarters for the management of the dynamically developing Silesian Park (formerly known as 'the Provincial Park of Culture and Leisure'). In 1963, after two earlier options had been rejected, a final location for this building was approved on one of the park's main pedestrian thoroughfares, connected to the Millennium Housing Estate by an underpass. The architects' brief was to design a building that would fulfil office, administrative, and official representative functions while ensuring that the individual zones could operate independently of one another. The completed building consists of three parts. The middle part is single-storey and serves as the entrance area and waiting room. Its extension is a flat roof supported by a massive curtain wall, on which a modern relief depicting General Jerzy Ziętek, the long-time post-war governor of

Silesia, is displayed. This part is linked to the two parts standing opposite it: the north part has two storeys and contains office space; the south part, also two storeys high, is a pavilion containing a spacious conference room directly linked to the director's office and a complex of three guest suites located on the floor above. The upper hall adjacent to the suites has access to the roof terrace above the main hall and the entrance area. The building's fragmented plan ensures highly favourable illumination of the rooms, which are double- or in some cases even triple-aspect.

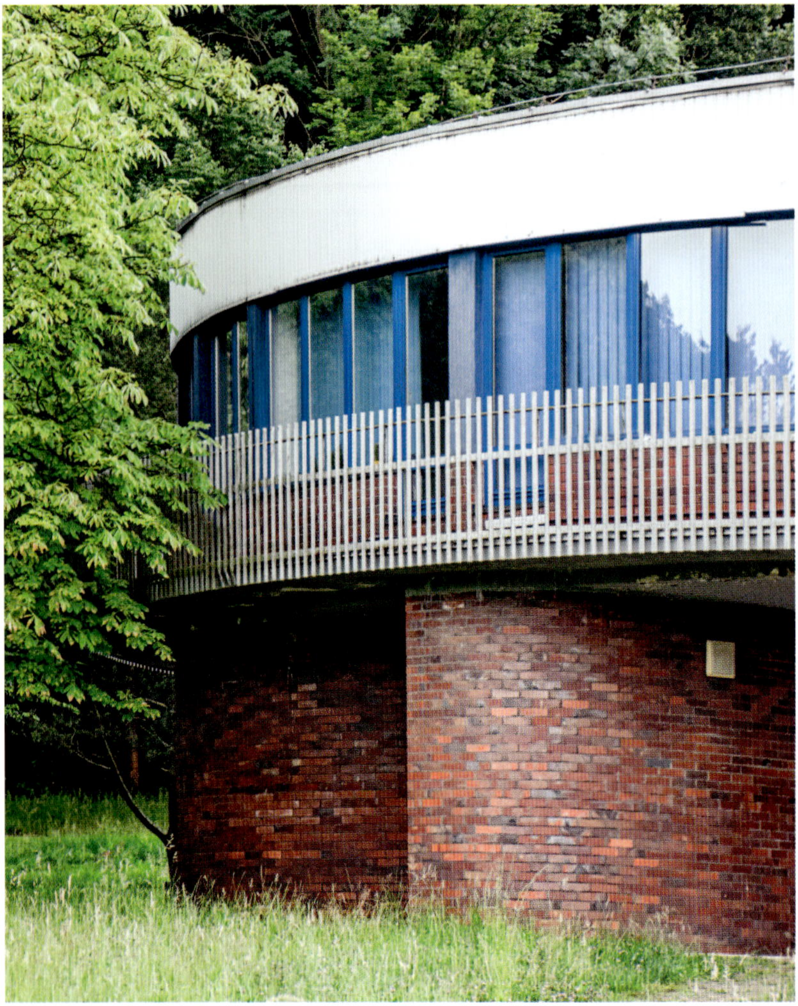

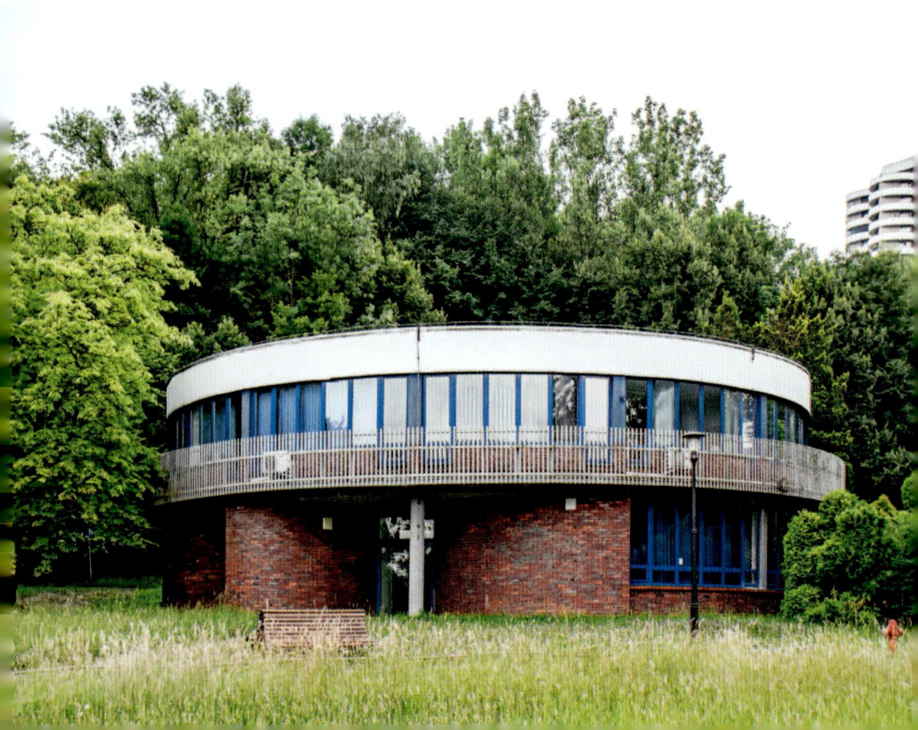

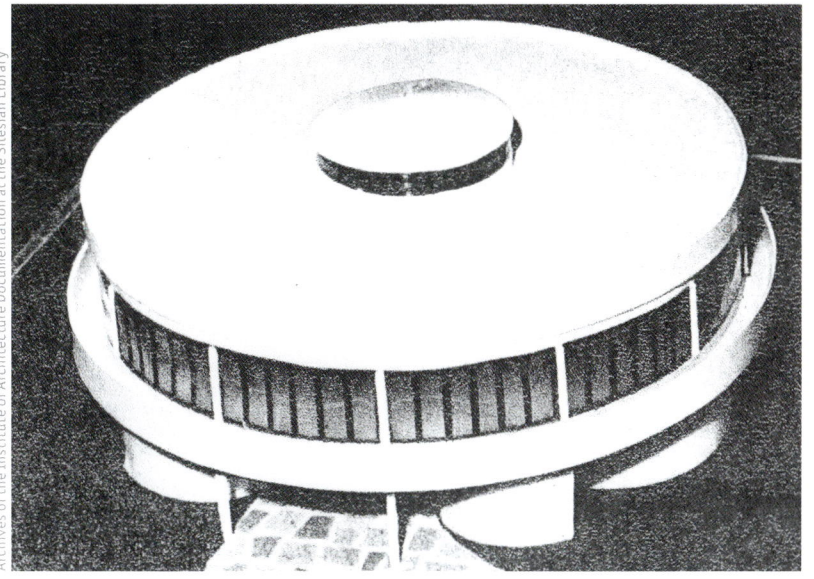

Pigeon Breeders Association Building

111 F

Chorzów, ul. Różana 6
*Henryk Buszko,
Aleksander Franta (PPBO)*
1969–1970

Not far from the park management building, beside an internal pedestrian and roadway called 'Aleja Różana' (Rose Avenue), is a distinctive compact,

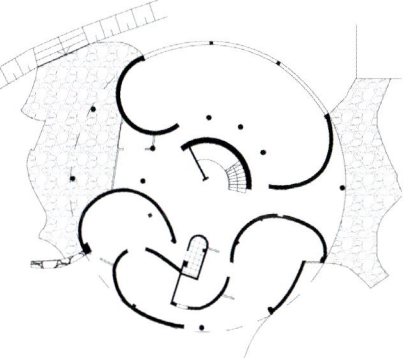

circular building which is the headquarters of the Katowice branch of the Polish Pigeon Breeders' Association. The building combines office, official representative, exhibition, and storage functions. Its two storeys differ considerably in their layouts: the ground floor consists of interpenetrating spaces inscribed between arc-like walls (a configuration which, seen as a horizontal projection, brings to mind an organic, avant-garde composition). A centrally located spiral staircase leads up into the orderly space of the upper floor, in which radially arranged office spaces surround the communication core. The building's exterior appearance today is not true to its original design: the joinery has been replaced, and its articulations and colours have been changed. On the upper floor, wall panels have been added under some of the windows, reducing the area of glazing. And the original black and white that are characteristic of these architects have been replaced with blue.

14

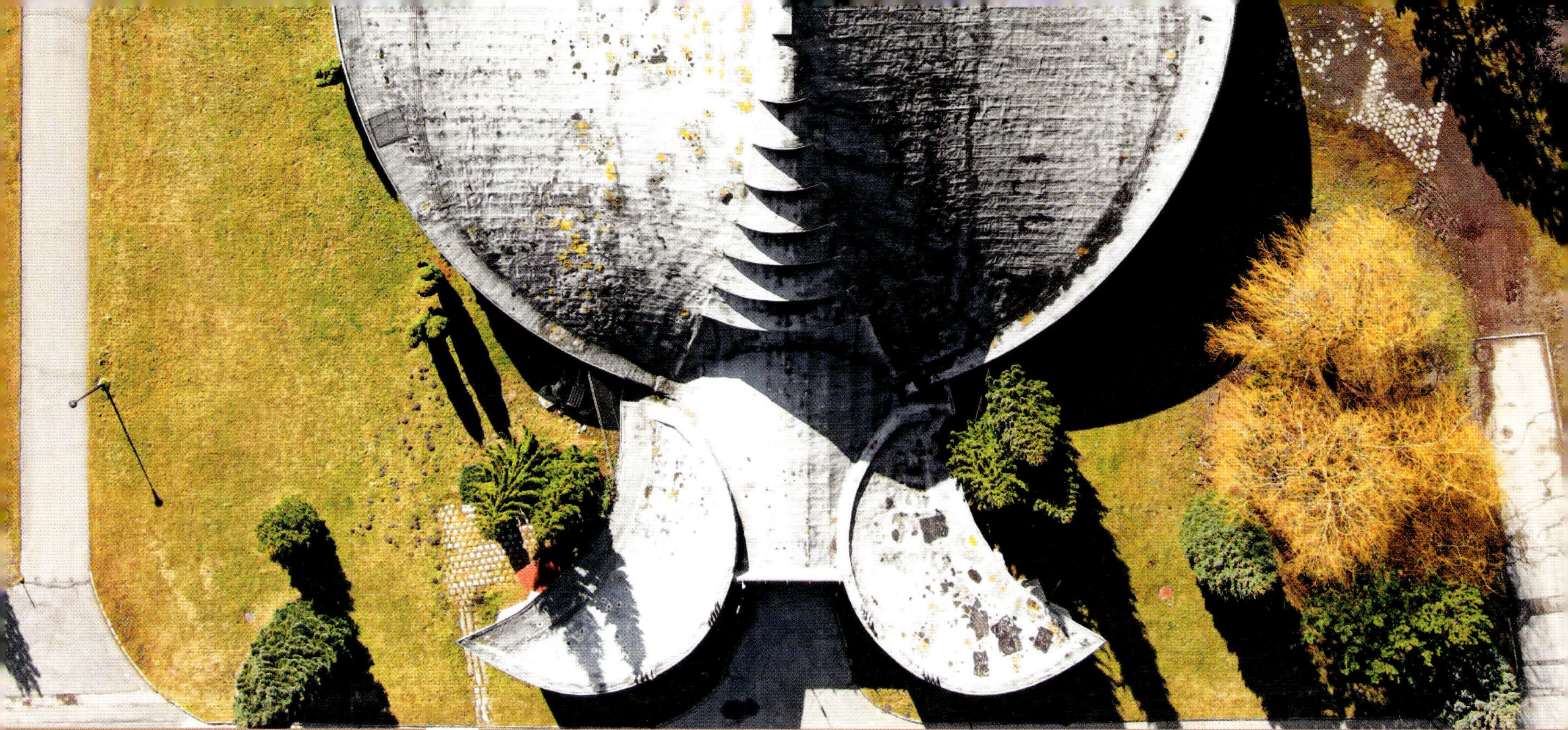

'Hat' exhibition hall

112 F

Chorzów, promenada
gen. Jerzego Ziętka 4
Jerzy Gottfried (Miastoprojekt)
1966–1968/
1983–1986

If you follow the main pedestrian avenue leading into the park, you see from afar a large building covered by a curved roof. This exhibition hall, originally known as 'the Hall of Flowers' (due to the fact that Poland's first international rose exhibition was held here in 1968), was designed by the architect Jerzy Gottfried in cooperation with the engineer Włodzimierz Feiferk using an innovative constructional approach. The main load-bearing structure is a so-called 'steel-reinforced concrete trestle', supporting a tent canopy stretched over it. The height of the hall at its highest point is 15 metres, and the exhibition area is more than 2000 square metres. The hall's current exterior and finishing materials are the result of reconstruction following a severe fire that destroyed the hall in 1982. The designer of the reconstruction was once again Jerzy Gottfried. The structure of the new building is almost identical to the original; however, the glazing of the side walls has been reduced and the glazed areas of the roof have been replaced with eyebrow windows.

Archives of the Institute of Architecture Documentation at the Silesian Library

Archives of the Institute of Architecture Documentation at the Silesian Library

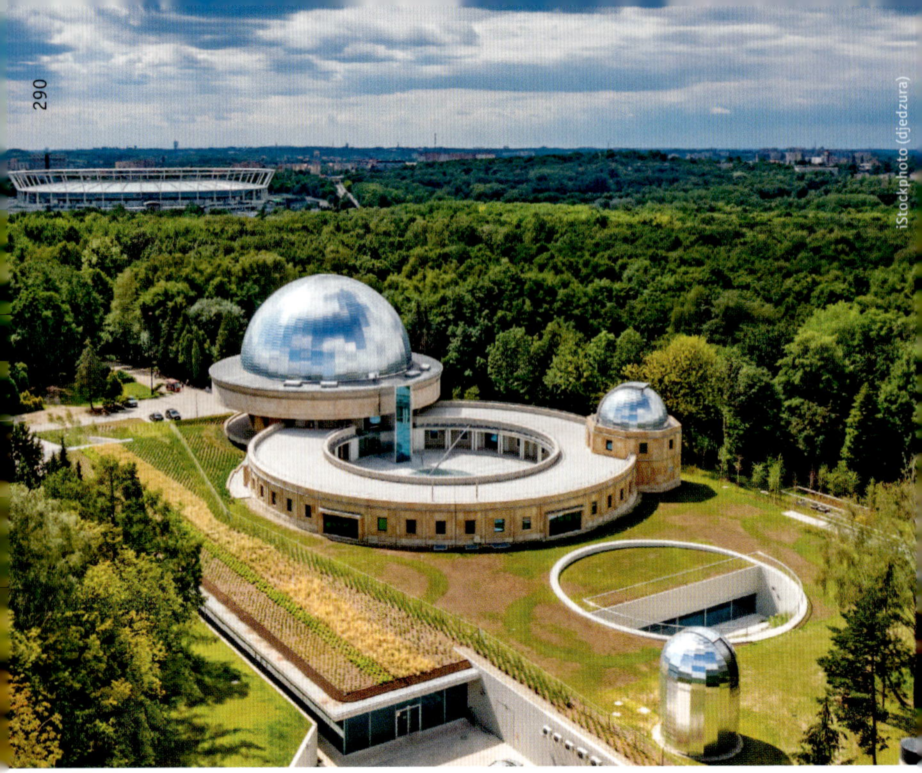
iStockphoto (djedzura)

Planetarium

113 A

Chorzów, al. Planetarium 4
Zbigniew Solawa
1953–1955

The Mikołaj Kopernik Silesian Planetarium in Chorzów is one of the most famous astronomical facilities in Poland. Its history and operations are an integral part of the region's cultural and scientific heritage. Construction of the planetarium began in 1953 (celebrated in the Polish People's Republic as the Year of Copernicus), and the official opening ceremony took place in 1955. The site assigned to the planetarium is in the central part of Silesian Park, which is also its highest point. The building was designed

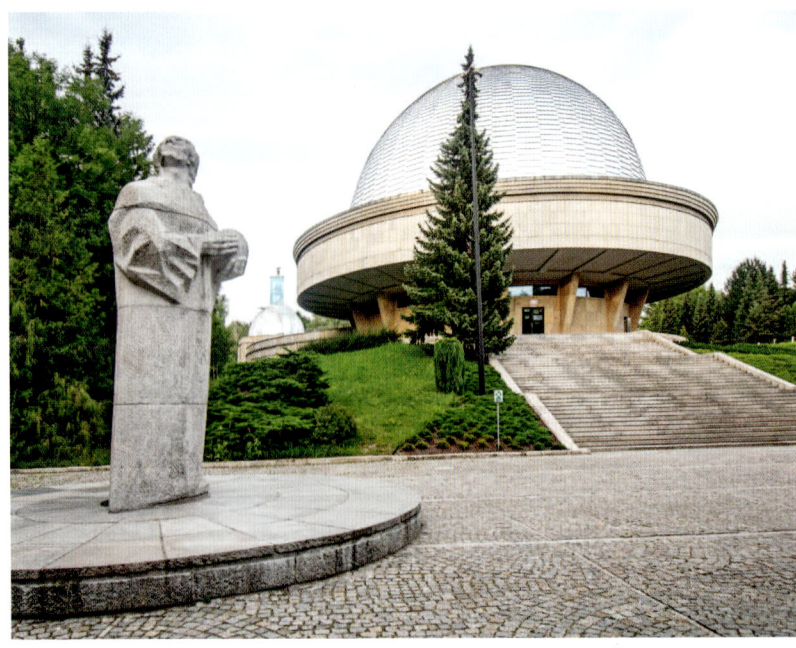

by the architect Zbigniew Solawa; the design of the dome itself was the work of the engineer Władysław Czaja. The planetarium complex consists of three interlocking buildings. The principal volume is covered by a dome beneath which is a projector made by the German Zeiss factory. This can display the appearance of the sky from any point on Earth, with the underside of the dome acting as a screen. Underneath is a 300-seat auditorium.

The second part is ring-shaped around an inner courtyard; this contains a series of administrative rooms and a conference room. Connected to it is the smallest building, which houses the astronomical observatory with a dome that opens to the sky. A four-year redevelopment and modernisation project was completed in 2022. An additional building, located mainly underground, provides space for interactive exhibitions.

Baildomb
residential building
ul. Złota 71
KWK Promes
2014–2020

114 B

Due to its attractive location in the vicinity of Silesian Park, a number of residential developments have been and continue to be built on Złota Street. One example of this kind of development is a zig-zag building located on a plot surrounded by pre-war brick workers' houses and a former clerical colony. The 'Baildomb' building owes its name to the Baildon Steelworks, founded in the 1820s by John Baildon in the Dąb district. The developer who built the residential development combined the name of the steelworks with this district's original name – 'Domb' – in a nod to the history of Katowice. The building has six above-ground storeys containing a total of 69 one- and two-storey flats (the latter are easily distinguishable when you look at the building from the outside because they are situated in massive volumes on the top storeys) with floor areas ranging from 29 to 142 square metres. On the side facing the street, a segment adjoining the residential part houses a service unit and a ramp leading to the underground garage.

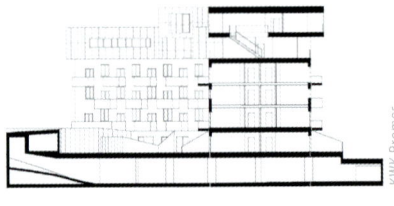

14

KWK Promes

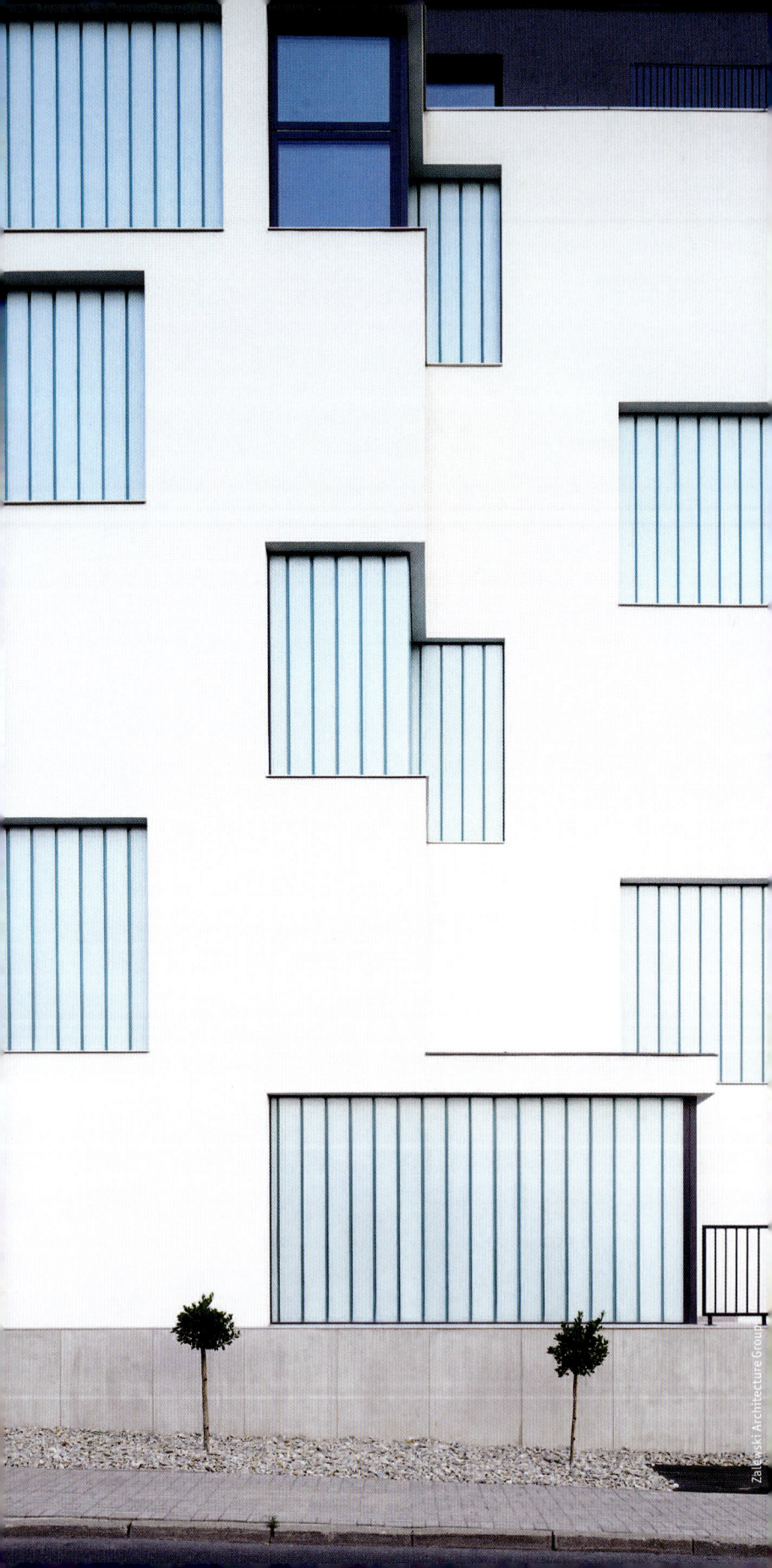

Zalewski Architecture Group

Złota 19 residential complex 115 B

ul. Złota 19
Zalewski Architecture Group
2015–2019

Almost at the same time as the 'Baildomb' development (014) was being built, construction was underway of an interesting complex of two five-storey residential buildings. Here two-room flats (with a floor area of 50 square metres) predominate, but there are also three-room flats (floor area: 70 square metres) at the corners and two-room flats with mezzanine floors (floor area: 100–150 square metres) on the top floors. Both buildings have a single-loaded corridor: the flats have a southeast exposure, while the corridors, connected by a single flight of stairs, are lit by a series of openings with profile glass panels overlooking the street. An interesting design solution ensures that the kitchenettes located deep inside the flats get enough light: above the kitchen worktops low-transparency glazing (which provides privacy for users of the kitchenettes) channels light from the bright corridors.

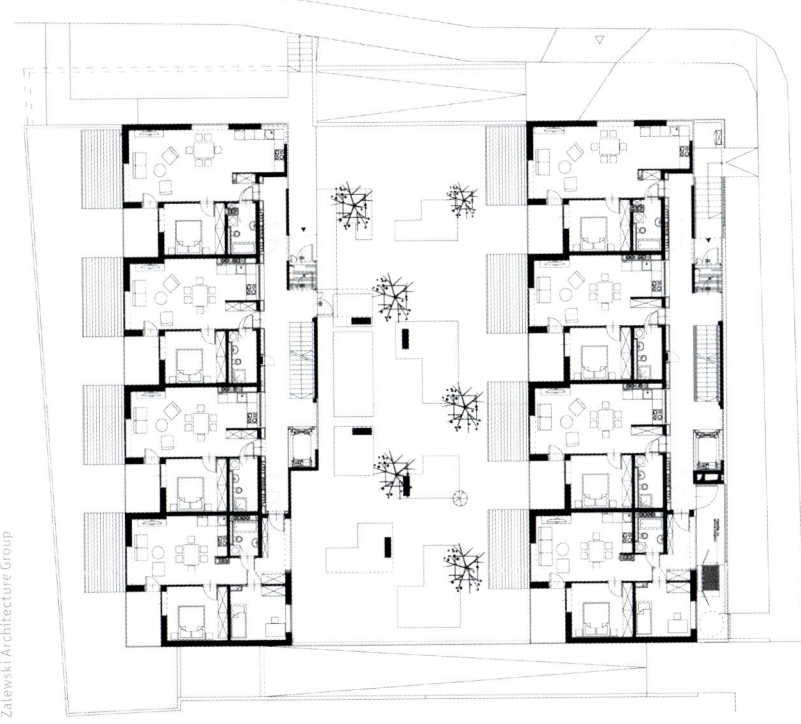

Zalewski Architecture Group

Lost Heritage
The Problem of How to Preserve Architecture from the Second Half of the Twentieth Century

At the beginning of the country's political and economic transformation in the 1990s, architecture from the communist period generally did not evoke positive associations in Poland. The burden of connotations of the former regime and the short temporal distance separating this architecture from the time of its creation led in many cases to significant neglect of original elements of buildings or to their removal, during uncontrolled modernisations, in favour of those considered modern and in line with prevailing fashion. As a result, many buildings have become unattractive in appearance, which has often led to their demolition. Another problem has been poor workmanship, including poor choice of construction and finishing materials. A further significant factor has been reduced comfort in the form of increasing heat loss due to the narrow external walls used during the communist period.

A significant reason for the transformation of Polish architecture in the second half of the twentieth century was the lack of systematic protection of this heritage. Although the first building from the times of the Polish People's Republic was entered in the register of monuments as early as 1991 (the Panorama Racławicka building, Wrocław; archs.: E. and M. Dziekoński, 1958–1980), it was not until more than two decades after the beginning of Poland's political and economic transition that efforts to protect the architecture created between 1945 and 1989 were intensified. These activities resulted in the registration of, for example, the Central Railway Station in Warsaw (1975; arch.: A. Romanowicz) and the High-Mountain Meteorological Observatory on Śnieżka (1974; arch.: W. Lipiński, W. Wawrzyniak). In the Silesian Voivodeship the sanatorium and spa complex in Ustroń Zawodzie District (1967–1990; archs.: H. Buszko, A. Franta) and two buildings in Rybnik – the Theatre of the Rybnik Land (1964; archs.: H. Buszko, A. Franta, J. Gottfried) and Okrąglak (1974; arch.: B. Meisel) – were listed in 2023. In Katowice the Palace of Youth complex (082) has been a monument since 2010; and the Art Exhibition Office pavilion (032) and the Silesian Insurgents Monument complex (037) were given this status in 2024.

The original interior design of Kosmos Cinema, 1960s; photo: J. Jarecki

However, a large amount of post-war architectural heritage has been lost as a result of interventions ranging from transformations to demolitions of buildings. In Katowice this can be seen, for example, on Korfantego Avenue, one of the city's main axes, which has lost important elements of its development, including Hotel Silesia (1971; arch.: T. Łobos; demolished: 2017), the Wedding Pavilion and Centrum services and retail pavilion (118), and the DOKP office skyscraper (119). Hotel Katowice (038) is currently being redeveloped. Reconstructions, which have resulted in the complete loss of many buildings' unique features, have particularly affected their interiors. Notable cases are the Zenit (028), Domus (040), and Skarbek (030) department stores. Kosmos (017), the city's first modern cinema, has also undergone a complete change of face. The interior design projects were designed by eminent artists and were in line with world trends of the time, but it is no longer possible to admire this work today. The same is true of the numerous neon signs created in Katowice in the 1960s and 1970s.

Another problem is interference with urban fabric that is coherent and was designed to produce a holistic impression. An example of such interference is the continuing overdevelopment of the Tysiąclecia (Millennium) Housing Estate (1958–1990; archs.: H. Buszko, A. Franta). The original development plan was designed to provide the residents not only with the optimal number of green areas, but also with conditions for natural ventilation of the estate. The building up of spaces that were intended as axes of air circulation has had a negative effect on residential comfort.

Nevertheless, the situation with preservation of heritage of the second half of the twentieth century is not all negative: prospects are currently improving. Recent initiatives (including the establishment of the Institute of Architecture Documentation of the Silesian Library in Katowice in 2018) have led to an increase in public awareness of recent architectural history and the legacy of architects active in the region. Workshops and series of walks are held to popularise the issue among not only residents of Katowice but also visitors from other regions of the country and worldwide.

Baildon Arena

116 B

Wojciech Zabłocki
1965–1969
demolished: 2003

Until 2003 at the corner of today's Żelazna Street and Chorzowska Street there stood a sports hall of striking, dynamic design. The initiative to build it came in the mid-1960s from the Vocational School Complex of the Baildon Steelworks, which argued that its pupils had nowhere suitable to practice sports or engage in recreation. The idea was eagerly taken up by the management of the steelworks, which became the main investor in and contractor for the project. Its design was entrusted to the architect and sportsman Wojciech Zablocki, whose achievements included several already completed sports facilities, such as the Olympic Training Centre in Warsaw. The new arena opened in 1969, and the building itself aroused widespread interest, especially since it had been built in parallel with Spodek Arena (021) at Katowice Roundabout. The auditorium had capacity for 1500 people. The grandstands were of reinforced concrete and the canopy of steel rod-and-beam construction. Over the years the hall hosted numerous sporting events and concerts. The facility's problems began in the second half of the 1990s, when one of the steel cables supporting the canopy snapped under the weight of snow, forcing the arena's closure. In 2001 Huta Baildon declared bankruptcy. The following year, the hall was sold to a private investor. In 2003 it was demolished.

Headquarters of the Regional State Railway Directorate ↓

117 B

Jerzy Gottfried
1965–1972
demolished: 2015

An important compositional element of downtown Katowice used to be an 18-storey office building, which was designed in the mid-1960s for the Regional State Railway Directorate and entered use in 1972. In view of its prominent location in the vicinity of Spodek Arena, which was under construction at the time (021), and the roundabout (at the junction of two major arteries), the design team led by Jerzy Gottfried strove to fit the new high-rise building harmoniously into this part of the city centre. Both the composition of its volumes and the façade design were intended to reinforce the impression of the building as a background for Spodek and the Monument to the Silesian Insurgents (037). The complex consisted of two parts: a 72-metre-high part (two cuboid, longitudinal segments offset in relation to one other along the north-south axis) and a low part (two-storey pavilions with an internal atrium). The high-rise section housed office complexes, which were configured innovatively for their time in the form of open spaces: this, in fact, was the first open-space office building in post-war Poland. The low-rise part housed catering facilities, including a canteen, a hotel for visiting employees, and a medical clinic. As the building had never been

All pictures: Archives of the Institute of Architecture
Documentation at the Silesian Library

thoroughly renovated, its visual appeal diminished over the decades. There was also less and less interest in renting offices from the companies to which the building had been made available in the 1990s. Even at the time of the building's sale to a private company, there were still plans for its redevelopment and modernisation. But in the end demolition work began in 2014. On the site of the once modern headquarters of the Directorate of Regional State Railways a complex of two KTW office buildings has now been erected (022).

Railway station 118 B

Wacław Kłyszewski, Jerzy Mokrzyński, Eugeniusz Wierzbicki
1959–1972
demolished: 2010–2011

With its original Brutalist aesthetics, the post-war railway station complex in Katowice was unique not only in Poland but also in Europe. The decision to build the station was taken at the end of the 1950s, when the infrastructure of the existing station located on Dworcowa Street proved insufficient to handle the heavy train traffic. That same year, an international competition for an urban-design and architectural project for the new station was held. This was won by a team of architects from Warsaw known as 'the Warsaw Tigers' with a proposal for a large, two-storey hall of original design – made of 16 reinforced-concrete cantilevers in the form of cups, the upper part of which formed the roof of a single-space hall. The cups were shaped in such a way that, when assembled, they could be glazed at their junctions, which was an effective way of providing light for the station interior. The building was connected by pedestrian routes with the areas north and south of it, thus linking the two sides of the inner city divided by the railway line. The station's foreground in the direction of today's 3-Maja Street was an overpass, under which the bus station was located. At present, Galeria Katowicka (049) stands on this site. The original station building was demolished in 2011. A partial reconstruction of the reinforced-concrete cupolas has been incorporated in the Galeria building.

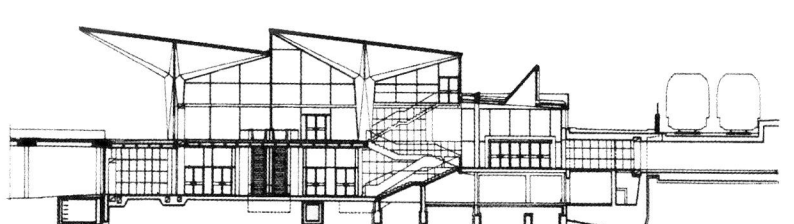

The Wedding Palace and Centrum services and commercial pavilion

119 **B**

Mieczysław Król
Wedding Palace: 1965–1968
Centrum pavilion: 1966–1972
demolished: 2011

Fronting the Superjednostka complex on today's Korfantego Avenue there used to be two two-storey pavilions of similar design: the Wedding Palace and the Centrum services and retail pavilion. The Palace of Weddings entered use first. In line with the trend promoted by the communist authorities, modern buildings had begun to be erected in cities for ceremonies such as civil weddings and secular baptisms. Katowice's Wedding Pavilion, located on Red Army Avenue (today's Korfantego Street), was one of the first buildings of its kind in post-war Poland. It consisted of two parts with separate entrances. Above the ground floor was suspended a glazed storey with a rectangular plan pierced by an internal atrium. At ground-floor level, the first part of the building looked out on a busy urban artery; this contained a reception hall with a staircase bifurcating in two directions. The hall had a black and white floor with an illusionistic composition of distorted squares. This was a popular place for commemorative wedding photographs. In addition to the wedding hall and baptismal hall, the upper floor housed a room for

banquets and a doctor's office. The interior was decorated with avant-garde bas-reliefs by prominent artists, including Jerzy Egon Kwiatkowski. This building had a smaller footprint than the Centrum services and retail pavilion. Built a few years later, Centrum had a functional programme

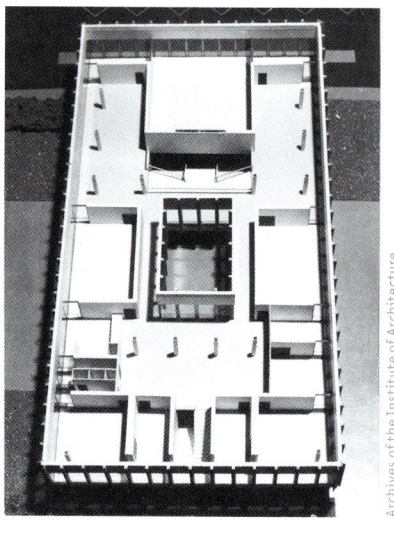

that included a fast-food bar capable of catering for 200 people at a time, a nightclub with dance floor, and a large shop with goods for children and young people with a 2200-square-metre display area.

Silesian Research Institute 120 E

Stanisław Kwaśniewicz
1968–1977
demolished: 2022

One of the most interesting examples of buildings in the Brutalist style in Katowice was the former headquarters of the Silesian Scientific Institute on Graniczna Street. Three storeys high with a massive, square-shaped body, this structure was an impenetrable fortress with exterior walls clad in sandstone panels of a light-grey colour. On the ground floor a central segment with a much smaller outline housed the principal and staff entrances and the main hall. This part of the building was surrounded by a deep arcade that provided parking for cars under a canopy. The second floor housed the administration offices and a publishing house, whose strip windows were visible from outside. The middle of this floor was occupied by a 120-seat conference room illuminated by two atria. On the top floor were researchers' offices and staff rooms with access to four spacious terraces and with openings to let sunlight into the atria located one floor below. The terraces also had a reinforced-concrete openwork pergola structure, designed for relaxing in during breaks from work. This user-friendly space contrasted sharply with how this floor was perceived when seen from outside – completely windowless (except for three small windows to provide illumination for the circulation nodes). All storeys were connected by three staircases: two staircases at the sides and a principal, central, spiral staircase, an impressive structure, located under the skylight. Unfortunately, the interesting architectural design was not matched by the technological capabilities of the time: the first technical problems began to emerge a few years after the Silesian Research Institute opened. These involved cracks and ingress of moisture, which was also due to poor drainage of the internal terraces. The building's deteriorating technical condition and the closure of the Silesian Institute of Science led to the building's abandonment. It stood empty until 2022, when it was demolished.

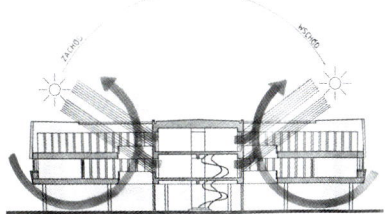

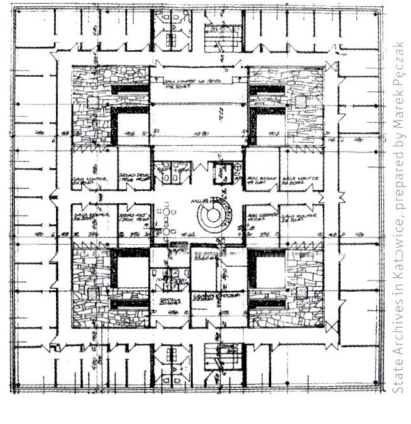

State Archives in Katowice, prepared by Marek Pęczak

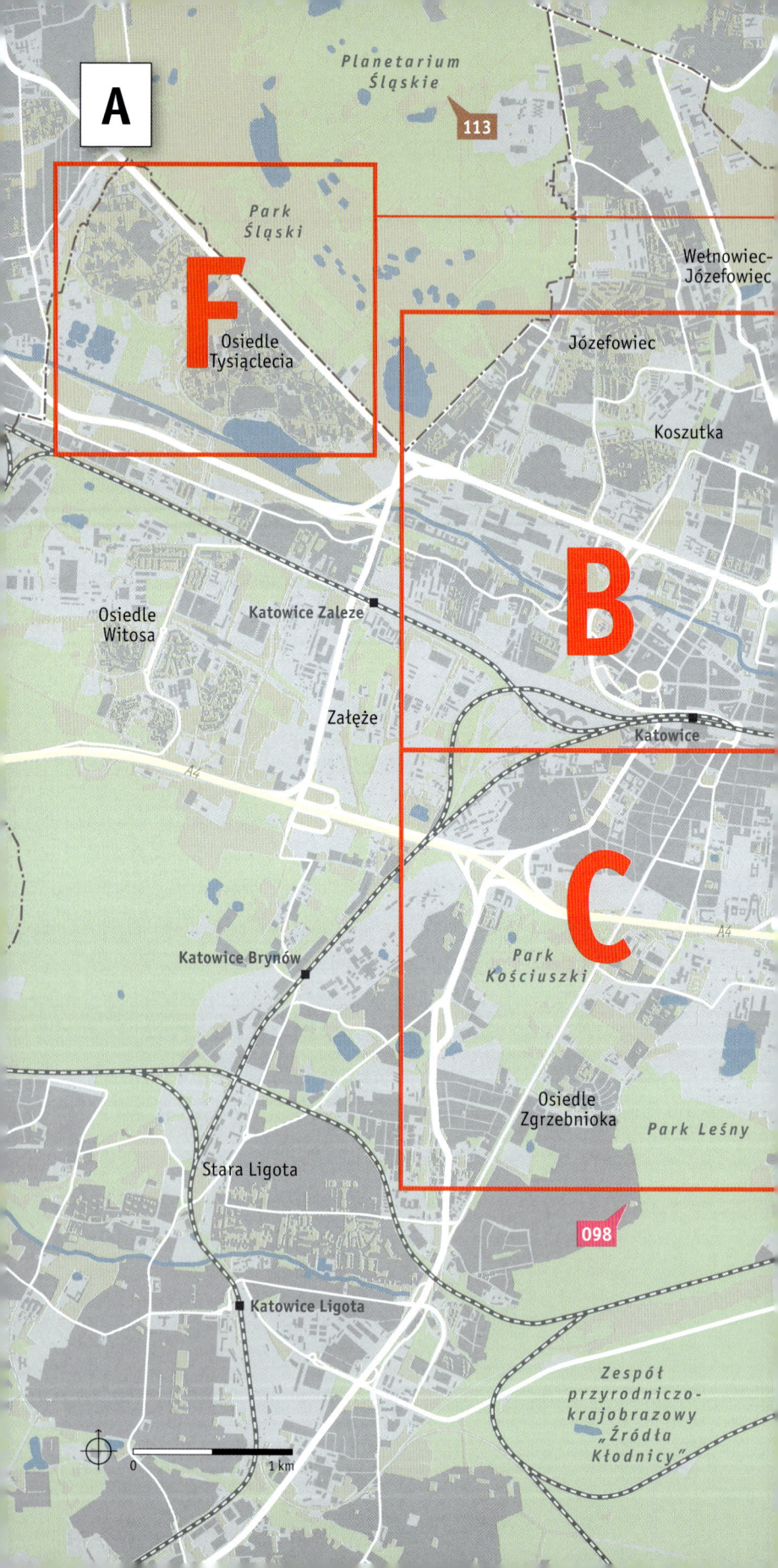

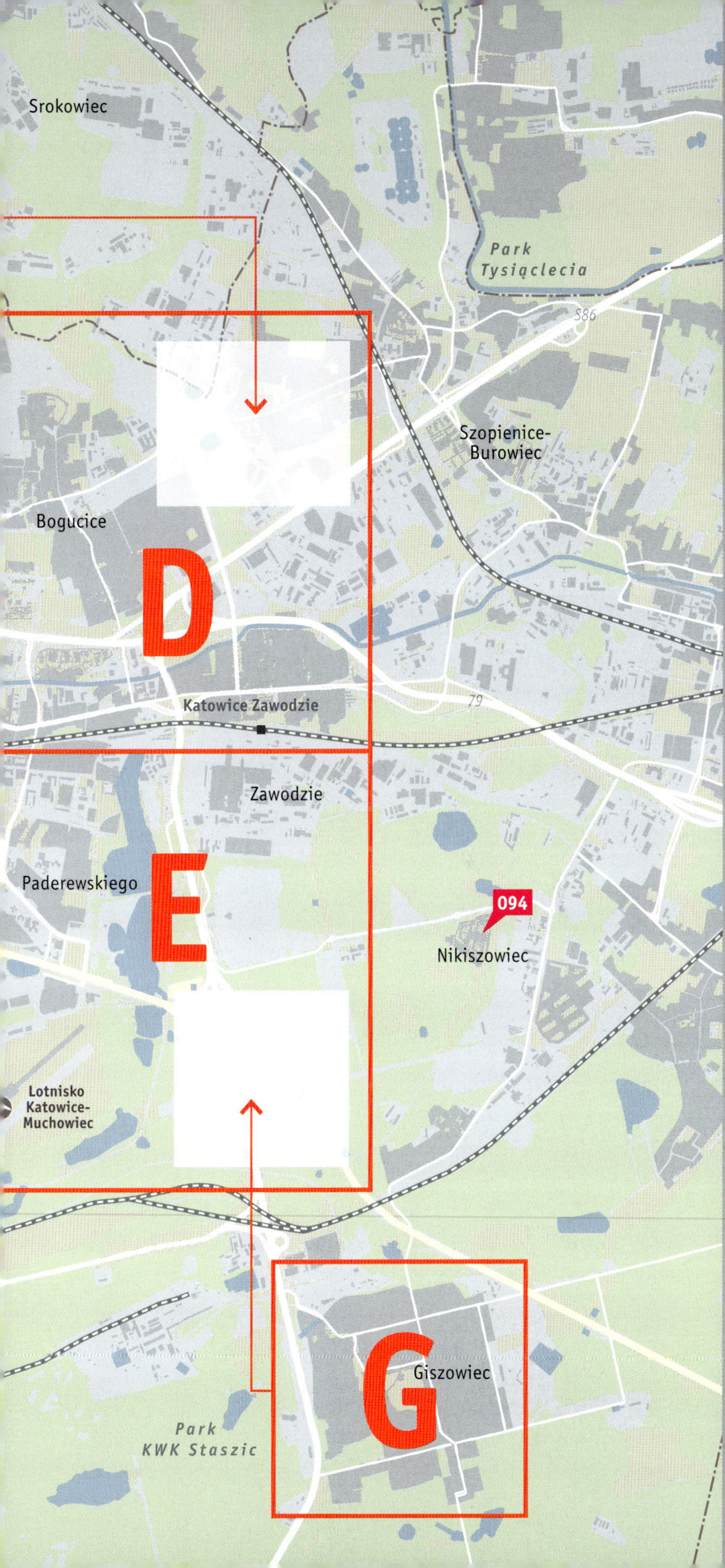

Srokowiec

Park Tysiąclecia

S86

Szopienice-Burowiec

Bogucice

D

Katowice Zawodzie

79

Zawodzie

Paderewskiego

E

094

Nikiszowiec

Lotnisko Katowice-Muchowiec

G

Giszowiec

Park KWK Staszic

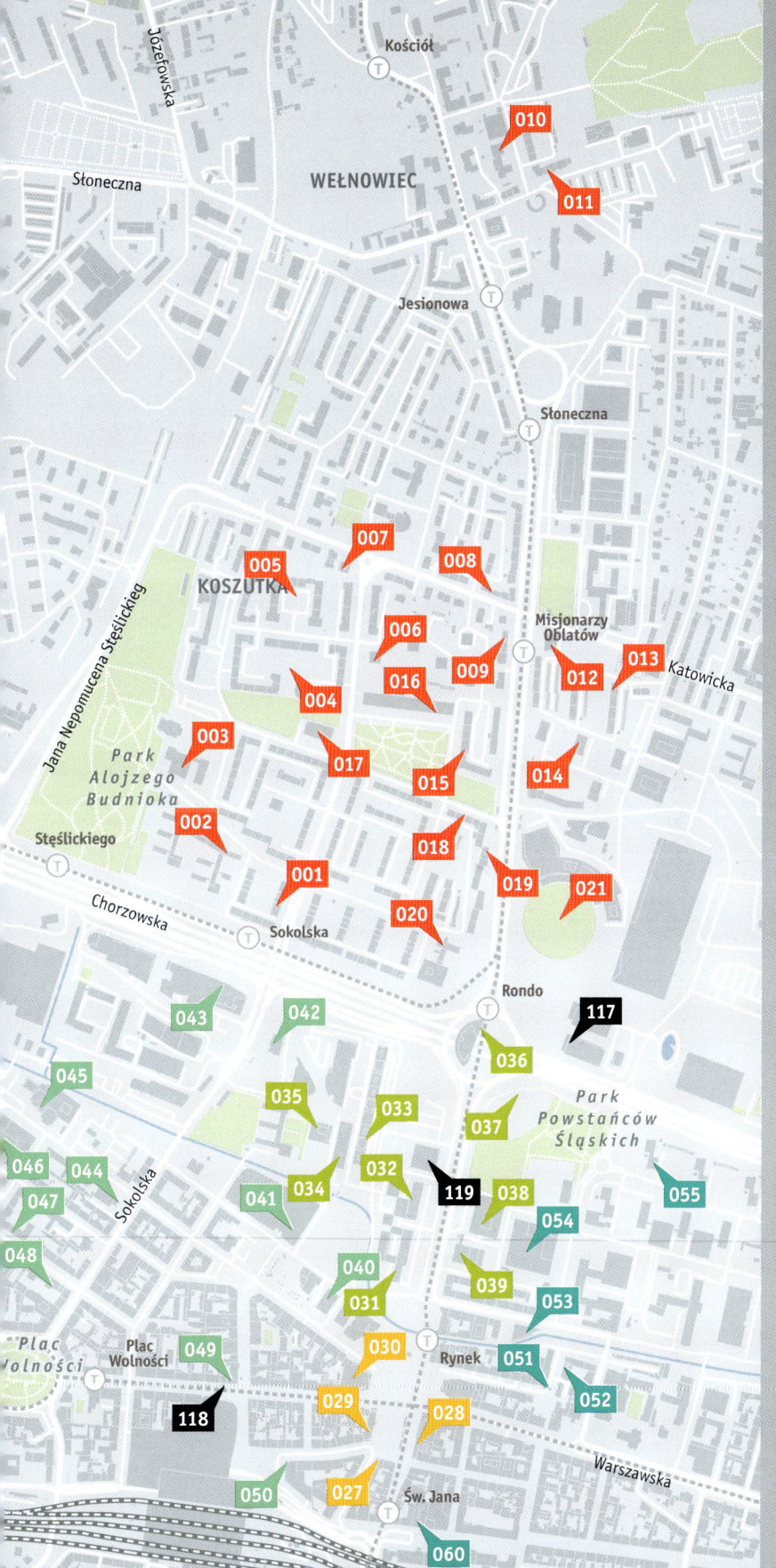

C

Raciborska

081

Adamskiego

080

Mikołowska

Poniatows

Aleja Górnośląska

078

Kościuszki
Szpital

100

Mikołowska

Park
Kościuszki

Kościuszki
Basen

099

Zgrzebnioka

Alfonsa Zgrzebnioka

095

BRYNÓW-OSIEK
ZGRZEBNIOK

Tadeusza Kościuszki

Brynowska

BRYNÓW

Gawronów

Gawronów

096

Drozdów

09

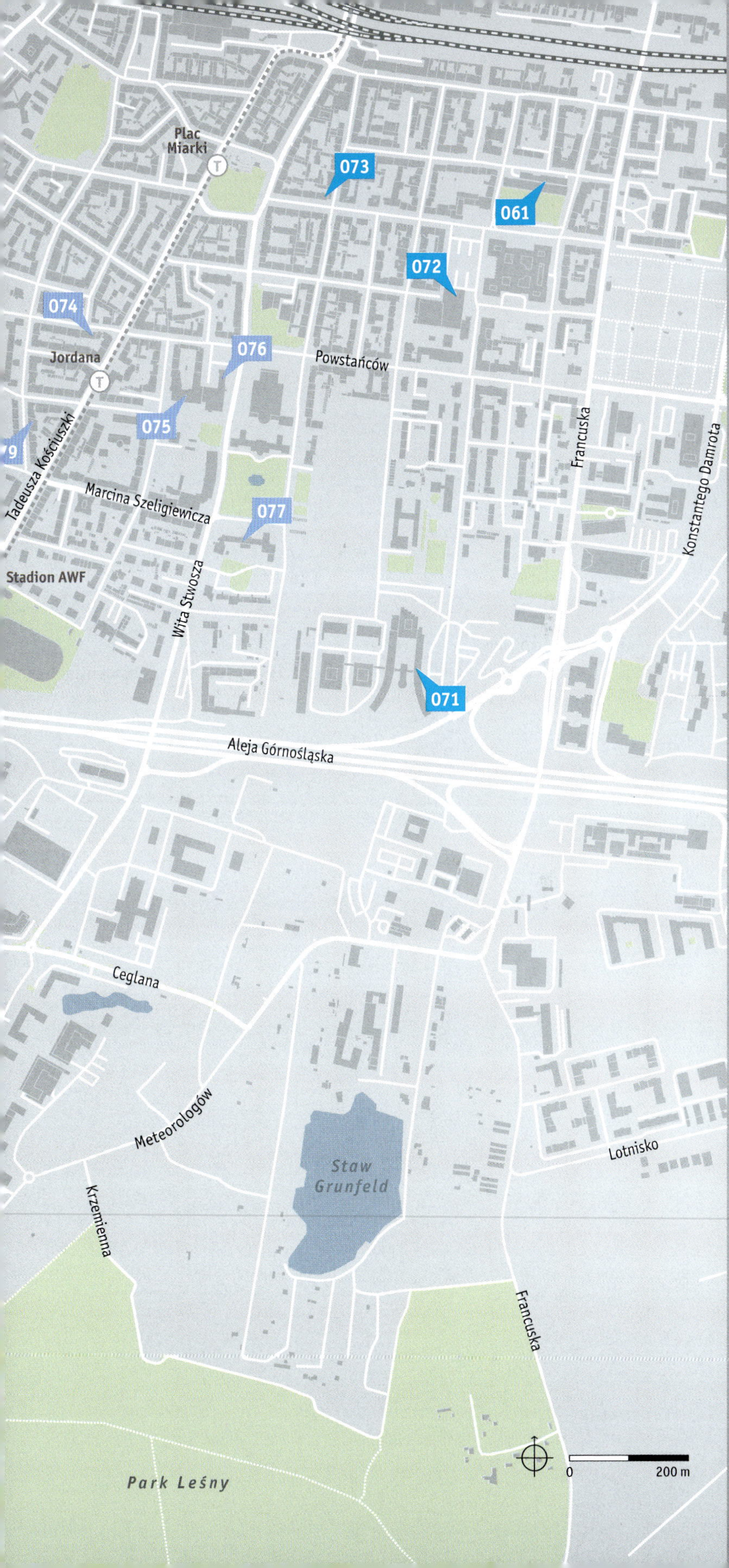

Plac
Miarki

073

061

072

074

Jordana

076

Powstańców

075

Tadeusza Kościuszki

9

Marcina Szeligiewicza

077

Francuska

Konstantego Damrota

Wita Stwosza

Stadion AWF

071

Aleja Górnośląska

Ceglana

Meteorologów

Staw
Grunfeld

Lotnisko

Krzemienna

Francuska

Park Leśny

0   200 m

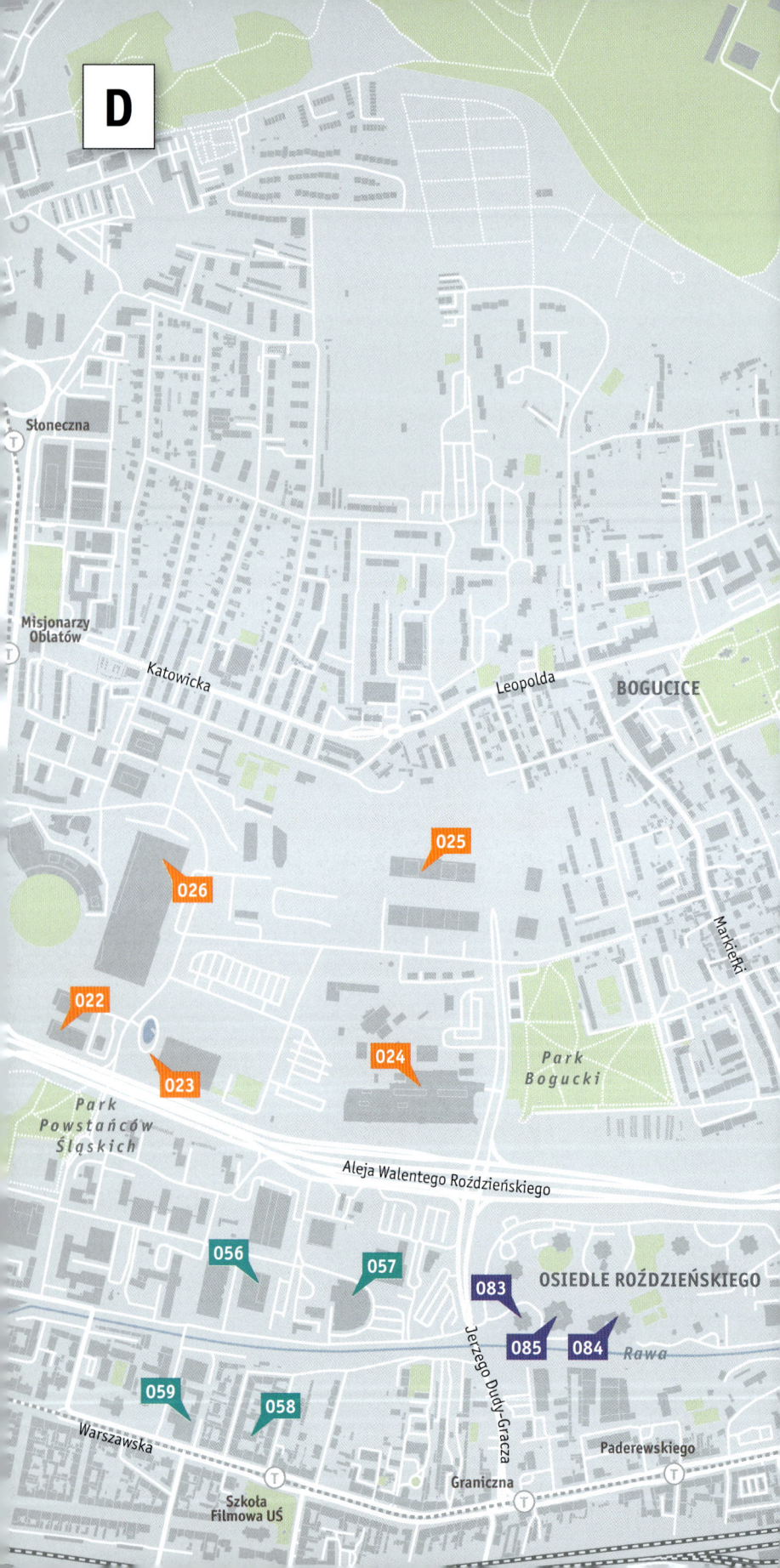

D

Słoneczna

Misjonarzy
Oblatów

Katowicka

Leopolda

BOGUCICE

Markiefki

025

026

022

023

024

*Park
Bogucki*

*Park
Powstańców
Śląskich*

Aleja Walentego Roździeńskiego

056

057

083

OSIEDLE ROŹDZIEŃSKIEGO

085   084   *Rawa*

Jerzego Dudy-Gracza

059

058

Warszawska

Paderewskiego

Graniczna

Szkoła
Filmowa UŚ

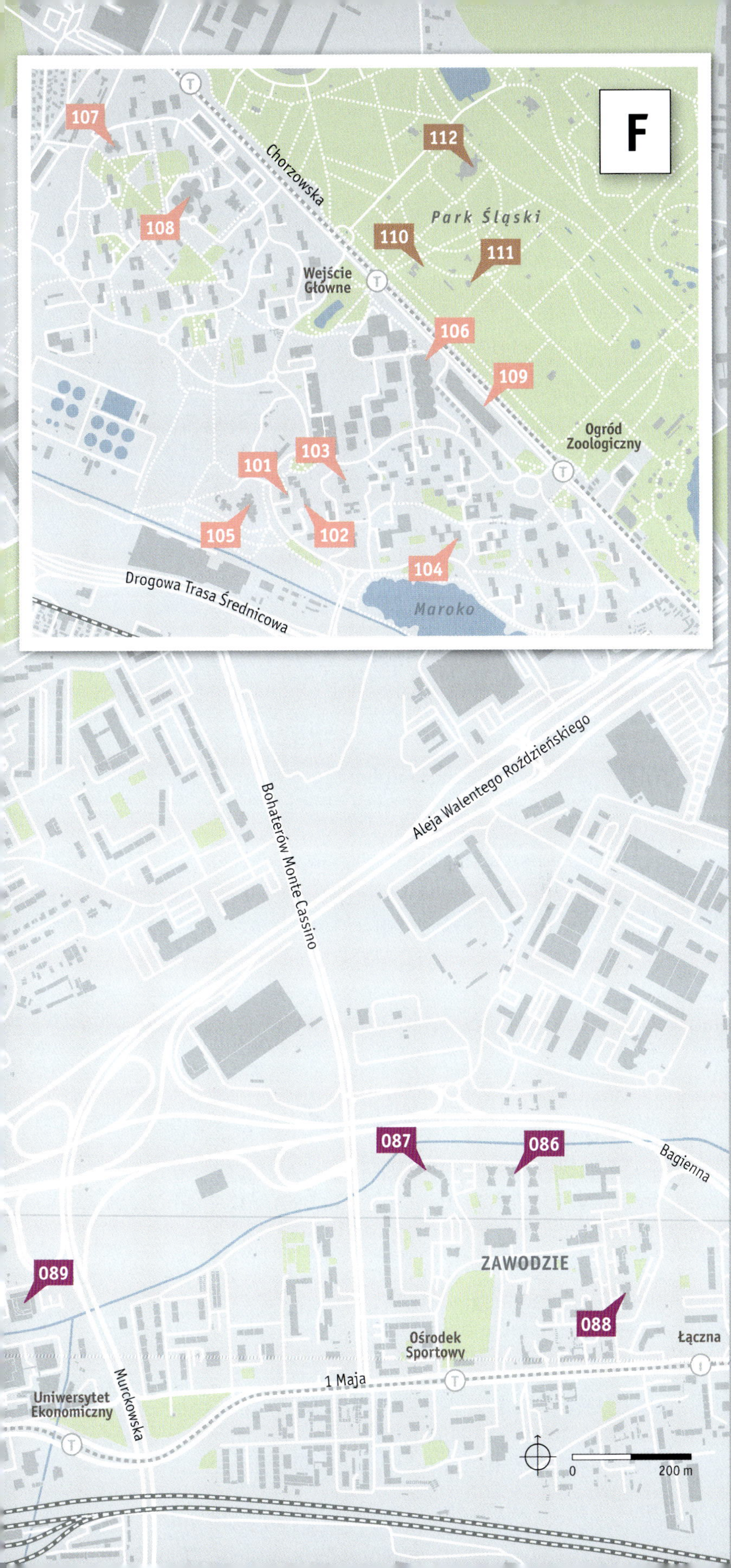

F

107

112

Park Śląski

108

110

111

Wejście
Głowne

106

109

Chorzowska

Ogród
Zoologiczny

101 103

105 102

104

Drogowa Trasa Średnicowa

Maroko

Aleja Walentego Roździeńskiego

Bohaterów Monte Cassino

087 086

Bagienna

089

ZAWODZIE

088

Ośrodek
Sportowy

Łączna

1 Maja

Uniwersytet
Ekonomiczny

Murckowska

0   200 m

E

063

062

064

065

Graniczna

120

068

069

067

Konstantego Damrota

Francuska

066

070

OSIEDLE
PADEREWSKIEGO

Graniczna

Ozdob

Aleja Górnośląska

OSIEDLE
PADEREWSKIEGO–MUCHOWIEC

Lotnisko

Francuska

Lotnisko
Katowice-Muchowiec

0   200 m

Staw
Sumi

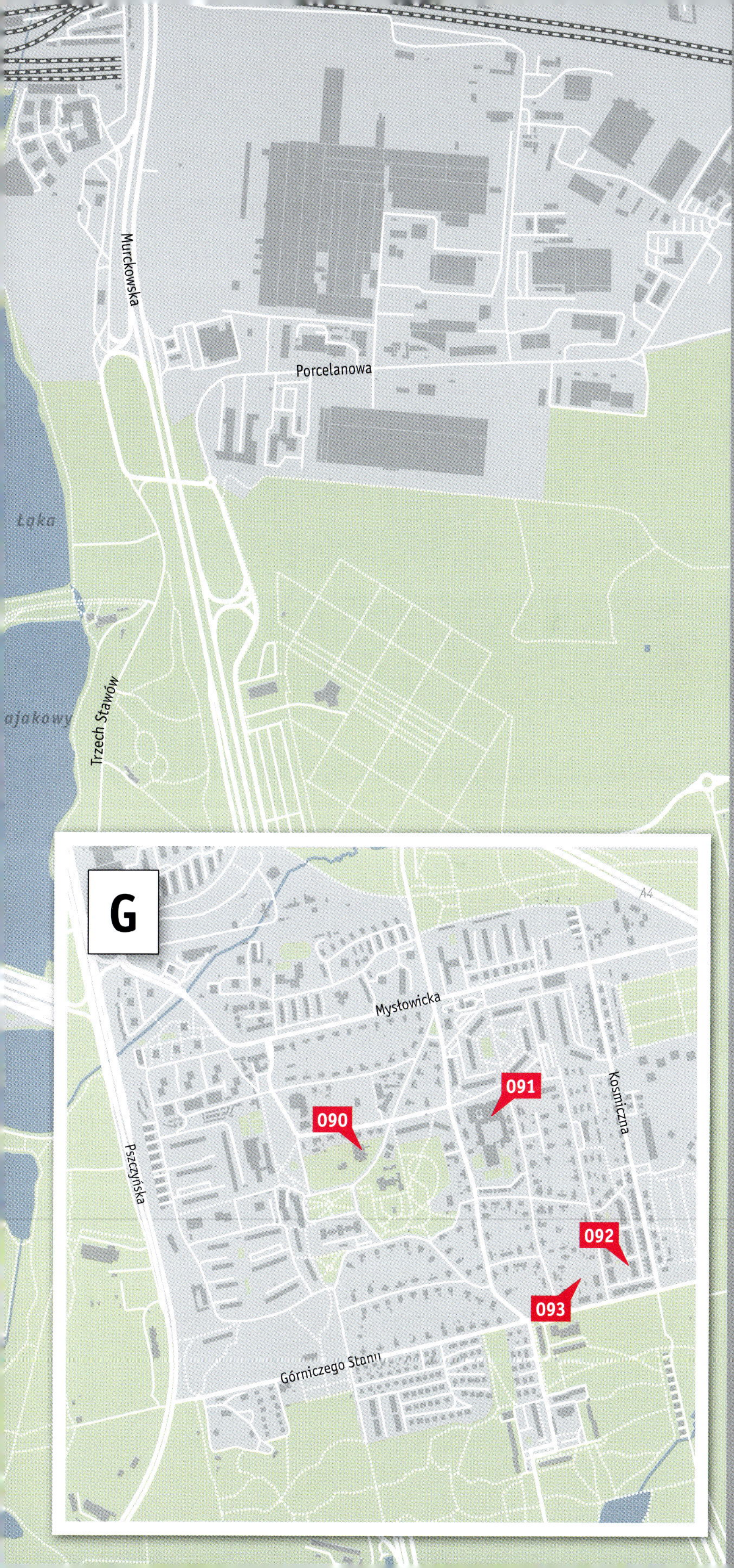

Murckowska

Porcelanowa

Łąka

Trzech Stawów

ajakowy

G

A4

Mysłowicka

Kosmiczna

Pszczyńska

090

091

092

093

Górniczego Stan··

Index of buildings

Chronological list arranged according to the project date.
Sorted by building type and project number.

Index of architects

Digits indicate project numbers

Author

Jakub Bródka
Born in 1995 in Katowice. Engineer
architect, graduate of the Faculty of
Architecture at the Silesian University
of Technology. Since 2020 he has been
a doctoral student at his alma mater
and at the University of Pisa, where
he conducts research into individual
forms of twentieth-century residential
architecture. He is also an academic
teacher and the author of several
architectural projects and studies.
As an employee of the Institute of
Architecture Documentation of the
Silesian Library, he actively documents
and researches the work of architects
active in the second half of the twentieth century in Upper Silesia. In 2024
he was awarded a scholarship by the
Minister of Science in recognition of
his research and publication achievements to date. In addition to his interest
in architecture and teaching, he is a
lover of classical music and skiing.

All the photos for which no
source is specified were taken by
Dominika Śliwińska.

Portrait photograph of the author
taken by Tomasz Celeban.

Unless otherwise indicated, floor
plans, section drawings, and site plans
were supplied by Jakub Bródka and
Michał Godziek.

The author in the course of archive queries, popularisation activities, and during cooperation with Dominika Śliwinska, who took most of the photographs for this book.

The *Deutsche Nationalbibliothek* lists
this publication in the *Deutsche National-
bibliografie*; detailed bibliographic data
are available at *http://dnb.d-nb.de*

ISBN 978-3-86922-896-9

© 2025 by DOM publishers, Berlin
www.dom-publishers.com

Proofreading
John Nicolson

Maps
Ee Dong Chen

Design
Masako Tomokiyo

Printing
Tiger Printing (Hong Kong) Co., Ltd.
www.tigerprinting.hk

ŚLĄSKA OKRĘGOWA IZBA ARCHITEKTÓW
RZECZYPOSPOLITEJ POLSKIEJ

Wydział Architektury
Politechniki Śląskiej